Manhattan

Test Prep & Admissions Consulting

MW01717354

# Turbocharge your GMAT: Geometry Guide

5th Edition (December 18th, 2012)

- ☐ *Coverage of all Geometry topics relevant for takers of the GMAT*
- ☐ *Intuitive and graphical explanations of concepts*
- ☐ *150 GMAT-like practice questions*
  - *Great collection of 700+ level questions*
  - *Ample questions with Alternate Approaches*
- ☐ *Mapped according to the scope of the GMAT*

www.manhattanreview.com

## Copyright and Terms of Use



10-Digit International Standard Book Number: (ISBN: 1629260215)
13-Digit International Standard Book Number: (ISBN: 978-1-62926-021-1)

Last updated on December 18, 2012.

Manhattan Review, 275 Madison Avenue, Suite 424, New York, NY 10025.
Phone: +1 (212) 316-2000. E-Mail: info@manhattanreview.com. Web: www.manhattanreview.com

## About the Turbocharge your GMAT Series

The Turbocharge Your GMAT series is designed to be clear and comprehensive. It is the set of tools you need to build the success you seek. Manhattan Review has created these guides to lead you through the complexities of the examination and achieve your best possible result. As so many students before you have discovered, our books break down the different test sections in a careful, clear manner and zero in on exactly what you need to know to raise your score. The complete series is designed to be your best GMAT test prep companion as you navigate the road to a successful outcome.

- ☐ **GMAT Math Study Guide (ISBN: 978-1-62926-013-6)**
- ☐ **GMAT Math Study Companion (ISBN: 978-1-62926-014-3)**
- ☐ **GMAT Verbal Study Guide (ISBN: 978-1-62926-015-0)**
- ☐ **GMAT Verbal Study Companion (ISBN: 978-1-62926-016-7)**
- ☐ **GMAT Math Essentials (ISBN: 978-1-62926-017-4)**
- ☐ **GMAT Number Properties (ISBN: 978-1-62926-018-1)**
- ■ **GMAT Geometry (ISBN: 978-1-62926-021-1)**
- ☐ **GMAT Arithmetic (ISBN: 978-1-62926-019-8)**
- ☐ **GMAT Algebra (ISBN: 978-1-62926-020-4)**
- ☐ **GMAT Word Problems (ISBN: 978-1-62926-028-0)**
- ☐ **GMAT Sets & Statistics (ISBN: 978-1-62926-029-7)**
- ☐ **GMAT Combinatorics & Probability (ISBN: 978-1-62926-030-3)**
- ☐ **GMAT Sentence Correction Guide (ISBN: 978-1-62926-022-8)**
- ☐ **GMAT Critical Reasoning Guide (ISBN: 978-1-62926-023-5)**
- ☐ **GMAT Reading Comprehension Guide (ISBN: 978-1-62926-024-2)**
- ☐ **GMAT Integrated Reasoning Guide (ISBN: 978-1-62926-025-9)**
- ☐ **GMAT Analytical Writing Guide (ISBN: 978-1-62926-026-6)**
- ☐ **GMAT Vocabulary Builder (ISBN: 978-1-62926-027-3)**

## About the Company

Manhattan Review's origin can be traced directly to an Ivy-League MBA classroom in 1999. While lecturing on advanced quantitative subjects to MBAs at Columbia Business School in New York City, Professor Dr. Joern Meissner was asked by his students to assist their friends, who were frustrated with conventional GMAT preparation options. He started to create original lectures that focused on presenting GMAT content in a coherent and concise manner rather than as a download of voluminous basic knowledge interspersed with so-called "tricks." The new approach immediately proved highly popular with GMAT students, inspiring the birth of Manhattan Review. Over the past 15+ years, Manhattan Review has grown into a multi-national firm, focusing on GMAT, GRE, LSAT, SAT, and TOEFL test prep and tutoring, along with business school, graduate school, and college admissions consulting; application advisory, and essay editing services.

## About the Founder

Professor Joern Meissner, the founder and chairman of Manhattan Review, has over twenty-five years of teaching experience in undergraduate and graduate programs at prestigious business schools in the USA, UK, and Germany. He created the original lectures, which are constantly updated by the Manhattan Review Team to reflect the evolving nature of GMAT, GRE, LSAT, SAT, and TOEFL test prep and private tutoring. Professor Meissner received his Ph.D. in Management Science from the Graduate School of Business at Columbia University (Columbia Business School) in New York City and is a recognized authority in the area of Supply Chain Management (SCM), Dynamic Pricing, and Revenue Management. Currently, he holds the position of Full Professor of Supply Chain Management and Pricing Strategy at Kuehne Logistics University in Hamburg, Germany. Professor Meissner is a passionate and enthusiastic teacher. He believes that grasping an idea is only half of the fun; conveying it to others makes it whole. At his previous position at Lancaster University Management School, he taught the MBA Core course in Operations Management and originated three new MBA Electives: Advanced Decision Models, Supply Chain Management, and Revenue Management. He has also lectured at the University of Hamburg, the Leipzig Graduate School of Management (HHL), and the University of Mannheim. Professor Meissner offers a variety of Executive Education courses aimed at business professionals, managers, leaders, and executives who strive for professional and personal growth. He frequently advises companies ranging from Fortune 500 companies to emerging start-ups on various issues related to his research expertise. Please visit his academic homepage www.meiss.com for further information.

## Manhattan Review Advantages

- **Time Efficiency and Cost Effectiveness**
  - The most limiting factor in test preparation for most people is time.
  - It takes significantly more teaching experience and techniques to prepare a student in less time.
  - Our preparation is tailored for busy professionals. We will teach you what you need to know in the least amount of time.

- **High-quality and dedicated instructors who are committed to helping every student reach her/his goals**

- **Manhattan Review's team members have combined wisdom of**
  - Academic achievements
  - MBA teaching experience at prestigious business schools in the US and UK
  - Career success

**Visit us at www.ManhattanReview.com and find out which courses are available close to *you*!**

## International Phone Numbers & Official Manhattan Review Websites

| | | |
|---|---|---|
| Manhattan Headquarters | +1-212-316-2000 | www.manhattanreview.com |
| USA & Canada | +1-800-246-4600 | www.manhattanreview.com |
| Australia | +61-3-9001-6618 | www.manhattanreview.com |
| Austria | +43-720-115-549 | www.review.at |
| Belgium | +32-2-808-5163 | www.manhattanreview.be |
| China | +86-20-2910-1913 | www.manhattanreview.cn |
| Czech Republic | +1-212-316-2000 | www.review.cz |
| France | +33-1-8488-4204 | www.review.fr |
| Germany | +49-89-3803-8856 | www.review.de |
| Greece | +1-212-316-2000 | www.review.com.gr |
| Hong Kong | +852-5808-2704 | www.review.hk |
| Hungary | +1-212-316-2000 | www.review.co.hu |
| India | +1-212-316-2000 | www.review.in |
| Indonesia | +1-212-316-2000 | www.manhattanreview.com |
| Ireland | +1-212-316-2000 | www.gmat.ie |
| Italy | +39-06-9338-7617 | www.manhattanreview.it |
| Japan | +81-3-4589-5125 | www.manhattanreview.jp |
| Malaysia | +1-212-316-2000 | www.manhattanreview.com |
| Netherlands | +31-20-808-4399 | www.manhattanreview.nl |
| Philippines | +1-212-316-2000 | www.review.ph |
| Poland | +1-212-316-2000 | www.review.pl |
| Portugal | +1-212-316-2000 | www.review.pt |
| Russia | +1-212-316-2000 | www.manhattanreview.ru |
| Singapore | +65-3158-2571 | www.gmat.sg |
| South Africa | +1-212-316-2000 | www.manhattanreview.co.za |
| South Korea | +1-212-316-2000 | www.manhattanreview.kr |
| Sweden | +1-212-316-2000 | www.gmat.se |
| Spain | +34-911-876-504 | www.review.es |
| Switzerland | +41-435-080-991 | www.review.ch |
| Taiwan | +1-212-316-2000 | www.gmat.tw |
| Thailand | +66-6-0003-5529 | www.manhattanreview.com |
| United Arab Emirates | +1-212-316-2000 | www.manhattanreview.ae |
| United Kingdom | +44-20-7060-9800 | www.manhattanreview.co.uk |
| Rest of the World | +1-212-316-2000 | www.manhattanreview.com |

 

# Contents

# Chapter 1

# Introduction

Dear Students,

Here at Manhattan Review, we constantly strive to provide you the best educational content for standardized test preparation. We make a tremendous effort to keep making things better and better for you. This is especially important with respect to an examination such as the GMAT. A typical GMAT aspirant is confused with so many test-prep options available. Your challenge is to choose a book or a tutor that prepares you for attaining your goal. We cannot say that we are one of the best, it is you who has to be the judge.

There are umpteen numbers of books on Quantitative Ability for GMAT preparation. What is so different about this book? The answer lies in its approach to deal with the questions. The book is meant to develop your fundamentals on one of the most scared topic on GMAT–Geometry.

You will find a lot of variety in the problems discussed. Alternate approaches to few tricky questions are worth appreciating. The book boasts of umpteen number of diagrams that represent scenarios while explaining concepts and explanations. You will find many 700+ level of questions in the book.

The Manhattan Review's 'Geometry' book is holistic and comprehensive in all respects. Should you have any queries, please feel free to write to me at info@manhattanreview.com.

Happy Learning!

Professor Dr. Joern Meissner
& The Manhattan Review Team

# Chapter 2

# Geometry Concepts

## 2.1 Lines

A **line** is assumed to extend indefinitely in both directions. There is one and only one line between two distinct points.

A **line segment** is the part of a line between two points called end points. A line segment is denoted by its end points. It is denoted by $\overline{XY}$.

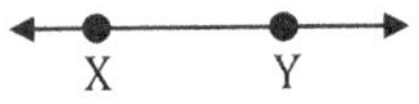


When a line segment is extended indefinitely in one direction, it is called a **ray**. A ray has one endpoint.

**Pairs of lines:** A pair of straight lines may be either:

- **Parallel:** Parallel lines are lines in the same plane that never intersect, even if extended infinitely.

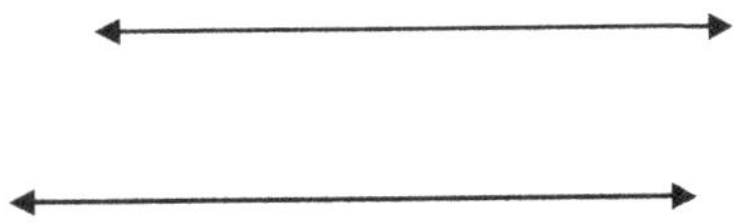

- **Intersecting:** A pair of lines in the same plane, if not parallel, must intersect at some point.

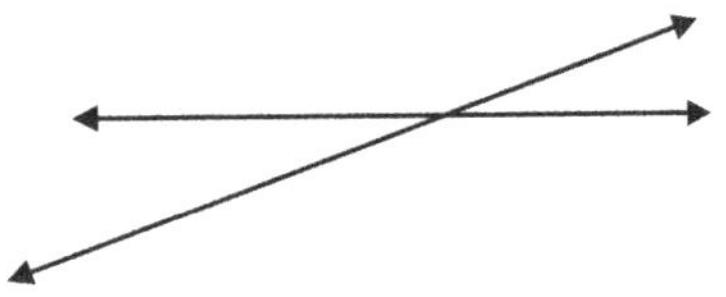

- **Perpendicular:** If the above lines intersect at right angles, then such lines are perpendicular to one another.

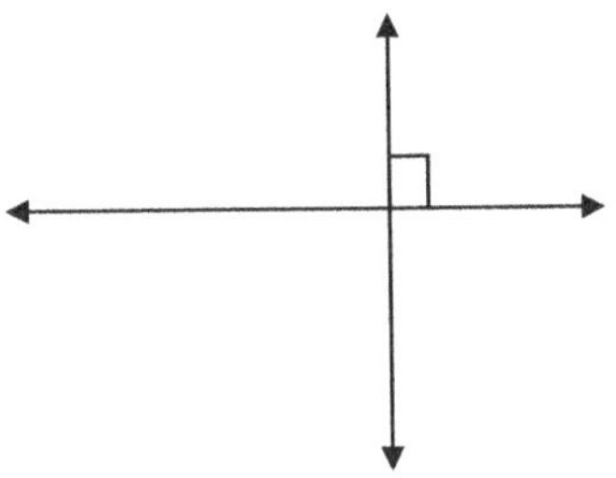

- **Skew:** Two lines in two different planes, which neither intersect each other, nor are parallel to each other, are termed skew.

 

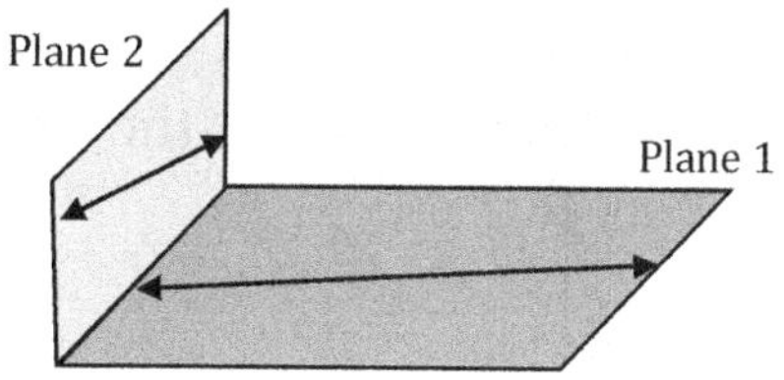
Plane 2
Plane 1

## 2.2 Angles

If two straight lines meet at a point they form an angle. The point is called the vertex of the angle and the lines are called the sides or rays of the angle.

Let us look at the important points associated with lines and angles:

| | |
|---|---|
| 1. An angle less than $90^o$ is **acute**. | 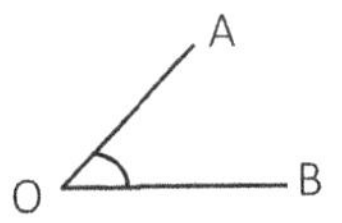 |
| 2. An angle equal to $90^o$ is **right angle**. | 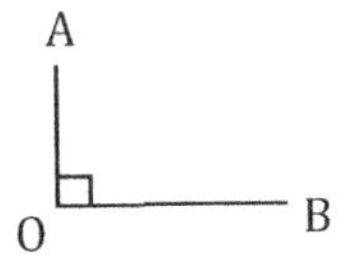 |
| 3. An angle greater than $90^o$ but less than $180^o$ is **obtuse**. | 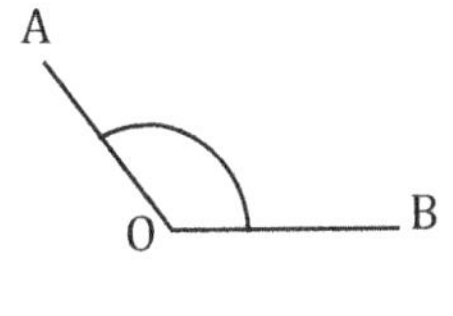 |
| 4. An angle of $180^o$ is a **straight angle**. | 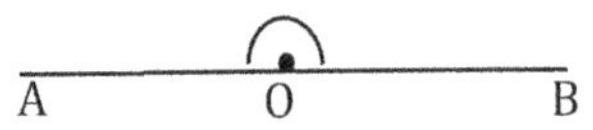 |
| 5. An angle greater than $180^o$ but less than $360^o$ is **reflex.** | 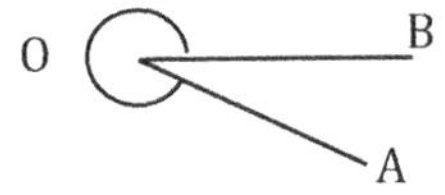 |
| 6. Two angles are **adjacent** if they have the same vertex with a common side and one angle is not inside the other.<br>• ∠BOC and ∠COD are adjacent<br>• ∠COD and ∠EOD are not adjacent | 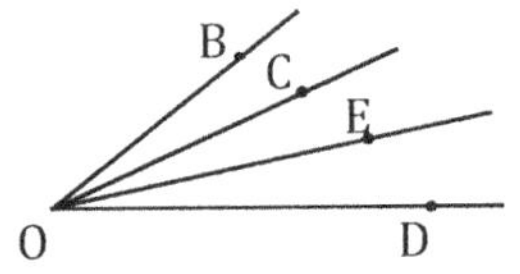 |
| 7. If the sum of two adjacent angles is $180^o$, then they are **supplementary**.<br>• ∠AOC and ∠DOC are supplementary. | 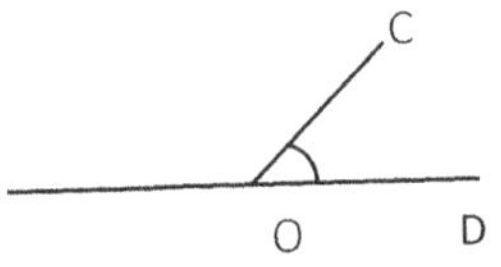 |

 

| | |
|---|---|
| 8. If the sum of two adjacent angles is $90^0$, then they are **complementary**.<br><br>• ∠BOC and ∠DOC are complementary. | 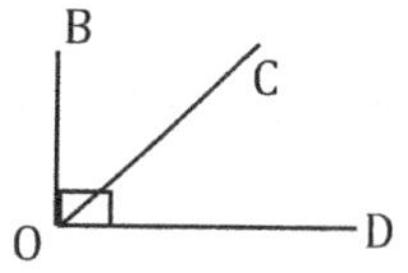 |
| 9. **Vertically Opposite Angles:** When two lines intersect, two pairs of vertically opposite angles are formed. Vertically opposite angles are equal.<br><br>• Here, ∠C and ∠A are equal.<br>• Similarly, ∠D and ∠B are equal. | 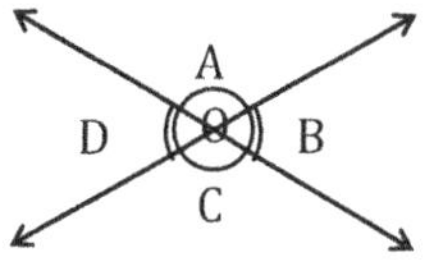 |
| 10. **Alternate and Corresponding Angles:** In the diagram below, AB and UV are parallel lines with DE as a transversal.<br>(Note: A transversal refers to any straight line that intersects a pair of straight line.)<br><br>This creates pairs of corresponding and alternate angle as shown below.<br><br>• Alternate angles are equal<br>∠ Q = ∠ S and ∠ P = ∠ R<br><br>• Interior angles on same side are supplementary<br>∠ P + ∠ S = ∠Q + ∠ R = ∠180°<br><br>• Corresponding angles are equal<br>∠N =∠S; ∠M =∠R; ∠P =∠T; ∠Q =∠U | 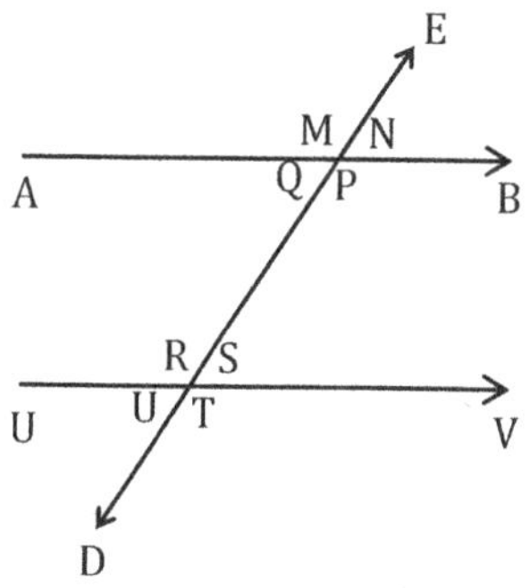 |

## 2.3 Triangles

A triangle is a figure bounded by three line segments in a plane. In the diagram, the line segments are AB, BC and CA, also called its sides; and A, B and C are called the vertices of the triangle. A triangle can also be called a 3-sided polygon.

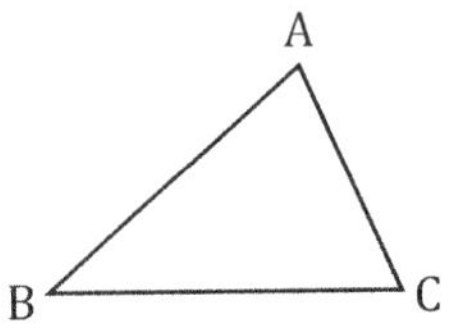


Let us look at the important points associated with triangles:

| | |
|---|---|
| 1. Sum of any two sides in a triangle is greater than the third side.<br><br>Also, any side is less than half of the perimeter of the triangle.<br><br>Note: What happens, if the sum of two sides is NOT greater than the third side?<br><br>Let us observe using the diagram below.<br><br>Let AB be one side of the triangle. Let the third vertex be C.<br><br>To determine the position of C, we draw arc with radius AC and BC with centres at A and B respectively. The point of intersection of the arc is the position of C.<br><br>If $AC + BC \not> AB$, then the arc never intersects as shown below.<br><br>Thus, there is no triangle at all!<br><br>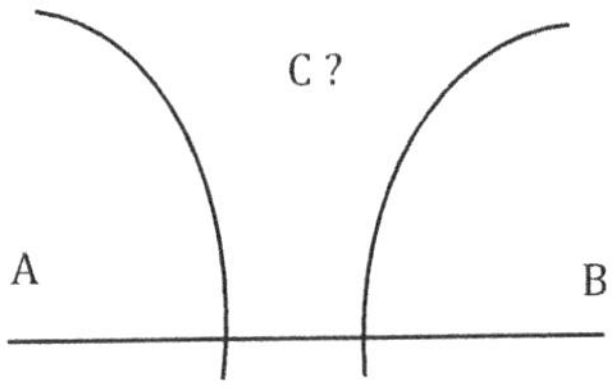 | Thus, in triangle ABC, we simultaneously have:<br><br>$AB + BC > AC \ldots$(i)<br>$AB + AC > BC \ldots$(ii)<br>$AC + BC > AB \ldots$(iii)<br><br>Let us choose any of the three inequalities above, say (i): adding AC to both sides:<br><br>$AB + BC + AC > AC + AC$<br><br>=> 2AC < Perimeter of the triangle<br><br>=> $AC < \frac{1}{2}$ * Perimeter of the triangle<br><br>Similarly, the inequalities for the other two sides follow. |

 

| | |
|---|---|
| 2. The greatest side in a triangle has the greatest angle opposite to it and vice-versa.<br><br>Similarly, the smallest side in a triangle has the smallest angle opposite to it and vice-versa. | 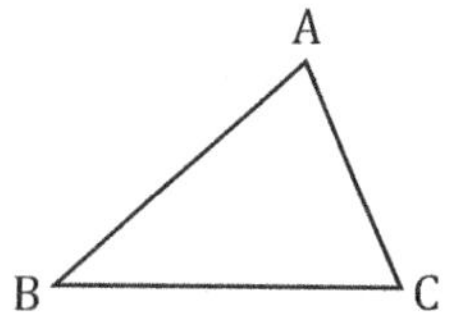<br>AB > BC > AC=>∠C > ∠A > ∠B |
| 3. Sum of the interior angles is $180^o$.<br><br>Sum of its exterior angles is $360^o$.<br><br>In the figure alongside, the interior angles are $i_a$, $i_b$ and $i_c$ and the exterior angles are $e_a$, $e_b$ and $e_c$.<br><br>Note: Have you ever wondered: Why is the sum of the interior angles of a triangle equal to $180^o$? (Find out - At the end of this chapter) | 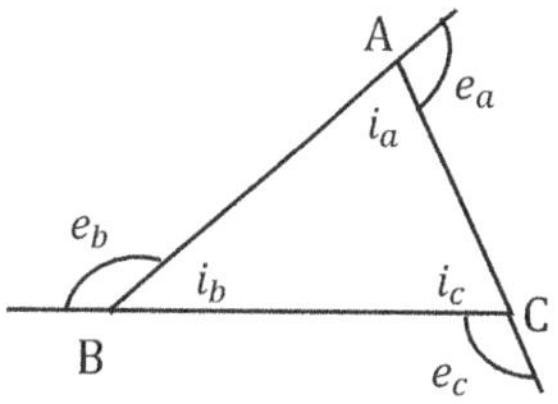<br>Thus, we have:<br><br>$i_a + i_b + i_c = 180^o$<br><br>$e_a + e_b + e_c$<br>$= 180^o - i_a + 180^o - i_b + 180^o - i_c$<br>$= 180^o * 3 - (i_a + i_b + i_c)$<br>$= 540^o - 180^o$<br>$= 360^o$ |
| 4. Any exterior angle in a triangle is equal to sum of the opposite interior angles. | This follows from the above rule #3. Let us see how:<br><br>Since $i_a + i_b + i_c = 180^o$, we have:<br><br>$i_a + i_b = 180^o - i_c$<br>$=> i_a + i_b = e_c$ |
| 5. A triangle with no two sides equal is called a **scalene** triangle. | 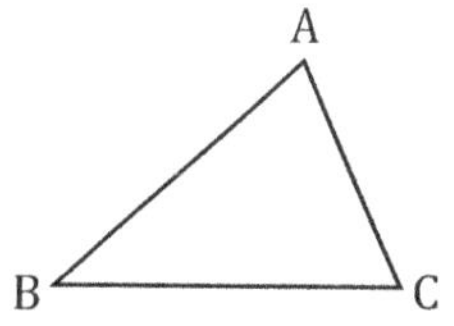<br>Here, AB ≠ BC ≠ CA, and ∠C ≠ ∠A ≠ ∠B |

| | |
|---|---|
| 6. If EXACTLY two sides of a triangle are equal, it is called an **isosceles** triangle.<br><br>The angles opposite to the equal sides are also equal.<br><br>**Note:** In an isosceles triangle, a perpendicular drawn from the vertex to the 'UNEQUAL' side bisects the side. | 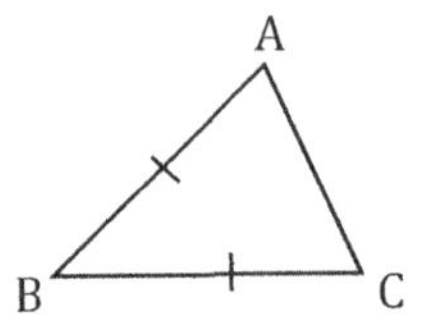<br>Here, AB = BC $\neq$ AC<br>=> $\angle C = \angle A \neq \angle B$<br>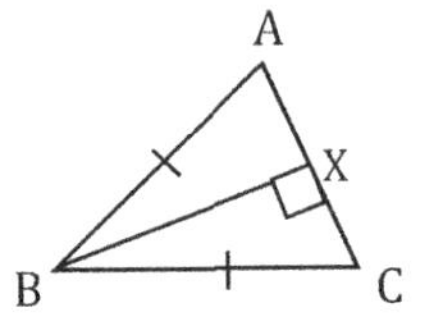<br>Here, BX $\perp$ AC => AX = CX and $\angle ABX = \angle CBX$ |
| 7. If all the three sides of a triangle are equal, it is called an **equilateral** triangle.<br><br>Each angle is equal to $60^{\circ}$.<br><br>• Height of an equilateral triangle $= \frac{\sqrt{3}}{2} *$ (Length of its side)<br>• Area of an equilateral triangle $= \frac{\sqrt{3}}{4} * (\text{Length of its side})^2$<br>• Perimeter of an equilateral triangle = 3* Length of its side | 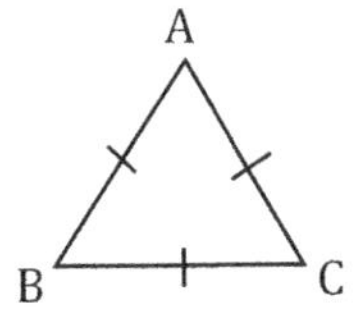<br>Here, AB = BC = CA<br><br>$\angle C = \angle A = \angle B = 60^{\circ}$ |

8. If ONE angle of a triangle is $90^\circ$, it is called a **right-angled** triangle.

   If ABC is right-angled at A, from Pythagoras' theorem we have:

   $AB^2 + AC^2 = BC^2$

   A few of the integer set of values of the sides AB, AC and BC satisfying Pythagoras' theorem are:

   - **3, 4, 5:** $3^2 + 4^2 = 5^2$
   - **6, 8, 10:** $6^2 + 8^2 = 10^2$
   - **5, 12, 13:** $5^2 + 12^2 = 13^2$
   - **7, 24, 25:** $7^2 + 24^2 = 25^2$
   - **8, 15, 17:** $8^2 + 15^2 = 17^2$

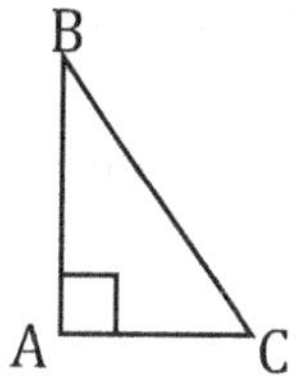


Another way of looking at Pythagoras' theorem:

The area of the square constructed on BC as its side equals the sum of areas of the squares constructed on AB and AC as the sides.

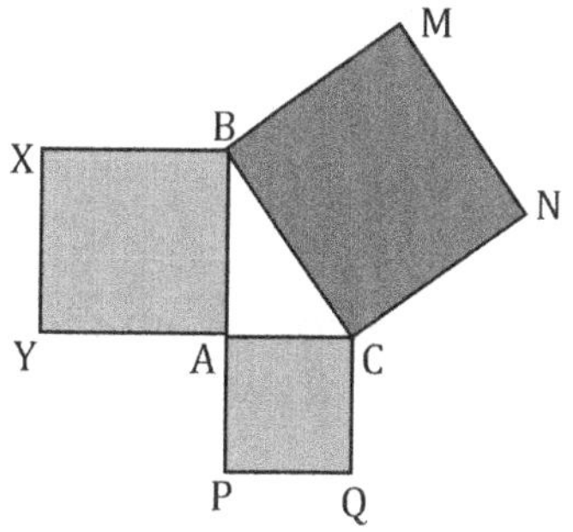


Thus, we have:

Area BMNC = Area ACQP + Area ABXY

9. If ALL the angles of a triangle are less than $90^\circ$, it is called an **acute-angled** triangle.

   Since $\angle A$, $\angle B$ and $\angle C$ are all acute, we have:

   - $AB^2 + AC^2 > BC^2$
   - $AB^2 + BC^2 > AC^2$
   - $AC^2 + BC^2 > AB^2$

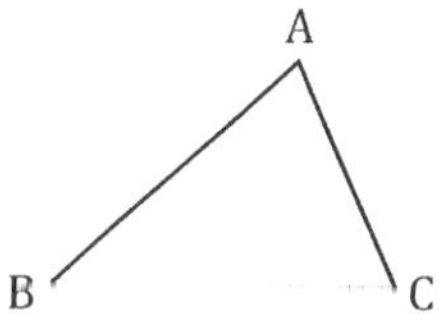


Here, $\angle C < 90^\circ, \angle A < 90^\circ$ and $\angle B < 90^\circ$

<table>
<tr>
<td>
10. If ONE angle of a triangle is more than $90^0$, it is called an obtuse-angled triangle.<br><br>
Since C is obtuse, we have:<br><br>
• $BC^2 + AC^2 < AB^2$
</td>
<td>
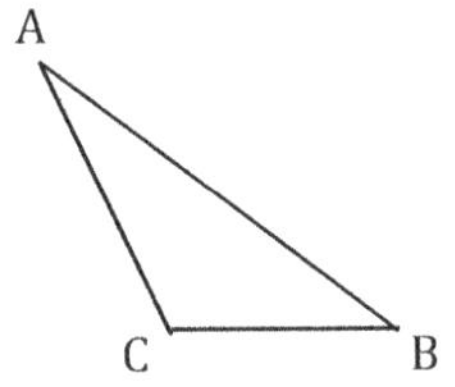

Here, $\angle C > 90^o$, $\angle A < 90^o$ and $\angle B < 90^o$
</td>
</tr>
<tr>
<td>
11. The medians of a triangle refer to the line segments drawn from a vertex bisecting the side opposite to the vertex.<br><br>
All three medians always intersect at a single point called the centroid. The centroid divides each median in the ratio 2:1 (2 units from the vertex and 1 unit from the side):<br><br>
• $\frac{AO}{OX} = \frac{BO}{OY} = \frac{CO}{OZ} = \frac{2}{1}$
</td>
<td>
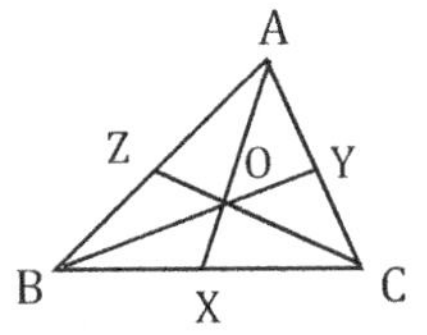

Here: AX, BY and CZ are the medians and O is the centroid of triangle ABC
</td>
</tr>
<tr>
<td>
12. The altitudes of a triangle refer to the perpendicular lines drawn from a vertex to the opposite side.
</td>
<td>
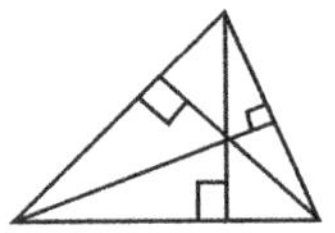
Here: AX, BY and CZ are the altitudes (also called 'heights') of triangle ABC.
</td>
</tr>
</table>

| | |
|---|---|
| 13. **Area** of a triangle:<br><br>• Area of $\triangle ABC = \frac{1}{2} * \text{Base} * \text{Height}$<br>$= \frac{1}{2} * BC * AD$<br>$= \frac{1}{2} AC * BE$<br>$= \frac{1}{2} AB * CF$<br><br>Thus, from the above, we have:<br>$BC * AD = AC * BE = AB * CF$<br><br>Thus, we have:<br><br>• $AD : BE : CF = \frac{1}{BC} : \frac{1}{AC} : \frac{1}{AB}$<br><br>Thus, the ratio of the altitudes equals the ratio of the reciprocals of the corresponding sides of a triangle. | 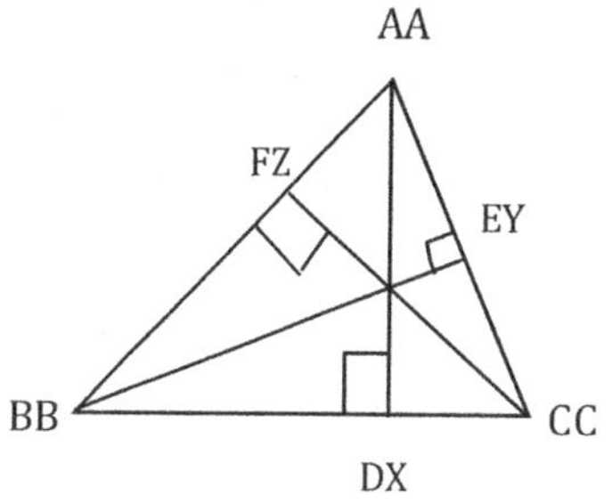<br> |
| 14. For triangles lying between the same set of parallel lines ($l$ and $m$), the ratio of the areas of the triangles equals the ratio of the corresponding bases of the triangles.<br><br>Since the triangles lie between the same set of parallel lines, their heights are the same, and hence, the ratio of their area equals the ratio of their bases. | 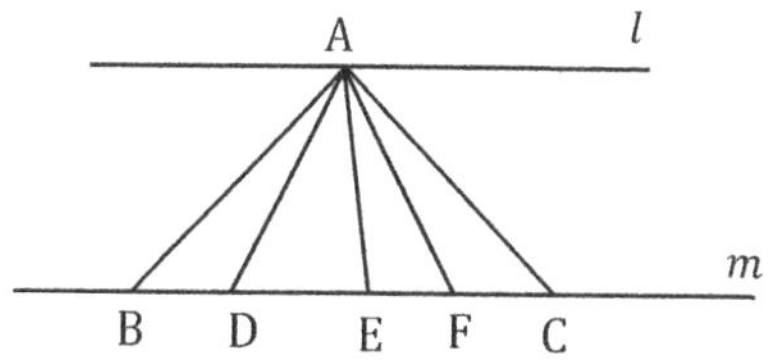<br><br><br>Here, lines from the vertex A are drawn to the base BC intersecting at D, E and F.<br><br>Thus, triangles ABD, ADE, AEF and AFC lie between the same parallel lines (hence, they have the same height)<br><br>=> Area of $\triangle ABD$ : Area of $\triangle ADE$: Area of $\triangle AEF$: Area of $\triangle AFC = BD : DE : EF : FC$ |

Let us now look into relations between different triangles. There are two important areas to focus on: Congruency and Similarity. Let us discuss them one by one:

**A. Congruent Triangles:** Two triangles are congruent if they are identical to each other in all aspects. Thus, the corresponding sides and angles of the triangles are equal.

There are four ways to prove congruency:

(a) **SAS** (Side-Angle-Side)

Triangle ABC ≅ Triangle XYZ if AB = XY; ∠A = ∠X; AC = XZ (Here the angle is the included angle)

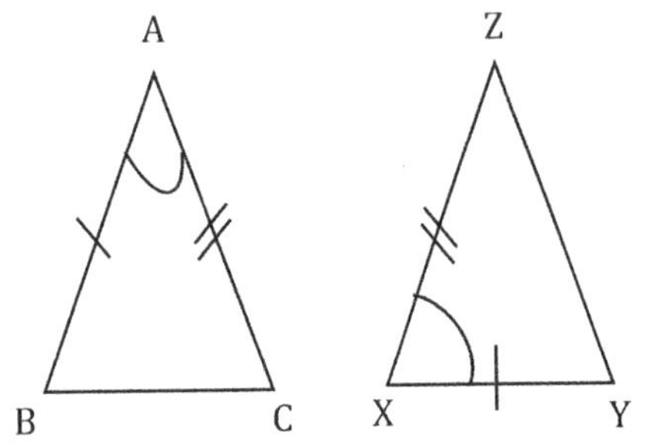


Note: Triangles MNP and DEF are NOT congruent:
Since: MN = DF; ∠N = ∠E; MP = DE
(∠N, ∠E are not the included angles)

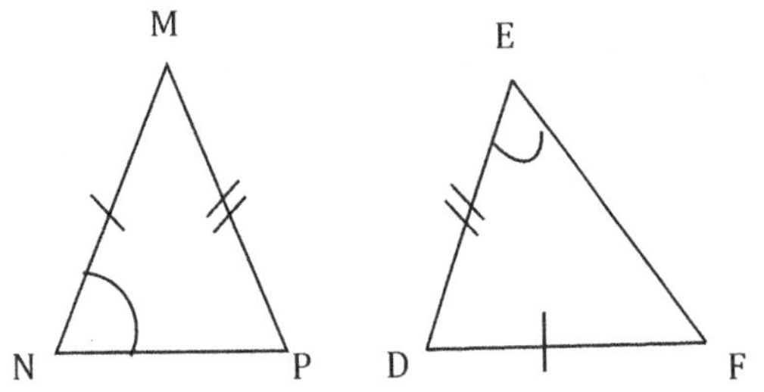


(b) **AAS** (Angle-Angle-Side)

Triangle ABC ≅ Triangle XYZ if ∠B = ∠Y; ∠C = ∠Z; AC = XZ.
Here, however, the side NEED NOT be the included side
(If two angles are equal, the third angle will also be equal)

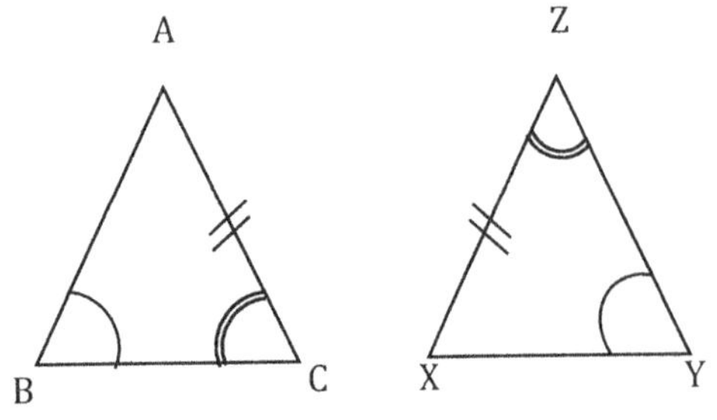


 

(c) **SSS** (Side-Side-Side)

Triangle ABC ≅ Triangle XYZ if AB = XY; AC = XZ; BC = YZ

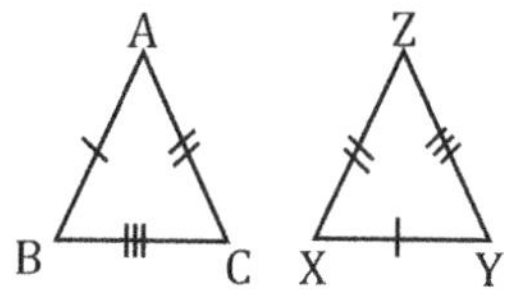


(d) **RHS** (Right angle-Hypotenuse-Side)

Triangle ABC ≅Triangle XYZ if $\angle B = \angle Y = 90^0$;
AC = XZ (hypotenuse); AB = XY.

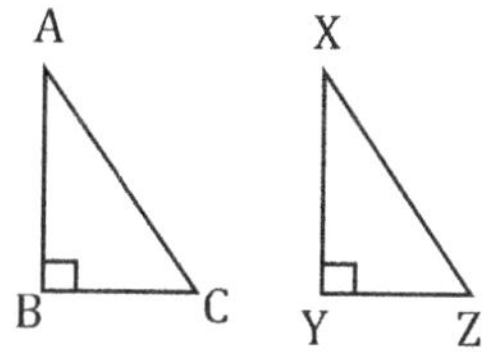


**B. Similar Triangles:** Similar triangles are similar in shape, need not have same size but are proportional i.e. the ratio of their sides is constant.

Two or more triangles can be called similar if:

(a) **AAA** (Angle-Angle-Angle)

Triangle ABC ~ Triangle XYZ if $\angle B = \angle Y$; $\angle C = \angle Z$
Note: Since $\angle A + \angle B + \angle C = \angle X + \angle Y + \angle Z = 180^0$
$\Rightarrow \angle A = \angle X$

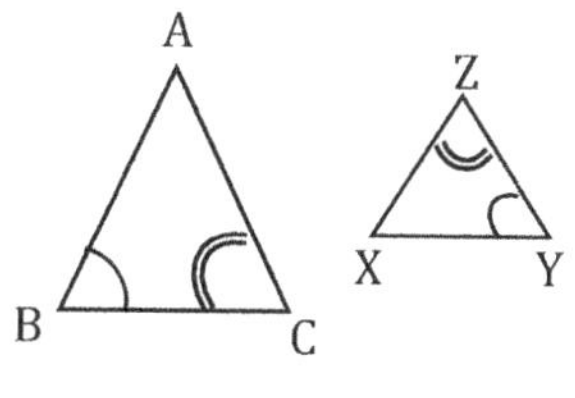


(b) **SAS** (Side ratio-Angle-Side ratio)

Triangle ABC ~ Triangle XYZ if $\angle A = \angle X$; $\frac{AB}{XY} = \frac{AC}{XZ}$
(Here the angle is the included angle)

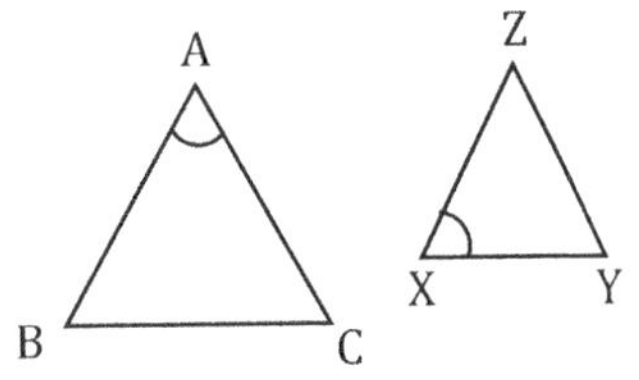


**Let us look at three important results for similar triangles:**

If two triangles are similar:

- Ratio of their corresponding sides equals the ratio of any corresponding length measure of the triangles; example: ratio of their altitudes or ratio of their medians, etc.
- Ratio of the areas of the triangles equals the SQUARE of the ratio of their corresponding sides:

  For any two similar triangles ABC and XYZ, we have:

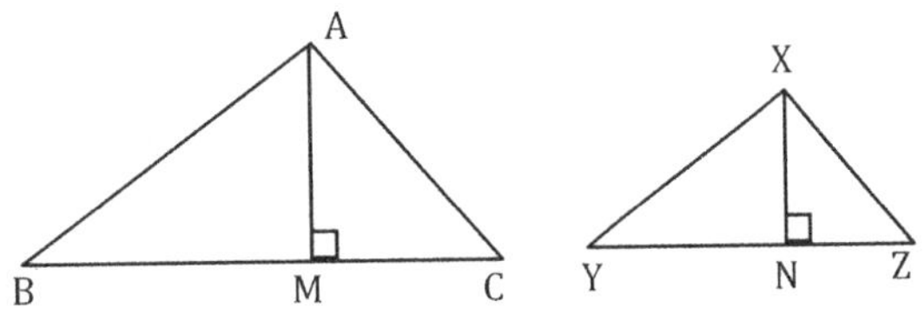


  Let the ratio of sides of the two triangles be $k$.
  Thus, we have:

$$\frac{AB}{XY}=\frac{BC}{YZ}=\frac{CA}{ZX}=\frac{AM}{XN}=k$$

$$\frac{(\text{Area of triangle ABC})}{(\text{Area of triangle XYZ})}=\left(\frac{\frac{1}{2}*BC*AM}{\frac{1}{2}*YZ*XN}\right)=\left(\frac{BC*AM}{YZ*XN}\right)=\left(\frac{BC}{YZ}\right)*\left(\frac{AM}{XN}\right)=k*$$

$$k=k^2$$

- Ratio of their perimeters of the triangles equals the ratio of their corresponding sides.

**A few important rules are now presented below. Effective use of these rules can reduce the time taken to solve a problem.**

(1) **Basic Proportionality Theorem:** A line parallel to one side of a triangle divides the other two sides proportionally i.e. it creates two similar triangles, one inside the

 

other, sharing a common vertex.

In triangle ABC, DE is drawn parallel to BC.

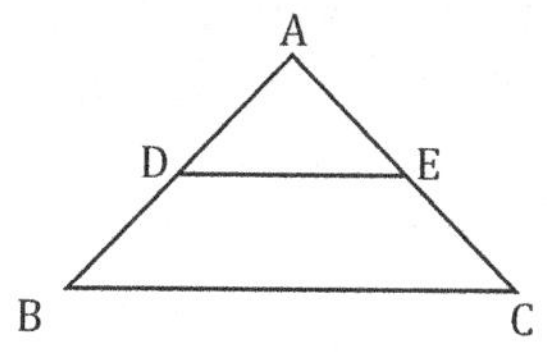


Thus, we have: $\triangle ABC \sim \triangle ADE$.

$$=> \frac{AD}{AB} = \frac{AE}{AC} => \frac{AD}{DB} = \frac{AE}{EC}$$

(2) **Mid-point Theorem:** The straight line joining the mid-points of two sides of a triangle is parallel to the third side and equal to half the third side.

(3) **Angle Bisector Theorem:** A bisector of any angle of a triangle will divide the opposite side in the same proportion as the two sides adjacent to the angle.

In $\triangle ABC$, AP is the angle bisector of $\angle A$. Thus, we have:

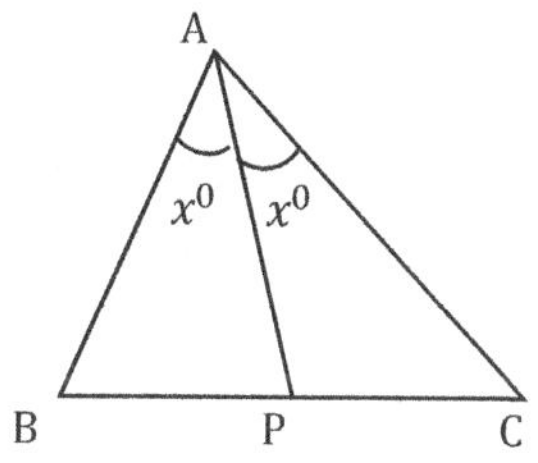


$$\frac{AB}{AC} = \frac{BP}{PC}$$

(4) **Right Triangles:**

- In any right triangle, the length of the median to the hypotenuse equals half the length of the hypotenuse.

  Here, AX is the median drawn to the hypotenuse BC.

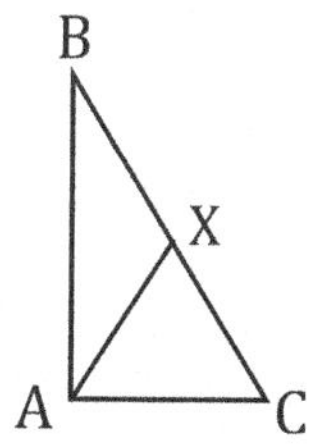


 

Thus, we have:

AX = BX = CX

- If AX is drawn ⊥ to the hypotenuse intersecting the hypotenuse BC at X, we have three similar triangles (AXB, CXA and CAB). Thus, we have the following relations:

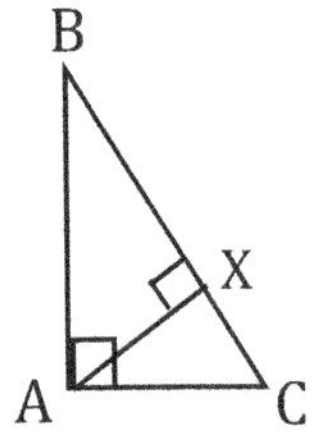


  - $AX^2 = BX*CX$ (from similarity of triangles AXB and CXA)
  - $AB^2 = BX*BC$ (from similarity of triangles AXB and CAB)
  - $AC^2 = CX*CB$ (from similarity of triangles CAX and CAB)
  - $AB * AC = AX * BC$ (equating area: $\frac{1}{2}*AB * AC = \frac{1}{2}*AX * BC$)

- 30 - 60 - 90 Triangle: Basically, a 30-60-90 triangle is half of an equilateral triangle.

  It can be seen that half of triangle XBC is the 30-60-90 triangle ABC.

  The ratio of the sides of a 30-60-90 triangle is shown:

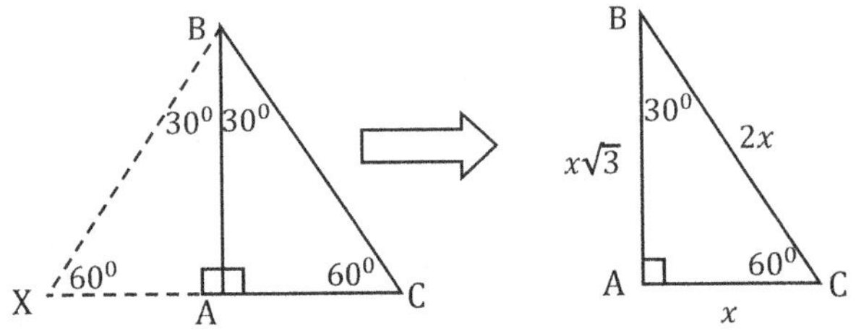


- 45 - 45 - 90 Triangle: Basically, a 45-45-90 triangle is half of a square. It can be seen that half of square ABXC is the 45-45-90 triangle ABC.

  The ratio of the sides of a 45-45-90 triangle is shown:

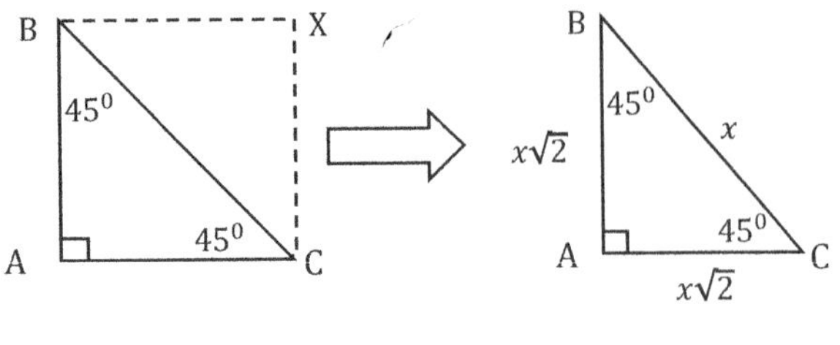

(5) **Maximum / minimum area and perimeter of triangles:**

- Among all triangles of the same area, the equilateral triangle has the minimum perimeter.
- Among all triangles of the same perimeter, the equilateral triangle has the maximum area.
- Among all isosceles triangles of the same area, the right-angled isosceles triangle has the minimum perimeter.
- Among all isosceles triangles of the same perimeter, the right-angled isosceles triangle has the maximum area.
- Among all triangles given the lengths of two sides, the triangle having those two sides perpendicular to one another has the maximum area.

Why is the sum of the interior angles of a triangle $180^\circ$?

In the triangle ABC, let us draw a line XY through A, parallel to BC.

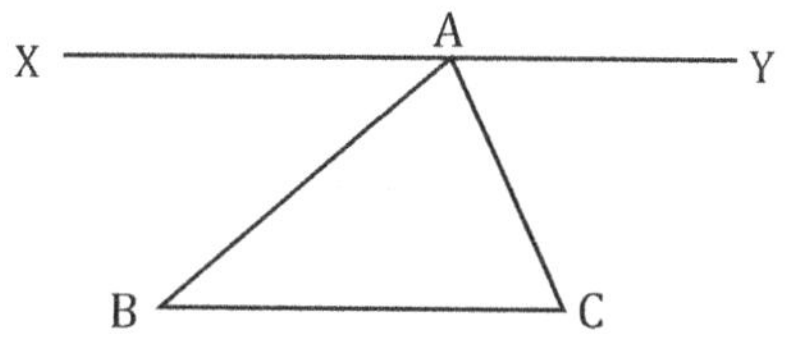


Thus, we have:

$\angle ABC = \angle XAB$, and $\angle ACB = \angle YAC$

Since XY is a straight line, we have:

$\angle XAB + \angle BAC + \angle YAC = 180^\circ$

$\Rightarrow \angle ABC + \angle BAC + \angle ACB = 180^\circ$

 

## 2.4 Polygons

A polygon is a closed figure bounded by line segments. Some common names of polygons:

A polygon with:

| | | |
|---|---|---|
| 3 sides = **triangle** | 6 sides = **hexagon** | 9 sides = **nonagon** |
| 4 sides = **quadrilateral** | 7 sides = **heptagon** | 10 sides = **decagon** |
| 5 sides = **pentagon** | 8 sides = **octagon** | Infinite sides = **circle** |

Nomenclature:

- A polygon with all sides equal AND all angles equal is called a **regular polygon**.
- A polygon with no interior angle greater than $180^\circ$ is called a **convex polygon**.
- A polygon with at least one interior angle greater than $180^\circ$ is called a **concave polygon**.

Let us look at the important points associated with polygons: If the number of sides of a polygon be $n$, we have:

<table>
<tr>
<td>1. Sum of all interior angles<br>$= (n-2) * 180^\circ$</td>
<td>Any polygon of $n$ sides can be broken down to $(n-2)$ non-overlapping triangles as shown:
<table>
<tr><td>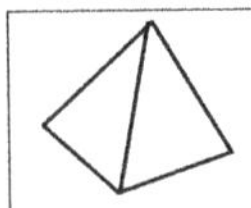</td><td>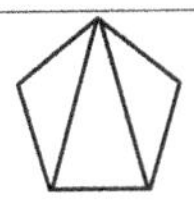</td><td>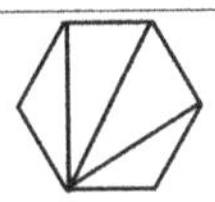</td></tr>
<tr><td>$n = 4$<br># of $\triangle$s<br>$= 4-2 = 2$</td><td>$n = 5$<br># of $\triangle$s<br>$= 5-2 = 3$</td><td>$n = 6$<br># of $\triangle$s<br>$= 6-2 = 4$</td></tr>
</table>
Thus, sum of interior angles is simply the sum of the angles of all $(n-2)$ triangles<br><br>$= (n-2) * 180^\circ$</td>
</tr>
<tr>
<td>2. Sum of all exterior angles<br>$= 360^\circ$</td>
<td>Sum of all exterior angles<br><br>= (Sum of all interior & exterior angles) - (Sum of interior angles)<br><br>$= n * 180^\circ - (n-2) * 180^\circ$<br><br>$= 360^\circ$</td>
</tr>
</table>

| | |
|---|---|
| 3. Number of diagonals $= \frac{n(n-3)}{2}$ | Number of diagonals<br><br>= (# of ways in which any two vertices of the polygon can be joined) - (# of sides)<br><br>$= C_2^n - n = \frac{n(n-1)}{2} - n$<br>$= \frac{n(n-3)}{2}$ |
| 4. Each interior angle of a regular polygon $= \frac{(n-2)*180^o}{n}$ | Each interior angle of a regular polygon<br>$= \frac{\text{Sum of all interior angles}}{\text{\# of angles}}$<br>$= \frac{(n-2)*180^o}{n}$ |
| 5. Each exterior angle of a regular polygon $= \frac{360^o}{n}$ | Each exterior angle of a regular polygon<br>$= \frac{\text{Sum of all exterior angles}}{\text{\# of angles}}$<br>$= \frac{360^o}{n}$ |
| 6. Area of a regular polygon $= \frac{1}{2}$ (perimeter) ($\perp$ from centre to a side) | Area of a regular polygon is simply the sum of the areas of $n$ triangles formed by joining the vertices to the centre of the polygon as shown:<br>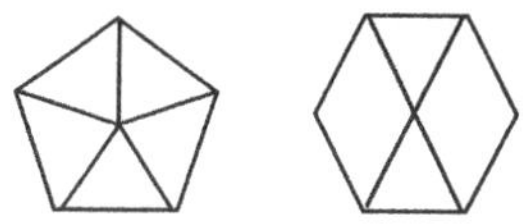<br>Thus, area of the polygon<br>$= n * \frac{1}{2} *$ (Side) $*$ ($\perp$ from centre to a side)<br>$= \frac{1}{2} *$ ($n*$Side) $*$ ($\perp$ from centre to a side)<br>$= \frac{1}{2}$ (perimeter) ($\perp$ from centre to a side) |

**Two special polygons:**

(1) **Regular Hexagon**: A regular hexagon is a polygon of six sides.

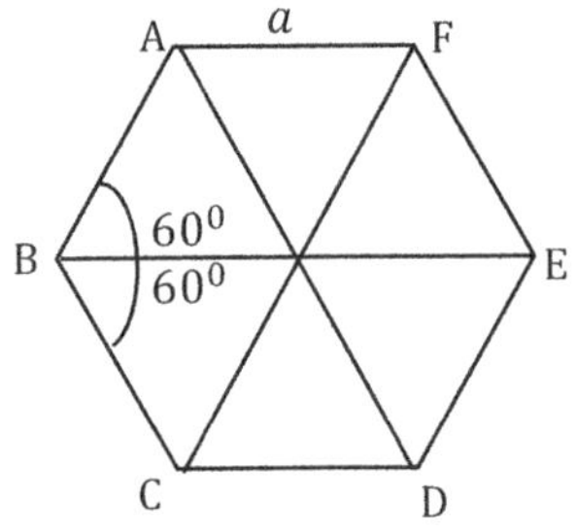


- All the six sides are of equal length
- Each interior angle is $120^0$
- Sum of Interior angles = $(6-2) \times 180^0 = 4 \times 180^0 = 720^0$
- It can be broken into six equilateral triangles

Thus, if each side of the regular hexagon is $a$, we have:

- **Perimeter = $6a$**
- **Area = $\frac{3\sqrt{3}}{2}a^2$**

(2) **Regular Octagon**: A regular octagon is a polygon of eight sides.

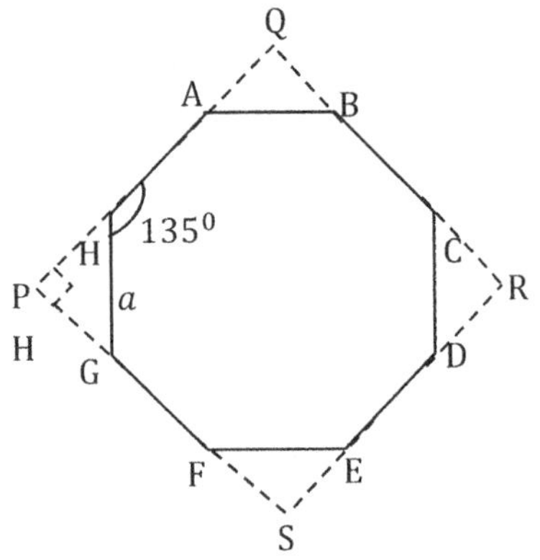


- All the eight sides are of equal length.
- Each interior angle is $135^0$
- Sum of Interior angles = $(8 - 2) * 180^0 = 6 * 180^0 = 1080^0$

To find the area, the dotted lines are constructed.

△PHG is right-angled isosceles (45-45-90).

 

Since GH = $a$, PH = PG = $\frac{a}{\sqrt{2}}$.

Thus, QA = PH = $\frac{a}{\sqrt{2}}$. Hence, QP = $a + \frac{2a}{\sqrt{2}} = a\left(1 + \sqrt{2}\right)$.

Area of octagon = Area of square PQRS – Area of 4 corner $\triangle$s

$$= PQ^2 - 4 \text{ x } \frac{1}{2} \text{ x PH x PG} = \left(a\left(1 + \sqrt{2}\right)\right)^2 - 4 \text{ x } \frac{1}{2} \text{ x } \left(\frac{a}{\sqrt{2}}\right)^2 = 2\left(1 + \sqrt{2}\right)a^2$$

Thus, if each side of the regular hexagon is $a$, we have:

- **Perimeter = 8$a$**
- **Area = 2 $\left(1+\sqrt{2}\right)$ $a^2$**

## 2.5 Quadrilateral

A quadrilateral has four sides and sum of all four angles is $360^o$.

Let us look at the properties of the main quadrilaterals:

(1) **Parallelogram:** The properties are given below:

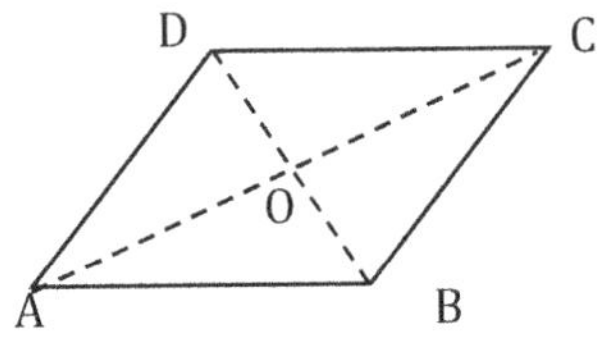


- Opposite sides are parallel and equal: $AB||CD$, $AB = CD$, $AD||BC$, $AD = BC$
- Opposite angles are equal: $\angle A = \angle C$, $\angle B = \angle D$
- Diagonals bisect each other: $AO = OC$, $BO = DO$
- Sum of any two adjacent angles $= 180^o$: $\angle A + \angle D = 180^o$, $\angle C + \angle B = 180^o$
- Straight lines joining the midpoints of adjacent sides of any quadrilateral form a parallelogram
- Area = Base * Height

(2) **Rectangle:** All the above properties of a parallelogram hold true for a rectangle. However, there are few additional properties:

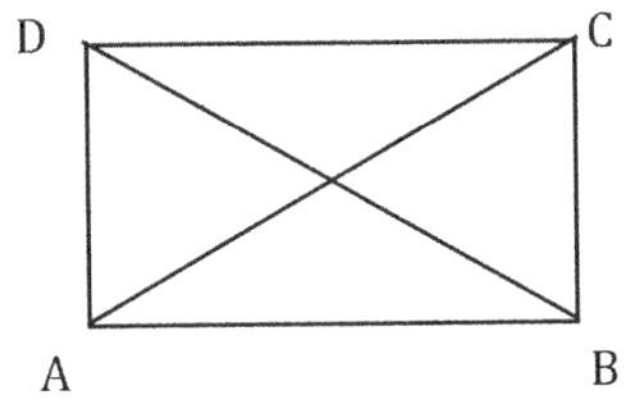


- All angles are equal and equal to a right angle: $\angle A = \angle B = \angle C = \angle D = 90^o$
- Diagonals are equal: $AC = BD$
- Perimeter = 2(Length + Breadth)
- Area = Length * Width
- Length of Diagonal $= \sqrt{\text{Length}^2 + \text{Breadth}^2}$

(3) **Rhombus:** All the properties of a parallelogram hold true for a rhombus. However, there are some additional properties:

 

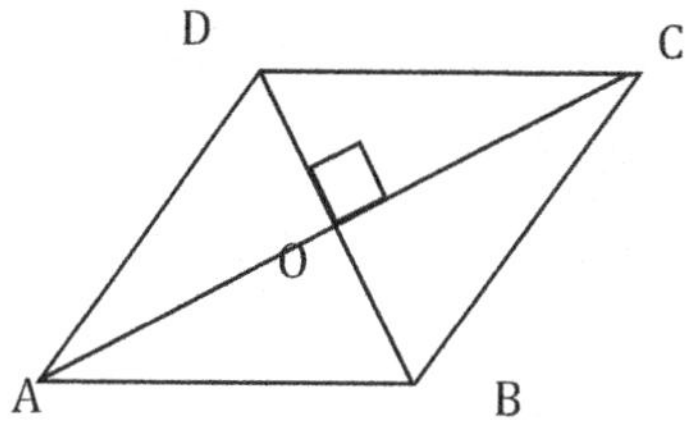


- All sides are equal: AB = BC = CD = DA
- The diagonals bisect each other at right angles: $\angle DOC = 90^{o}$
- The diagonals bisect the angles at the vertex: $\angle BAC = \angle DAC$, etc.
- Area = $\frac{1}{2}$ ∗ (Product of the diagonals) $= \frac{1}{2} * AC * BD$

**Note**: Area of any quadrilateral having diagonals perpendicular to one another can be calculated as $\frac{1}{2}$ ∗ (Product of the diagonals)

(4) **Square:** All the properties mentioned above for all the figures hold true for a square.

Thus, we have:

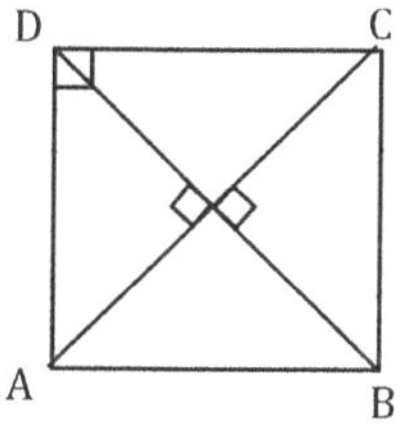


- All sides are equal: AB = BC = CD = DA
- All angles are right angles.
- The diagonals are equal and bisect each other at right angles.
- Perimeter of a square = $4a$, where $a$ is the length of a side.
- Length of a diagonal = $a\sqrt{2}$
- Area = $(\text{Side})^2 = \frac{1}{2} * (\text{Diagonal})^2 = a^2$

(5) **Trapezium:** A trapezium has only one pair of opposite sides parallel.

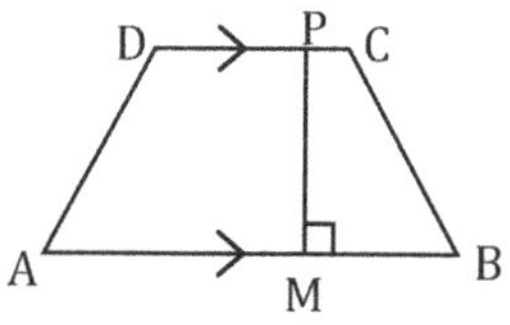

- Area $= \frac{1}{2} * (\text{Sum of} \parallel \text{sides}) * (\text{Distance between} \parallel \text{sides}) = \frac{1}{2} * (AB + CD) * MP$

**Maximum / minimum area of quadrilaterals:**

- Among all quadrilaterals with the same area, the square has the least perimeter.
- Among all quadrilaterals with the same perimeter, the square has the greatest area.

 

## 2.6 Circles

Let us look at the important points associated with circles:

| | |
|---|---|
| 1. Tangent is perpendicular to the radius i.e. AB ⊥ OA<br><br>2. Perpendicular from the centre bisects the chord i.e. OZ bisects XY<br><br>3. Similarly, if Z is the mid-point of XY, then OZ is perpendicular to XY | 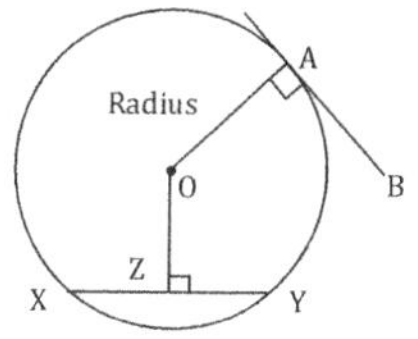<br>O: Centre of the circle, OA: Radius AB: Tangent, XY: Chord |
| 4. Tangent segments drawn to a circle from an external point are equal i.e. PR = PQ | 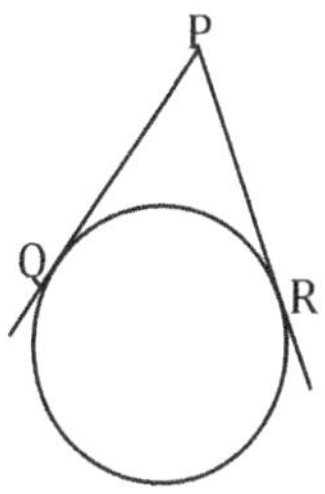 |
| 5. Angle subtended at the centre by an arc (QR) is equal to twice the angle made by the same arc at any other point on the remaining circumference<br><br>=> $\angle QOR = 2 * \angle QPR$ | 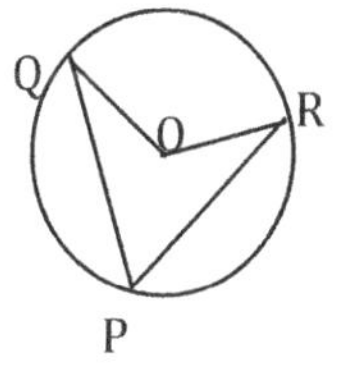 |
| 6. The angle between a tangent (QP) and a chord (RP) at the point of contact (P) is equal to the angle in the alternate segment<br><br>=> $\angle QPR = \angle PSR$<br><br>7. As a result of the above, triangles PRQ and SPQ are similar, which gives us:<br><br>$PQ^2 = SQ * RQ$ | 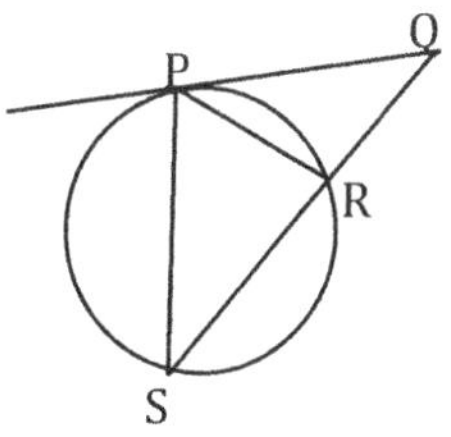 |

 

| | |
|---|---|
| 8. If two chords intersect:<br><br>AE * BE = CE * DE | 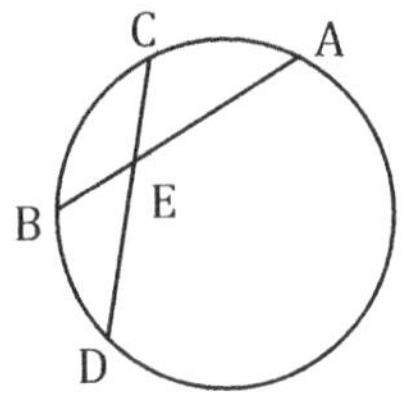 |
| 9. Area of a circle of radius $r = \pi r^2$<br><br>10. Circumference of the above circle = $2\pi r$<br><br>11. Length of the arc subtending angle $\theta$ at the centre of a circle of radius $r$<br><br>$= \left(\frac{\theta}{360}\right) * 2\pi r$<br><br>12. Area of the sector formed by the above arc<br><br>$= \left(\frac{\theta}{360}\right) * \pi r^2$<br>$= \frac{1}{2} * r * \left\{\left(\frac{\theta}{360}\right) * 2\pi r\right\}$<br>$= \frac{1}{2} * r *$ (Length of arc)<br><br>13. Perimeter of the sector above<br><br>= (Length of the arc) + (2 * Radius)<br><br>$= \left(\frac{\theta}{360}\right) * 2\pi r + 2r$ | 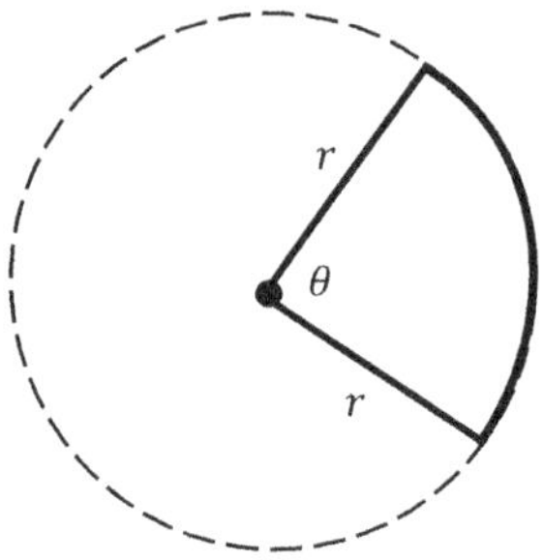 |

**Maximum / minimum area of any polygon:**

- Among all polygons with the same perimeter, the circle has the maximum area.
- Among all polygons with the same area, the circle has the least perimeter.

## 2.7 3-D Geometry

We will consider different solid shapes in this section.

First let us understand what we mean by a prism and a pyramid.

**Right Prism:** A prism is a shape that has the same uniform cross-section at any point of its height. A right prism is a prism whose lateral edges are perpendicular to the base.

- **Volume of a prism** = Area of base * Height
- **Lateral surface area** = Perimeter of base * Height
- **Total surface area** = Lateral surface area + Base area(s)

Examples of prisms: Triangular prism, Rectangular prism (Cuboid/Cube), Circular prism (Cylinder), etc.

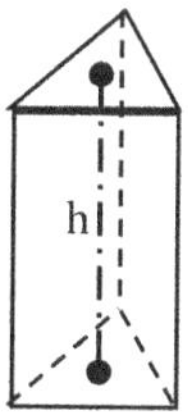

Triangular Prism

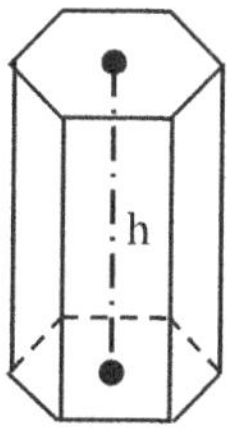

Hexagonal Prism

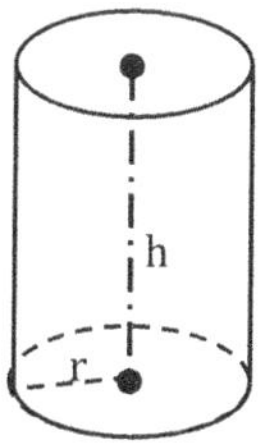

Circular Prism

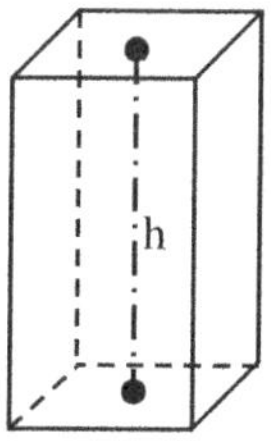

Rectangular Prism

**Right Pyramid:** A pyramid is a shape whose area of cross-section decreases at a uniform rate till it converges to a point, called the vertex. A pyramid whose base is a regular polygon, the center of which coincides with the foot of the perpendicular dropped from the vertex on base is called right pyramid.

- **Volume of a pyramid** = $\frac{1}{3}$ * Area of base * Height
- **Lateral surface area** = $\frac{1}{2}$ * Perimeter of base * Slant height
- **Total surface area** = Lateral surface area + Base area

Examples of pyramids: Triangular pyramid, Rectangular pyramid, Circular pyramid (Cone), etc.

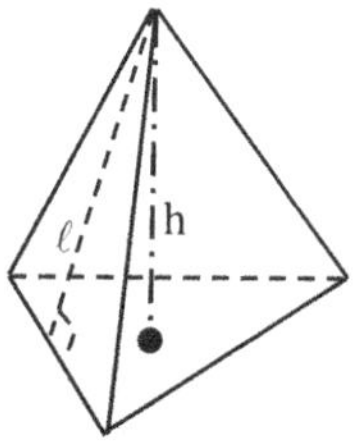

Triangular pyramid

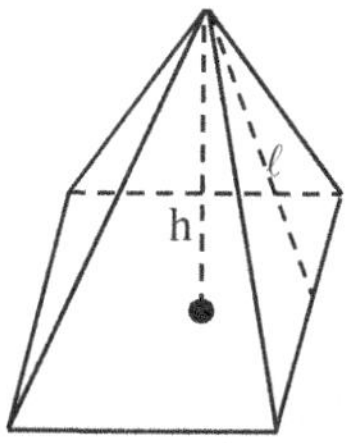

Square pyramid

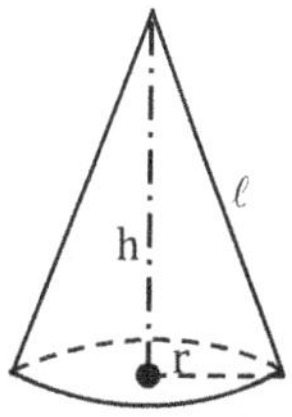

Circular pyramid

 

**Few important 3-D figures:**

(1) **Cuboid:** A cuboid is a prism having six rectangular faces.

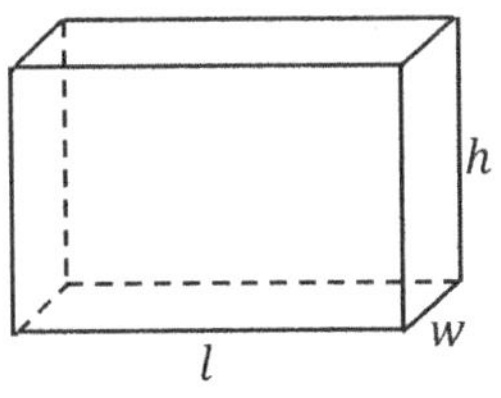


- **Volume** = $l * w * h$, where $l$ = length, $w$ = width, $h$ = height

  = $\sqrt{\text{Product of areas of the mutually perpendicular faces}}$

  = $\sqrt{(lw)(wh)(lh)} = lwh$

- **Area of four walls** = $2(l + w) * h$
- **Total surface area** = $2(lw + wh + lh)$
- **Body Diagonal** = $\sqrt{(l^2 + w^2 + h^2)}$

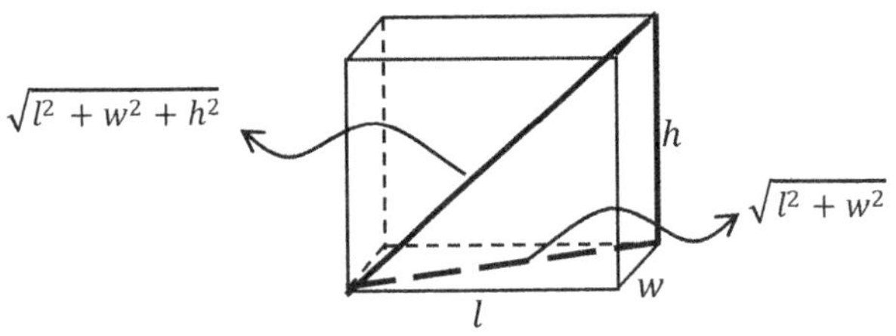


The 'Body Diagonal' is the longest line joining any two vertices of the cuboid.

(2) **Cube:** A prism whose every face is a square is called a cube.

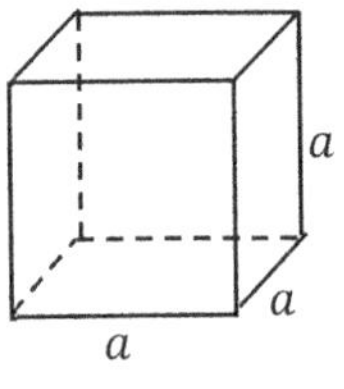


- **Volume** = $a^3$,where $a$ = edge of the cube
- **Total surface area of the cube** = Area of 6 squares of area $a^2 = 6a^2$
- **Body Diagonal of a cube** = $a\sqrt{3}$

 

(3) **Cylinder:** If a rectangle is revolved about one of its sides as the axis, the solid thus formed is a right circular cylinder.

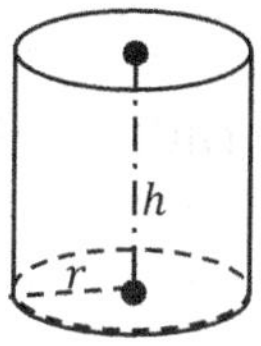


- **Volume** = $\pi r^2 h$, where r = radius of base, h = height
- **Curved surface area** = $2\pi r h$
- **Total surface area** = $2\pi r\,(r + h)$
- **Longest distance between two points** = $\sqrt{(2r)^2 + h^2}$

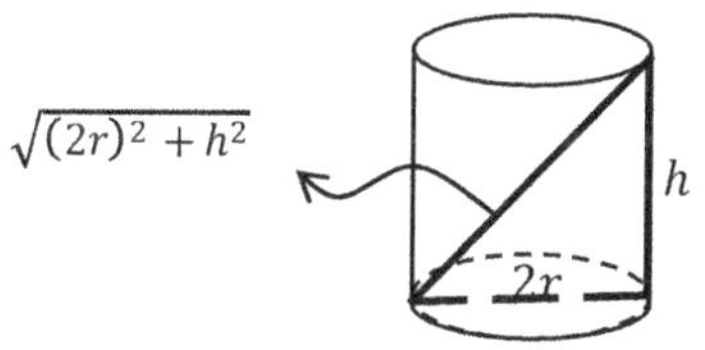


(4) **Cone:** If a right triangle is revolved about one of its sides containing the right angle as the axis the solid formed is called a cone.

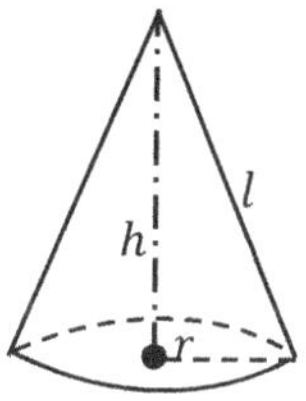


- **Volume** = $\frac{1}{3}\pi r^2 h$, where $r$ = radius of base, $h$ = height
- **Curved surface area** = $\pi r l$ where $l$ = slant height = $\sqrt{(r^2 + h^2)}$
- **Total surface area** = $\pi r(r + l)$

(5) **Sphere:** When a circle is revolved about its diameter, the solid thus formed is called a sphere.

- **Volume** = $\frac{4}{3}\pi r^3$, where $r$ = radius of the sphere
- **Surface area** = $4\pi r^2$

**Note:** The GMAT seldom asks you questions applying the formulae for volume or surface area of the sphere, cone or pyramids in general. However, you should remember that the volume of a cone is proportional to $r^2h$ and that for the sphere is proportional to $r^3$.

**Solids inside other solids:**

(1) If a largest possible sphere is circumscribed by a cube of edge '$a$', the radius of the sphere $= \frac{a}{2}$

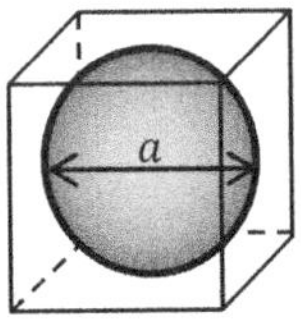


(2) If a largest possible cube is inscribed in a sphere of radius '$r$', then the diameter of the sphere equals the body diagonal of the cube (AB)

$=> 2r = \sqrt{3} * \text{(Side of the cube)}$

$=> \text{Side of the cube} = \frac{2r}{\sqrt{3}}$

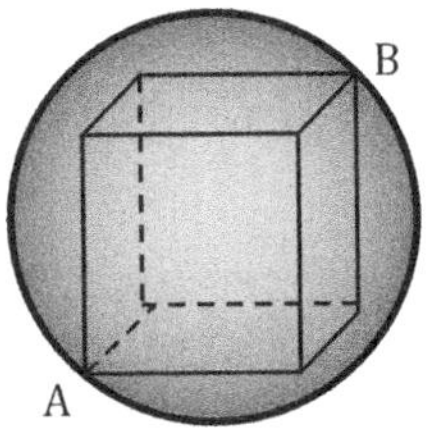


(3) If a largest possible sphere is inscribed in a cylinder of radius '$r$' and height '$h$', then:

- If $h > r$: Radius of sphere $= r$

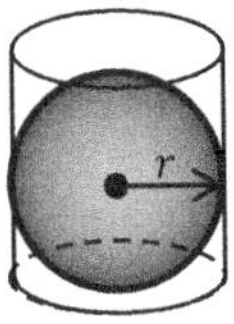


- If $r > h$: Radius of sphere $= \frac{h}{2}$

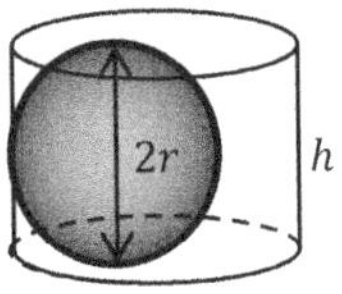


 

## 2.8 Co-ordinate Geometry

**Rectangular axes:** The figure shows the XY Cartesian plane. The line XOX′ is called the X-axis and YOY′ the Y-axis. A point P $(x, y)$ in the plane denotes the X-value or ***abscissa*** $(x)$and the Y-value or the ***ordinate*** $(y)$ of point P.

The plane is divided into four equal parts by the two axes; these parts are called **Quadrants** (I, II, III, and IV).

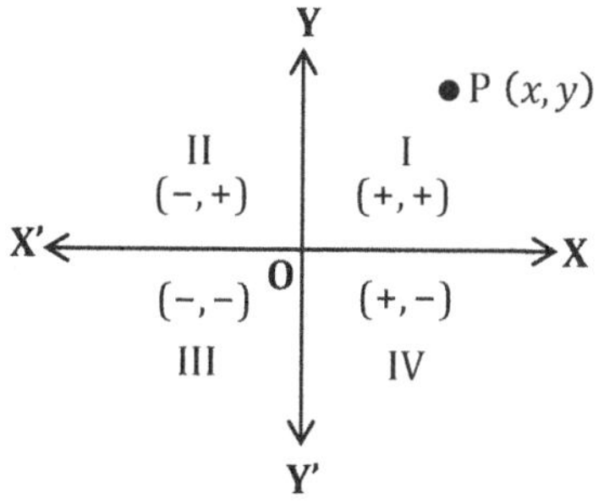


**Let us have a look a few important formulae in coordinate geometry:**

1. **Distance between Two Given Points:**

The distance between any two points P $(x_1, y_1)$ and Q $(x_2, y_2)$:

$PQ = \sqrt{PM^2 + QM^2}$

$=> \boldsymbol{PQ = \sqrt{(x_2 - x_1)^2 + (y_2 - y_1)^2}}$

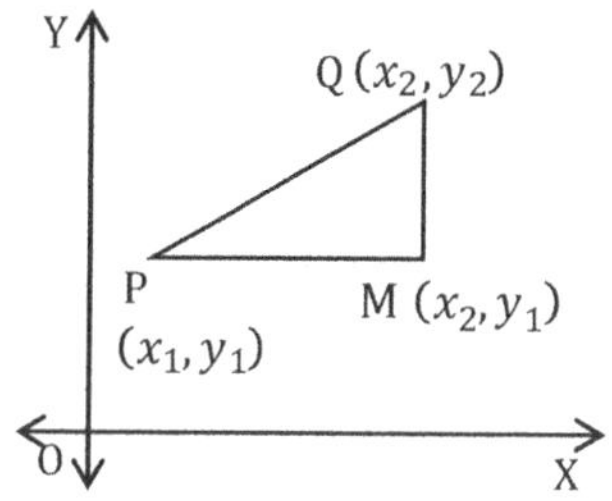

2. **Section Formulae:**

- **Internal Ratio**: If P divides the line joining A $(x_1, y_1)$ and B $(x_2, y_2)$ internally in the ratio of $m : n$, i.e. $\frac{AP}{PB} = \frac{m}{n}$, we have:

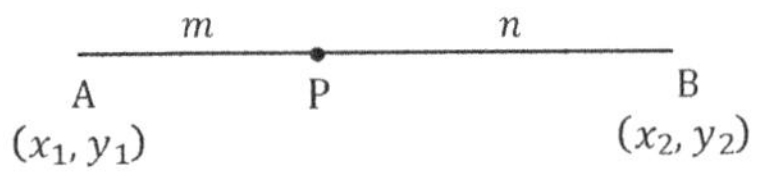


  Coordinates of P:

  $$\left(\frac{mx_2+nx_1}{m+n}, \frac{my_2+ny_1}{m+n}\right)$$

  **Mid-Point:** Mid-point of a line joining the points $(x_1, y_1)$ & $(x_2, y_2)$:

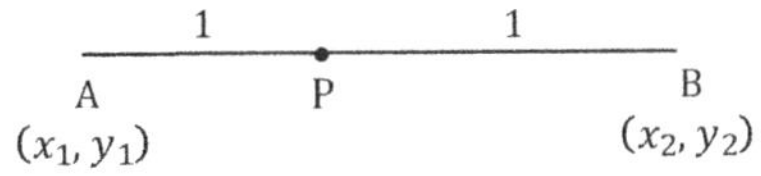


  $$\left(\frac{x_1+x_2}{2}, \frac{y_1+y_2}{2}\right)$$

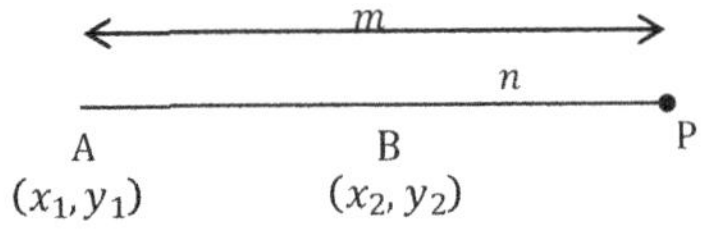


- **External Ratio**: If P divides the line joining A $(x_1, y_1)$ and B $(x_2, y_2)$ externally in the ratio of $m : n$, i.e. $\frac{AP}{PB} = \frac{m}{n}$, we have:

  Coordinates of P:

  $$\left(\frac{mx_2-nx_1}{m-n}, \frac{my_2-ny_1}{m-n}\right)$$

**Important points:**

- The X-axis divides the line joining the points $(x_1, y_1)$ and $(x_2, y_2)$ in the ratio $y_1 : y_2$
- The Y-axis divides the line joining the points $(x_1, y_1)$ and $(x_2, y_2)$ in the ratio $x_1 : x_2$

3. **Slope of the line joining two points:**

The slope of the line joining the two points P $(x_1, y_1)$ and Q $(x_2, y_2)$ is given by:

$\boldsymbol{m = tan\ \theta = \frac{y_2 - y_1}{x_2 - x_1}}$; where$\theta$ = angle subtended by the line at X-axis, measured anti-clockwise

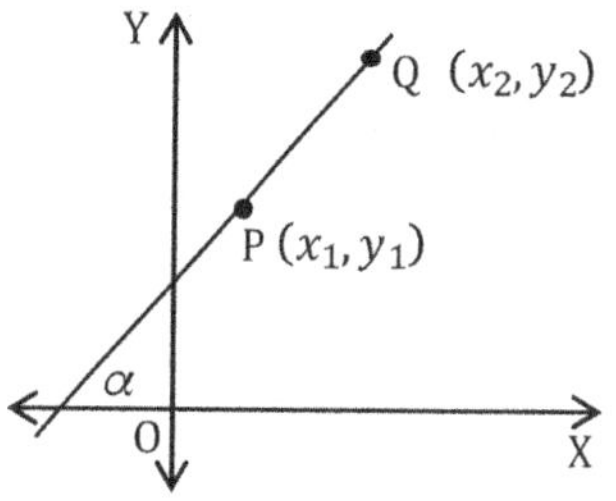


**Important points:**

- The slope of a line parallel to X-axis is zero and that of a line parallel to Y-axis is undefined (infinite).
- The equation of a straight line parallel to the X-axis is $y = a$, where $a$ is a constant.
- The equation of a straight line parallel to the Y-axis is $x = b$, where $b$ is a constant.

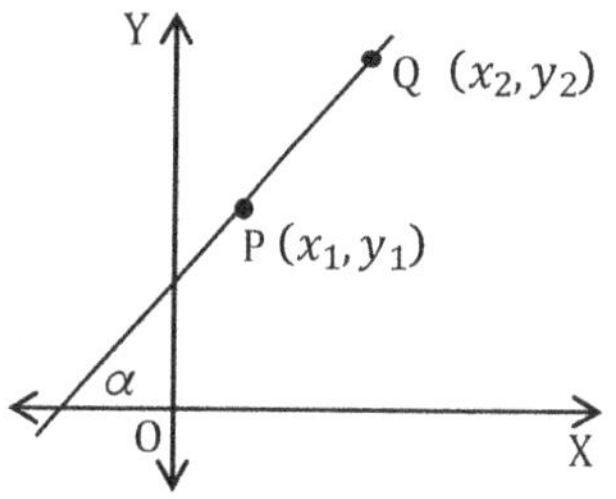


Two major aspects of coordinate geometry are straight lines, circles and parabola. Let us discuss them one by one.

A. **Straight Line:** The straight line is represented by the first degree equation $ax + by = k$, where $a$, $b$ and $k$ are constants and $a$, $b$ are not simultaneously zero.

Note: If $k$ = 0tr, then the line passes through the "Origin (0, 0)".

(a) **Equation of a line passing through two points:**

The equation of a line passing through two points $(x_1, y_1)$ and $(x_2, y_2)$ is:

$$\boldsymbol{\frac{y - y_1}{y_1 - y_2} = \frac{x - x_1}{x_1 - x_2}}$$

$$=> \frac{y - y_1}{x - x_1} = \frac{y_1 - y_2}{x_1 - x_2} => \frac{y - y_1}{x - x_1} = m$$

$$=> \boldsymbol{(y - y_1) = m(x - x_1)}$$

(b) **Equation of a line in Slope Intercept Form:**

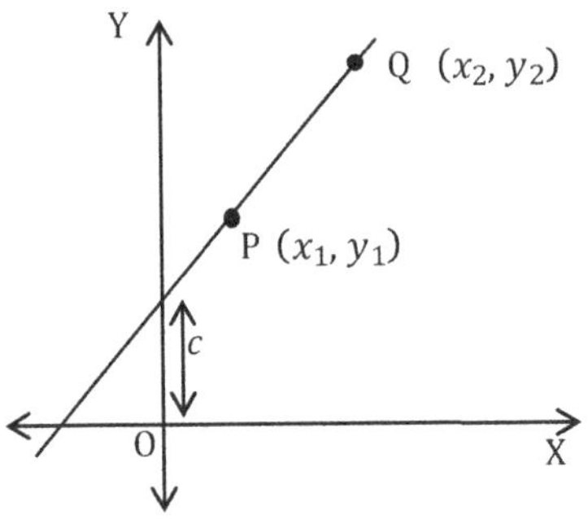


We have: $(y - y_1) = m(x - x_1)$

$=> y - y_1 = mx - mx_1 => y = mx + (y_1 - mx_1)$

$=> \boldsymbol{y = mx + c}$

Here, $c = y_1 - mx_1$ is the intercept made by the line on the Y-axis.

**Some important points:**

- Two lines are PARALLEL if their SLOPES are EQUAL

  Thus, a line parallel to $y = mx + c$ would be $y = mx + c'$
  Similarly, a line parallel to $ax + by = k$ would be $ax + by = k'$
  Similarly, if two lines: $y = m_1x + c$ & $y = m_2x + c'$ are parallel, then: $\boldsymbol{m_1 = m_2}$

- Two lines are PERPENDICULAR if the PRODUCT of their SLOPES is **−1**.

  Thus, a line perpendicular to $y = mx + c$ would be $y = \left(-\frac{1}{m}\right)x + c'$
  Similarly, a line perpendicular to $ax + by = k$ would be $bx - ay = k'$
  Similarly, if two lines: $y = m_1x + c$ & $y = m_2x + c'$ are perpendicular, then: $\boldsymbol{m_1 * m_2 = -1}$

(c) **Equation of a line in Intercept Form:**

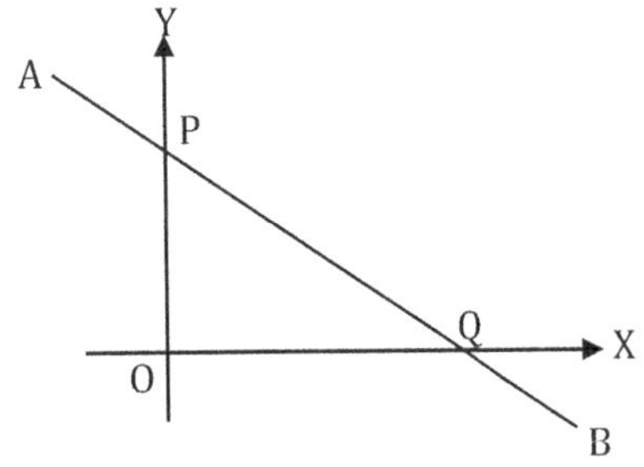


 

General equation of a line: $ax + by = k$

This equation can be modified as follows:

$$ax + by = k \Rightarrow \frac{ax}{k} + \frac{by}{k} = 1 \Rightarrow \frac{x}{\left(\frac{k}{a}\right)} + \frac{y}{\left(\frac{k}{b}\right)} = 1$$

Here $\left(\frac{k}{a}\right)$ and $\left(\frac{k}{b}\right)$ are the X and Y intercepts as represented by the points P and Q respectively. If the intercepts are taken as '$m$' and '$n$' respectively, we have:

$$\frac{x}{m} + \frac{y}{n} = 1$$

**Note:** The AREA of the triangle formed by the line and the axes is $\left(\frac{mn}{2}\right)$ square units.

(d) **Distance of a point from a line:**

Perpendicular distance of $(x_1, y_1)$ from $ax + by = k \Rightarrow ax + by - k = 0$, is:

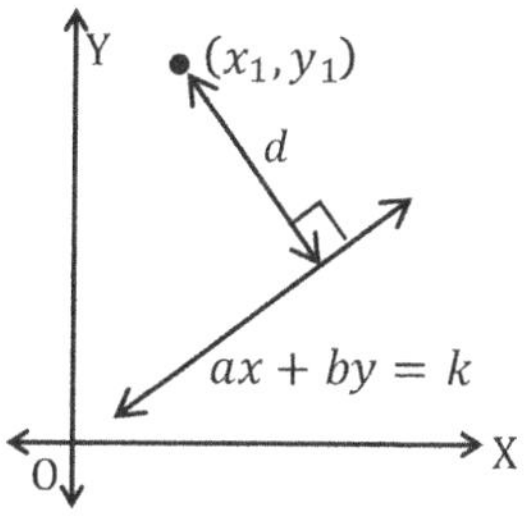


$$d = \left|\frac{ax_1 + by_1 - k}{\sqrt{a^2 + b^2}}\right|$$

Note: The use of the above formula is rarely required. One may use it effectively to find the length of the side of a square, etc.

**B. Circle:** Let P $(x, y)$ be a point on the circle having radius $r$ with centre at Origin $(0, 0)$.

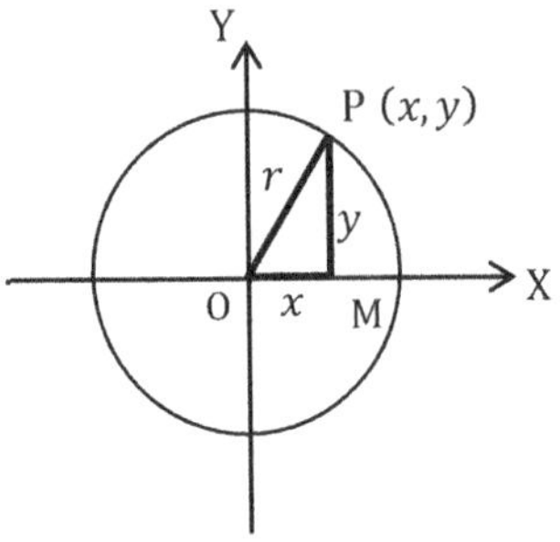


Applying Pythagoras' theorem in triangle PMO, we have:

$\boldsymbol{x^2+y^2=r^2}$, which is the equation of the circle

**C. Parabola:** Parabolic graphs are basically the graph of quadratic functions.
The general quadratic expression is: $y = ax^2 + bx + c$, where $c$ is the Y-intercept.
We can broadly classify quadratic expressions in the following six main categories:

$ax^2 + bx + c \ (a > 0)$

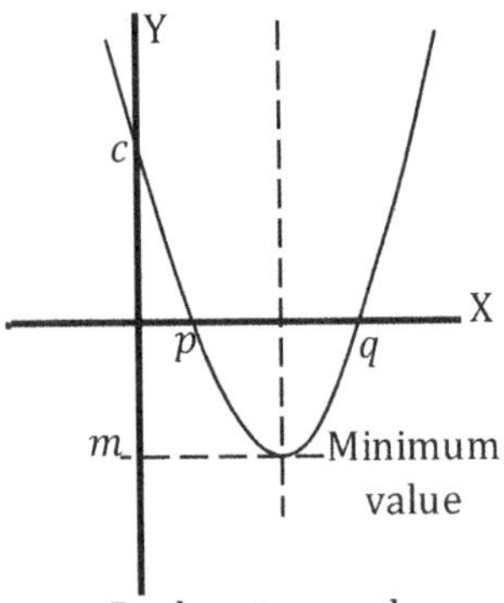


Real roots $p$ and $q$
Value of $m$ is negative

$ax^2 + bx + c \ (a > 0)$

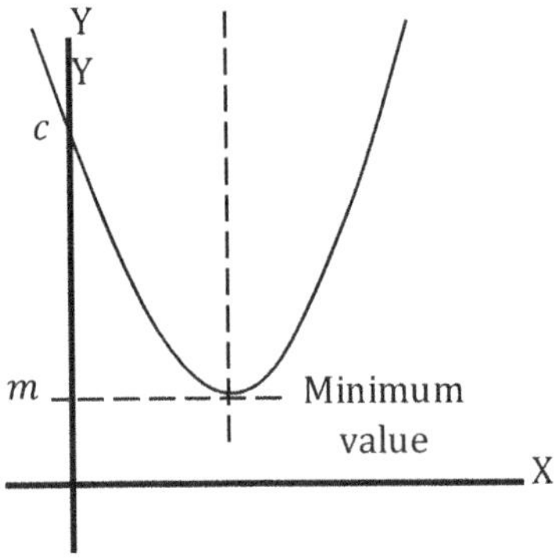


Imaginary roots
Value of $m$ is positive

$ax^2 + bx + c \ (a > 0)$

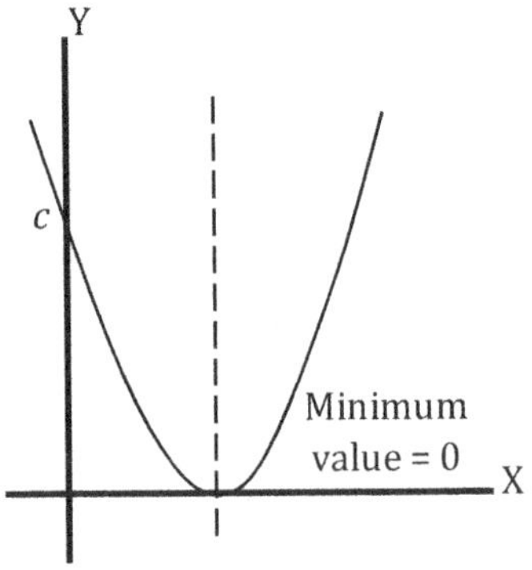


Single real root
Value of $m$ is zero

$ax^2 + bx + c \ (a < 0)$

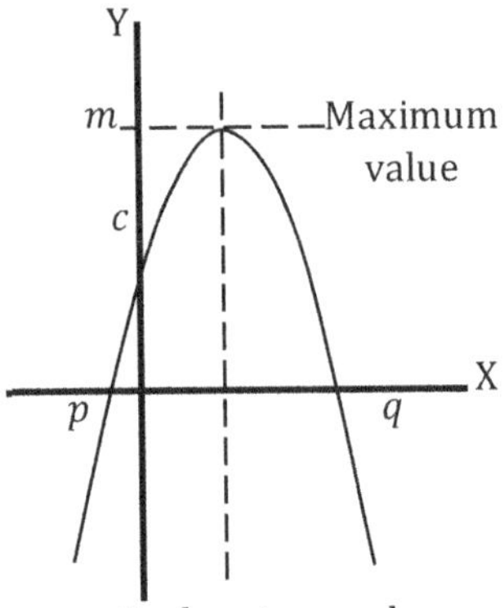


Real roots $p$ and $q$
Value of $m$ is positive

$ax^2 + bx + c \ (a < 0)$

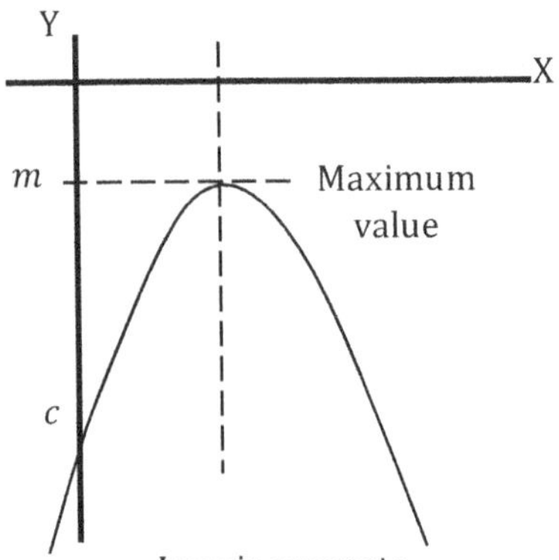


Imaginary roots
Value of $m$ is negative

$ax^2 + bx + c \ (a < 0)$

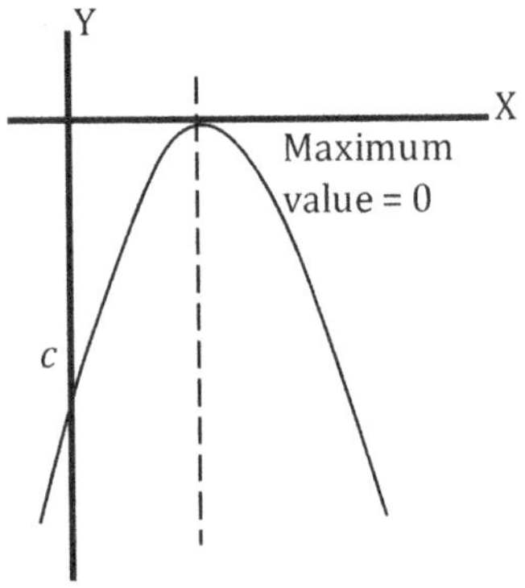


Single real root
Value of $m$ is zero

 

**A few points to keep in mind:**

(1) **Position of a point with respect to a line/region:**
Let us understand this with an example.

Let us say, we have a line: $2x + 3y = 5$ and two points $(3, -4)$ and $(2, 1)$.

We need to determine whether the points lie on the same side of the line or on opposite sides of the line.

- **First point**: We substitute $x = 3, y = -4$ on the LHS of the equation of the line and compare the LHS and RHS.

  Thus, we have: LHS $= 2 * 3 + 3 * (-4) = -6 <$ RHS

- **Second point**: We substitute $x = 2, y = 1$ on the LHS of the equation of the line and compare the LHS and RHS.

  Thus, we have: LHS $= 2 * 2 + 3 * 1 = 7 >$ RHS

Since the two points have different inequalities, they lie on opposite sides of the line. However, had they resulted in the same inequality, they would have been on the same side of the line.

(2) **Intersection of two lines:** To find the intersecting point of two lines, we need to solve them simultaneously. Let us understand this with two examples.

- Intersection of two straight lines: Let the two straight line equations be $2x + 3y = 13$ and $4x - y = 5$

  Multiplying the second equation with '3' and adding to the first equation, we eliminate $y$ and get: $14x = 28 \Rightarrow x = 2$. Substituting $x = 2$ in the second equation, we have: $y = 4 * 2 - 5 = 3$

  Thus, the two straight lines intersect at $(2, 3)$.

- Intersection of a straight line and a parabola: Let the equation of the straight line be $x + y = 4$ and that of the parabola (quadratic) be $y = x^2 + 2$.

  Substituting $y = 4 - x$, obtained from the first equation, in the second, we have: $4 - x = x^2 + 2 \Rightarrow x^2 + x - 2 = 0 \Rightarrow (x + 2)(x - 1) = 0 \Rightarrow x = -2$ or 1 If $x = -2 : y = 4 - (-2) = 6$ and if $x = 1 : y = 4 - 1 = 3$

  Thus, the two lines intersect at $(-2, 6)$ and $(1, 3)$.

(3) **Slope of lines depending upon orientation:**

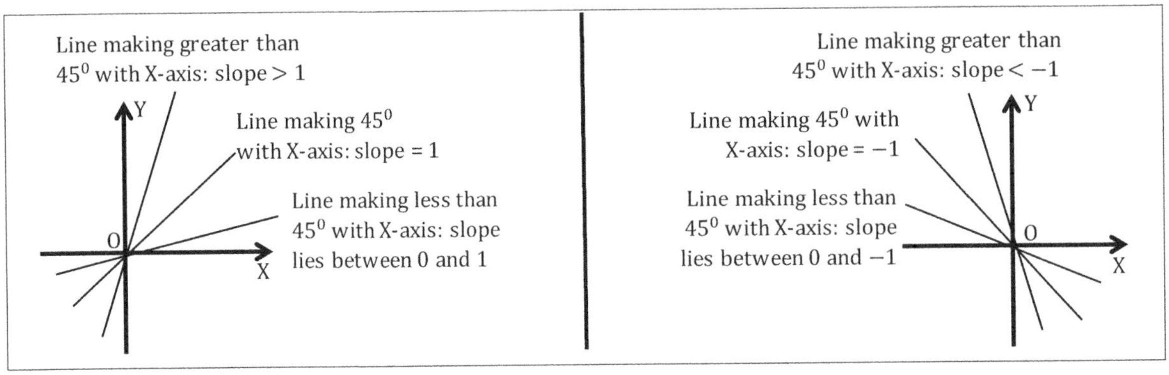
Line making greater than
$45^0$ with X-axis: slope > 1
Y
Line making $45^0$
with X-axis: slope = 1
Line making less than
$45^0$ with X-axis: slope
lies between 0 and 1
O
X
Line making greater than
$45^0$ with X-axis: slope < −1
Y
Line making $45^0$ with
X-axis: slope = −1
Line making less than
$45^0$ with X-axis: slope
lies between 0 and −1
O
X

 

## 2.9 Concept questions

### 2.9.1 Lines and Angles

(1) In the figure given below, line AB is parallel to line CG and $\angle FEC = 123^o$. If BE = CE and $\angle GCD = 75^o$, find $\angle ABF$.

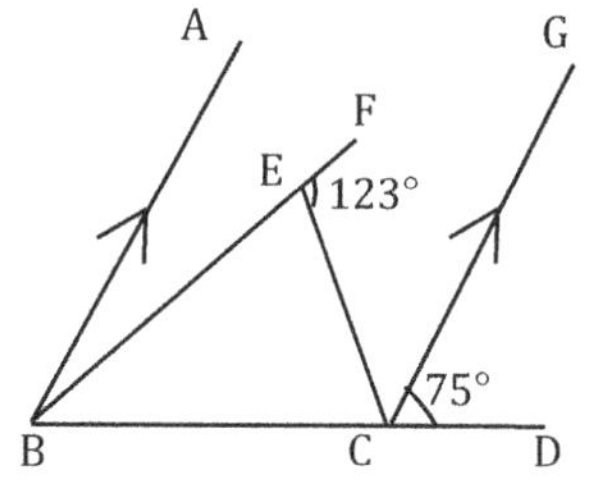


In the problem, we see a pair of parallel lines AB and CG.

Also, we see an external angle of triangle BEC, which is isosceles
(given that BE = CE)

Thus, the main three things we should focus on are:

- Are there any corresponding or alternate angles?
- Which angles of the isosceles triangle are equal?
- External angle of a triangle equals the sum of opposite interior angles

Let us now solve the problem.

We know that:

AB || CG
=> $\angle GCD = \angle ABC = 75^o$ (Corresponding angles)

Now, BE = CE
=> $\angle EBC = \angle ECB$ (Angles opposites to equal sides would be equal)

Also, $\angle FEC = \angle CBE + \angle ECB$
(External angle of a triangle equals the sum of opposite interior angles)

=> $123^o = 2\angle EBC$
=> $\angle EBC = 61.5^o$
=> $\angle ABF = 75^o - 61.5^o = 13.5^o$

(2) In the figure, if PQ = PR = RS, ST = RT and $\angle STU = 120^o$, what is the value of $x$?

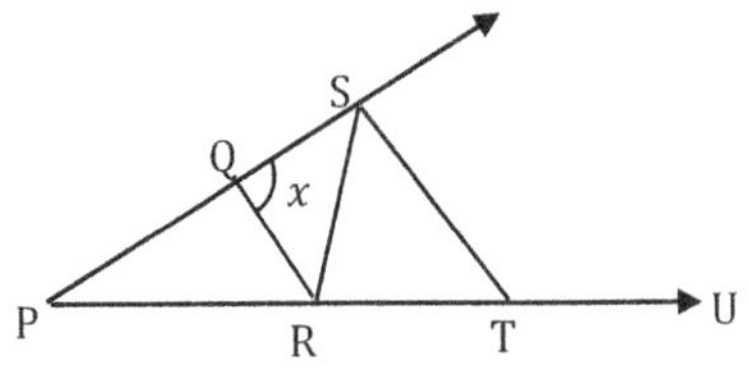


In the problem, we see a number of lines equal.

Thus, the main things we should focus on are:

- Are there any isosceles triangles?
- Are there any equilateral triangles?

Let us now solve the problem.

$\angle STR = 180^o - 120^o = 60^o$

Since ST = RT, triangle TSR is isosceles

$$=> \angle TSR = \angle TRS = \frac{(180^o - 60^o)}{2} = 60^o$$

Note: Triangle STR is thus equilateral

$\angle SRP = 180^o - 60^o = 120^o$

Since RS = PR, triangle SRP is isosceles

$$=> \angle RPS = \angle RSP = \frac{(180^o - 120^o)}{2} = 30^o$$

Again, since PQ = PR, triangle QRP is isosceles

$$=> \angle RQP = \angle QRP = \frac{(180^o - 30^o)}{2} = 75^o$$

Since $x$ is the external angle of triangle PQR:

$=> x = \angle RPQ + \angle QRP = 30^o + 75^o = 105^o$

(3) In the given figure, AB is parallel to CD and BC is parallel to DF, if $\angle ABC = 45^o$ and EDF = $40^o$, then find the measure of CDE.

 

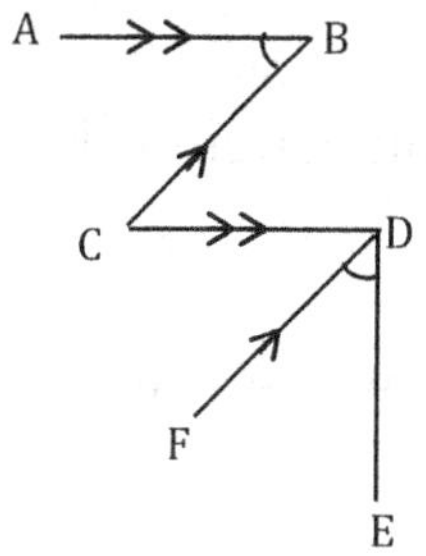


In the problem, we see two pairs of parallel lines.

Thus, the main thing we should focus on is:

- Are there any corresponding or alternate angles?

Let us now solve the problem.

It is given that: ABC = $45^{\circ}$

=> BCD = $45^{\circ}$ (Alternate angles, AB parallel to CD)

=> CDF = $45^{\circ}$ (Alternate angles, BC parallel to FD)

It is given that: EDF = $40^{\circ}$

=> CDE = $45^{\circ} + 40^{\circ} = 85^{\circ}$

 

### 2.9.2 Triangles

(4) How many different triangles with a perimeter of 15 can be constructed that have sides as integer values?

In the problem, we see that the perimeter of a triangle is known and we need to find possible triangles.

Thus, the main things we should focus on are:

- Relation of a side of triangle and the perimeter
- Sum of any two sides of the triangle must be greater than the third side

Let us now solve the problem.

Perimeter = 15

Since each side of a triangle is less than half the perimeter, we have:
Each side must be less than $\frac{15}{2} = 7.5$

Thus, the maximum length of a side is 7 cm (Since the sides are integers).

Also, sum of any two sides must be greater than the third side.

Thus, the sides of the possible triangles are:
(7,7,1), (7,6,2), (7,5,3), (7,4,4), (6,6,3), (6,5,4), (5,5,5)

Thus, there are seven different triangles possible.

(5) If ray CX bisects $\angle$ACB, which of the following is true?

A) BC = BX B) BC < BX
C) BC > BX D) AX = BX

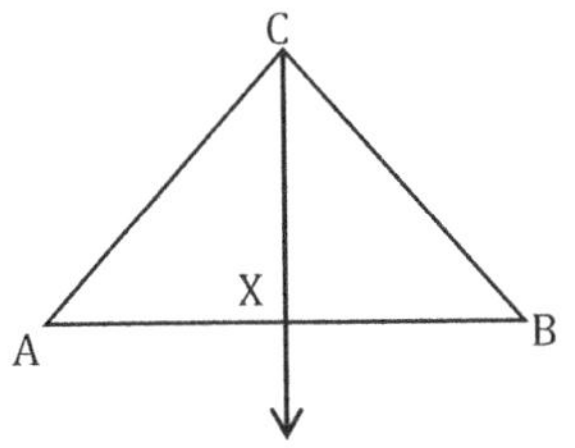

In the problem, we see that there is an angle bisector.

Also, we need to choose an option which states an inequality or equality.

Thus, the main three things we should focus on are:

- Is there any isosceles triangle which we can use to prove the equality?
- Since there is an inequality in the options, we should focus on the inequality regarding the sides of a triangle
- Can we compare the angles of a triangle and from there derive the inequality of the sides?

Let us now solve the problem.

$\angle CXB$ is the exterior angle of $\Delta ACX$

=> $\angle ACX = \angle BCX$

Hence, $\angle CXB = \angle ACX + \angle CAX$

=> $\angle CXB > \angle ACX$

=> $\angle CXB > \angle BCX$

=> $BC > BX$
(Since the largest side of a triangle is opposite to the largest angle of the triangle)

Hence, option (C) is the correct answer.

(6) If each side of $\Delta ACD$ has length 3 and if AB has length 1, then what is the area of region BCDE?

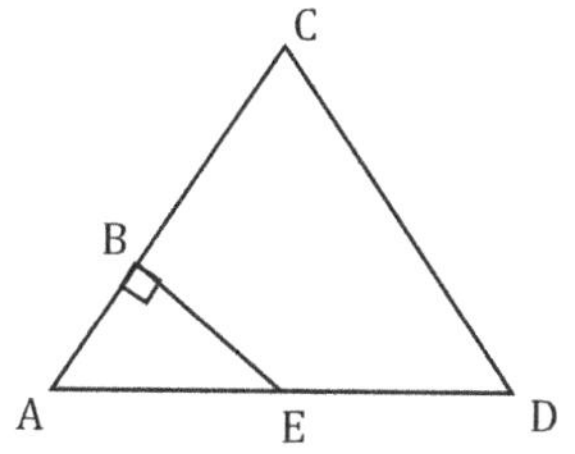


In the problem, we see that there is an equilateral triangle

Also, we need to find the area of a region.

Thus, the main two things we should focus on are:

- Area of the equilateral triangle
- Is there a 30-60-90 triangle present (since such a triangle can be easily obtained from an equilateral triangle)?

Let us now solve the problem.

Triangle ACD is equilateral => $\angle CAE = 60^o$

Thus, in right-angled triangle ABE:

$\angle BEA = 180^o - 90^o - 60^o = 30^o$

Thus, triangle ABE is a 60-90-30 triangle

$=> BE = \sqrt{3} * AB = \sqrt{3}$

=> Area of BCDE = (Area of ACD) - (Area of ABE)

$$= \frac{\sqrt{3}}{4} * 3^2 - \frac{1}{2} * AB * BE$$

$$= \frac{9\sqrt{3}}{4} - \frac{\sqrt{3}}{2} = \frac{7\sqrt{3}}{4}$$

(7) If, in the triangle alongside, $\frac{PS}{PR} = \frac{3}{7}$ and ST = 5, find QR. Also find the ratio of the areas of triangle PST and quadrilateral RQST.

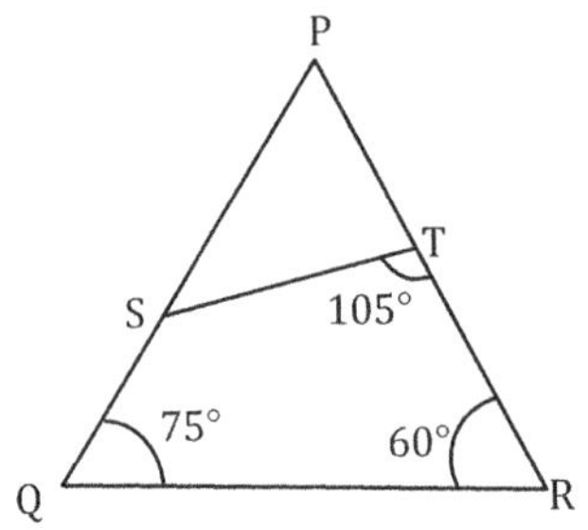


In the problem, we see that the ratio of sides of two triangles is given.

 

Also, we need to find the ratio of areas and also find one side.

Thus, the main things we should focus on are:

- Is there any similar triangle?
- How to determine the side ratio of the similar triangles?

Let us now solve the problem.

In $\Delta PQR$, $\angle QPR = 180^o - 75^o - 60^o = 45^o$

In quadrilateral RTSQ, $\angle TSQ = 360^o - (105^o + 75^o + 60^o) = 120^o$

$=> \angle PST = 180^o - 120^o = 60^o$

$\angle PTS = 180^o - 105^o = 75^o$

Thus, triangles PQR and PTS are 45-75-60 triangles, hence they are similar.

$$=> \frac{PS}{PR} = \frac{ST}{QR} => \frac{3}{7} = \frac{5}{QR}$$

$$=> QR = \frac{35}{3} = 11.67$$

Since triangles PQR and PTS are similar:

$$\frac{\text{Area of triangle PST}}{\text{Area of triangle PRQ}} = \left(\frac{PS}{PR}\right)^2 = \left(\frac{3}{7}\right)^2 = \frac{9}{49}$$

$$=> \frac{\text{Area of triangle PST}}{\text{Area of quadrilateral RQST}} = \frac{9}{49 - 9} = \frac{9}{40}$$

(8) A, B, C are the vertices of a triangle of area 60. Let AD be the median from A on BC and BY be the median from B on AD. If BY is extended to meet AC in E, what is the area of the triangle AYE?

In the problem, we see that there is some information regarding medians of a triangle.

Also, the area of the triangle is given.

Thus, the main thing we should focus on is:

- Median bisects the side and hence, also divides the triangle in equal areas.

Let us now solve the problem.

We know that a median is a line drawn from the vertex which bisects the opposite side.

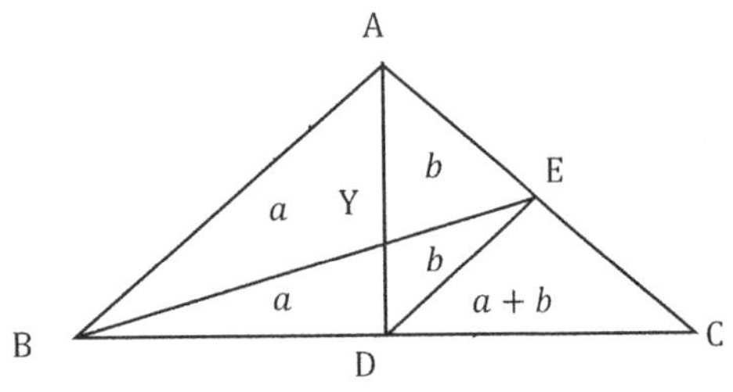


Thus, a median divides the triangle in two equal areas as well (since the ratio of the area of the two triangles created by the median is simply the ratio of the bases of the triangles, i.e. 1 : 1)

Since AD is a median:

Area of ABD = Area of ACD = $\frac{\text{Area ABC}}{2} = \frac{60}{2} = 30$

Since BY is median:
Area of ABY = Area of BYD = $a$ (assumed)

=> $2a = 30$ => $a = 15$

Again, EY is the median in triangle AED. Thus:
Area AEY = area DEY = $b$ (assumed)

Again, DE is the median in triangle BEC. Thus:
Area BED = Area DEC = $(a + b)$

Area ABC = 60
=> $3a + 3b = 60$

=> $45 + 3b = 60$

=> $b = 5$

Thus, area of triangle AYE is 5.

 

(9) If $AX_1 = X_1Y_1 = Y_1Z_1 = Z_1W_1 = W_1B$, AB = 9 and area of Δ ABC is 150, what is the area of $Z_1W_1W_2Z_2$?

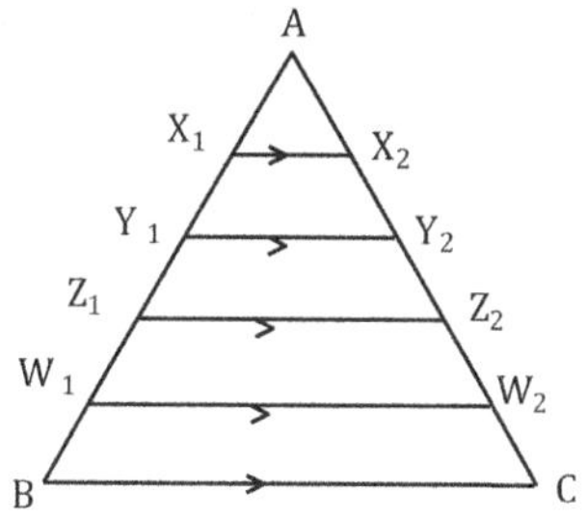


In the problem, we see that there are parallel lines drawn in a triangle.

Also, we need to find the area of a region in the triangle.

Thus, the main things we should focus on are:

- Which are the similar triangles?
- What is the ratio of the sides of the similar triangles?
- Area ratio equals the square of side ratio for similar triangles.

Let us now solve the problem.

$$AX_1 = X_1Y_1 = Y_1Z_1 = Z_1W_1 = W_1B = \frac{1}{5}(9) = 1.8$$

Area of $Z_1W_1W_2Z_2$ = (Area of $AW_1W_2$) - (Area of $AZ_1Z_2$)

Since $X_1X_2$ parallel to $Y_1Y_2$ parallel to $Z_1Z_2$ parallel to $W_1W_2$ parallel to BC, we have:

Triangles $AZ_1Z_2$ and ABC are similar

$$=> \frac{AZ_1}{AB} = \frac{AZ_2}{AC} = \frac{3}{5}$$

$$=> \frac{(\text{Area of triangle } AZ_1Z_2)}{(\text{Area of triangle ABC})} = \left(\frac{3}{5}\right)^2 = \frac{9}{25}$$

$$=> \text{Area of } AZ_1Z_2 = \frac{9}{25} * 150 = 54$$

Similarly, triangles $AW_1W_2$ and ABC are similar

 

$$=> \frac{AW_1}{AB} = \frac{AW_2}{AC} = \frac{4}{5}$$

$$=> \frac{(\text{Area of triangle } AW_1W_2)}{(\text{Area of triangle } ABC)} = \left(\frac{4}{5}\right)^2 = \frac{16}{25}$$

$$=> \text{Area of } AW_1W_2 = \frac{16}{25} * 150 = 96$$

$$=> \text{Area of } Z_1W_1W_2Z_2 = 96 - 54 = 42$$

(10) In the figure, BD =12. Find the length of the angle bisector of $\angle A$.

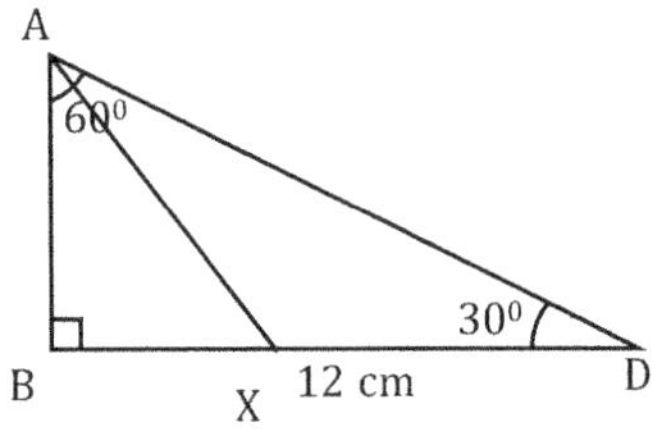


In the figure, we see that there is a 30-60-90 triangle.

Also, we need to find the length of a side in the triangle.

Thus, the main thing we should focus on is:

- Relation between the sides of a 30-60-90 triangle.

Let us now solve the problem.

In the 30-90-60 triangle ABD:

$$AB = \frac{BD}{\sqrt{3}} = 4\sqrt{3}$$

Since AX is an angle bisector, $\angle BAX = \frac{60^o}{2} = 30^o$

$=> \angle AXB = 60^o$

Thus, ABX is a 30-60-90 triangle

$$=> BX = \frac{4\sqrt{3}}{\sqrt{3}} = 4$$

 

=> AX = 2 * BX = 8

Note: If you observed carefully, there is a 30-60-90 triangle inside another 30-60-90 triangle!

 

### 2.9.3 Quadrilaterals

(11) In a quadrilateral ABCD, the sides and diagonals are related as

A) AB + BC + CD + DA = AC + BD

B) AB + BC + CD + DA < AC + BD

C) AB + BC + CD + DA = AC × BD

D) AB + BC + CD + DA > AC + BD

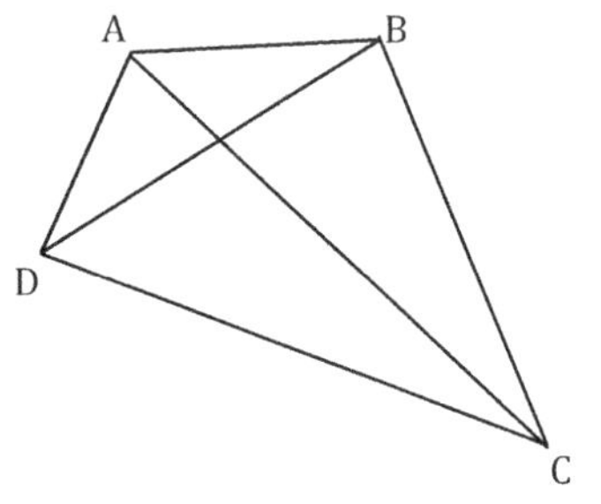


In the problem, we see that we need to find the inequality satisfying the sides and diagonals of a quadrilateral.

Thus, the main things we should focus on are:

- Since there is no direct result known for the inequality of the sides and diagonals of a quadrilateral, we should break the quadrilateral into triangles and use the side inequality of a triangle.
- Which triangles to consider?

Let us now solve the problem.

Let us use the side inequality rule in the following triangles:

In triangle ABD: AB + DA > BD

In triangle BDC: BC + CD > BD

In triangle ABC: AB + BC > AC

In triangle ADC: CD + DA > AC

Adding: 2(AB + BC + CD + DA) > 2(AC + BD)

=> AB + BC + CD + DA > AC + BD

 

Hence, option (D) is the correct answer.

(12) ABCD is a square of side 1cm. Equilateral triangles AQD and BPC are drawn inside the square. Find the length of PQ.

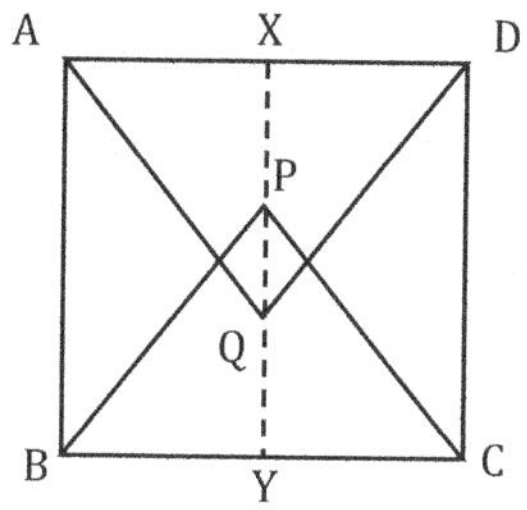


In the problem, we see information regarding a square and two equilateral triangles.

Also, we need to find the length of a line.

Thus, the main things we should focus on are:

- Relation for the height of an equilateral triangle and its sides.
- How to relate the equilateral triangle to the square?

Let us now solve the problem.

We can see from the diagram that: QX + PY – PQ = XY = AB

=> Height of $\triangle$AQD + Height of $\triangle$BPC – PQ = Side of square ABCD

=> PQ = 2*(Height of one equilateral triangle) – (Side of square)

$$= 2\left(\frac{\sqrt{3}}{2}\right)(1) - 1 = \sqrt{3} - 1$$

(13) In a quadrilateral ABDC as shown in the figure, diagonal AD is the perpendicular bisector of diagonal BC. If $\angle ABD = 105^\circ$, $\angle BDC = 60^\circ$ and BD = DC = 12, find the area of ABDC.

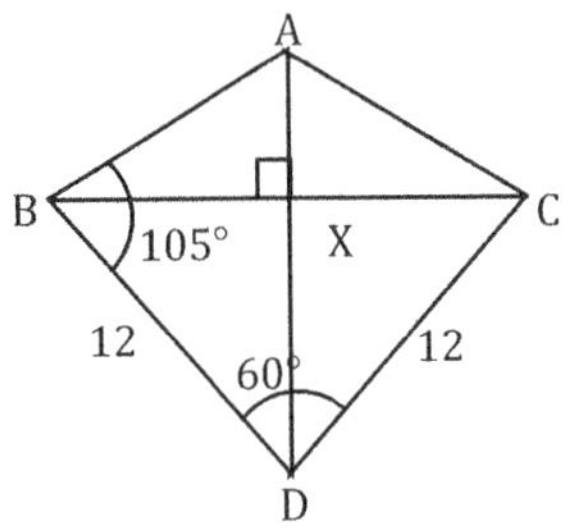


In the problem, we see that there is a $60^o$ angle.

Also, we need to find the area of the quadrilateral.

Thus, the main things we should focus on are:

- Is there an equilateral triangle or a 30-60-90 triangle?
- Since the area of a quadrilateral cannot be directly determined, how do we break it into triangles whose areas can be easily determined?
- Since there is a $105^o$ angle as well, and $105^o = 60^o + 45^o$, is there a 45-45-90 triangle too?

Let us now solve the problem.

Since BD = DC, and $\angle BDC = 60^o$, $\Delta BDC$ is equilateral.

$=> \angle ABC = 105^o - 60^o = 45^o$

Since AD is the perpendicular bisector of diagonal BC:

Triangles ABX and ACX are congruent
(AX is common, BX = CX, $\angle AXB = \angle AXC = 90^o$ => "SAS")

$=> \angle ACB = \angle ABC = 45^o$

Hence, $\angle BAC = 180^o - 45^o - 45^o = 90^o$

Thus, ABC is 90-45-45 triangle => $AB = AC = \frac{BC}{\sqrt{2}} = \frac{12}{\sqrt{2}} = 6\sqrt{2}$

Area ABDC = Area BDC + Area ABC

$= \frac{\sqrt{3}}{4}(12)^2 + \frac{1}{2}\left(6\sqrt{2}\right)^2$

 

$= 36\sqrt{3} + 36$

(14) The parallel sides of a trapezium are 60 and 77. The other sides are 25 and 26. What is the approximate area of the trapezium?

A) 1460 B) 1640 C) 1850 D) 2200

In the problem, we see that the sides of a trapezium are given and we need to determine its area.

Thus, the main things we should focus on are:

- How to determine the height of the trapezium?
- Since the trapezium is not isosceles, dropping perpendiculars from the vertices of the smaller parallel side to the loner one would make the calculation difficult since we would need to solve for Pythagoras' theorem twice.
- In the above event, the problem would take a very long time to solve. So, is there an alternative method?
- Since the non-parallel sides are very close, can we assume them to be equal and then approximate the answer?

Let us now solve the problem.

Let the trapezium be ABCE.

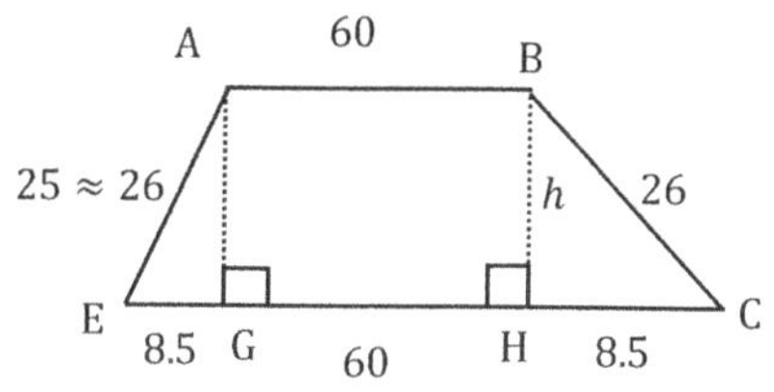


GH = AB = 60

We assume AE to be 26.

Thus, triangles AEG and BCH are congruent

$$=> EG = CH = \frac{77 - 60}{2} = 8.5$$

From right-angled triangle BHC:

$h^2 = \sqrt{26^2 - 8.5^2} \approx \sqrt{676 - 72} = \sqrt{604} \approx \sqrt{600}$, i.e. between $\sqrt{24^2}$ and $\sqrt{25^2}$

$=> h \approx 24.5$

Thus, approximate area of trapezium ABCE

$=> \frac{1}{2}(60 + 77) * 24.5 = \frac{1}{2} * 137 * \frac{49}{2} = 137 * \frac{49}{4} \approx 137 * 12 = 1644$

Hence, option (B) is the correct answer.

**Alternate Approach:**

Note: This method uses the formula for Area of a triangle = $\sqrt{s(s-a)(s-b)(s-c)}$, where $s = \frac{a+b+c}{2}$, and $a, b, c$ are the sides of a triangle.

The use of this formula is NOT required in GMAT, and this approach is shown only for academic interest.

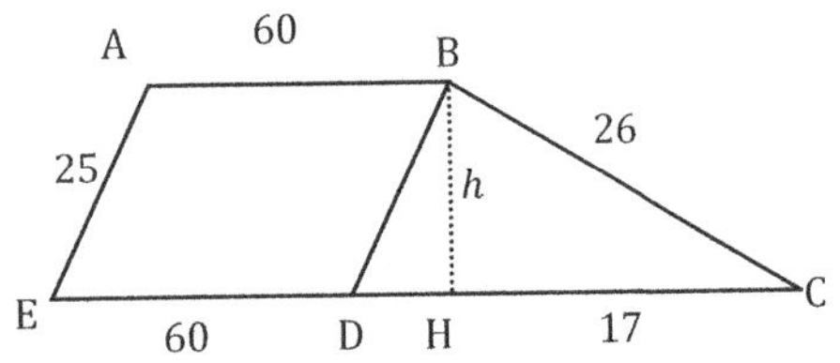


We complete the parallelogram ABDE as shown.

Thus, ED = AB = 60 => DC = 77 - 60 = 17

BD = AE = 25

Semi-perimeter of triangle BDC = $\frac{25 + 17 + 26}{3} = 34$

Equating area of triangle BDC:

$\frac{1}{2} * 17 * h = \sqrt{34 * (34 - 25) * (34 - 26) * (34 - 17)}$

$= \sqrt{34 * 9 * 8 * 17} => h = 24$

Thus, area of trapezium = $\frac{1}{2}(60 + 77) * 24 = 1644$.

 

Note: Observe how close the approximate calculation method is to the actual – In fact, they are equal!!

(15) ABCD is a square. E, F, G and H are the midpoints of the sides taken in order. J and K are the midpoints of HG and GF, respectively. L is a point on EF such that LF $= \frac{1}{4}$ EF. What is the ratio of the area of triangle LJK to that of square ABCD?

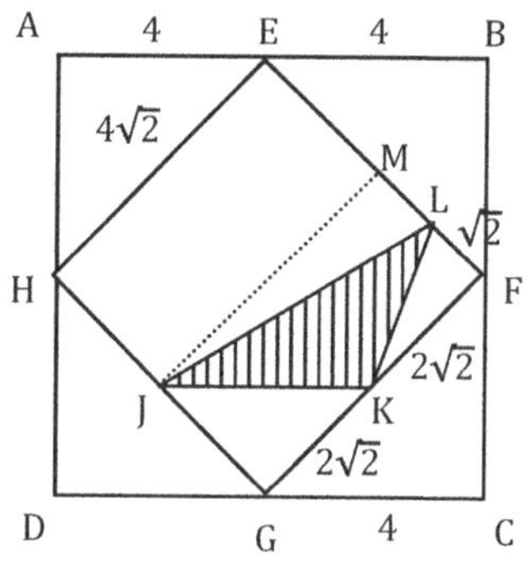


In the problem, we see information regarding squares.

Also, we need to find the ratio of areas.

Thus, the main things we should focus on are:

- Relate the area of the triangle to that of the square.
- Since dimensions are not given, we may choose any convenient value.

Let us now solve the problem.

Let the side of square be 8

(Actual dimension doesn't matter since we need a ratio)

=> Area of square ABCD = 64

Since AB = 8 => AE = $\frac{8}{2} = 4$

EFGH is a square with side $4\sqrt{2}$
(Pythagoras' theorem in $\triangle$BEF)

This is so, because, the figure obtained by joining midpoints of the sides of a square (here, ABCD) is also another square.

 

Thus, area of $\Delta JKL$

= Area JMFG - (Area JLM + Area LKF + Area JKG)

$= \frac{1}{2}$ Area EFGH - (Area JLM + Area LKF + Area JKG)

$$= \frac{1}{2}\left(4\sqrt{2} * 4\sqrt{2}\right) - \frac{1}{2}\left(4\sqrt{2} * \sqrt{2} + 2\sqrt{2} * \sqrt{2} + 2\sqrt{2} * 2\sqrt{2}\right) = (16 - 10) = 6$$

=> (Area of triangle LJK) : (Area of square ABCD) = 6 : 64 = 3 : 32.

(16) Two squares, with side lengths $A$ and B ($B > A$), are placed together such that the right side of square with side $A$ touches the left side of square with side $B$ and their bases are collinear. A diagonal is drawn from the bottom left corner of square with side $A$ to the top right corner of square with side $B$. What is the area below the diagonal in square with side $A$, in terms of $A$ and $B$?

A) $\frac{A^2B}{2(A+B)}$

B) $\frac{B}{2}(A+B)$

C) $\frac{A}{2}(A+B)$

D) $\frac{AB^2}{2(A+B)}$

In the problem, we see information regarding squares.
Also, we need to find the area of a triangle.

Thus, the main thing we should focus on is:

- How to determine the base and height of the triangle?

Let us now solve the problem.

Referring to the diagram given below,

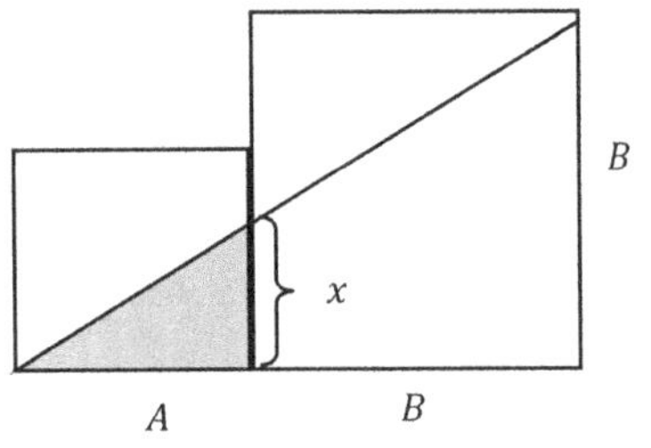


From similar triangles, we have:

$$\frac{x}{B} = \frac{A}{A+B} \Rightarrow x = \frac{AB}{A+B}$$

 

Required area $= \frac{1}{2}A * x = \frac{1}{2}A\left(\frac{AB}{A+B}\right) = \frac{A^2B}{2(A+B)}$

Hence, option (A) is the correct answer.

(17) In the figure given below, if the perimeter of $\Delta$ABC is '$x$' then what is the perimeter of the hexagon?

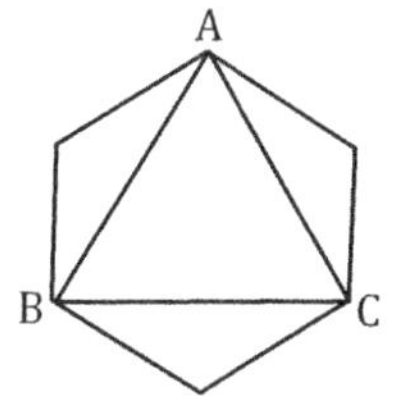


In the problem, we see information regarding a regular hexagon and an equilateral triangle.

Thus, the main things we should focus on are:

- Relate the equilateral triangle and the hexagon
- Find means of calculating the side of the hexagon, noting that a regular hexagon consists of six smaller equilateral triangles.

Let us now solve the problem.

Perimeter of equilateral triangle ABC = $x$

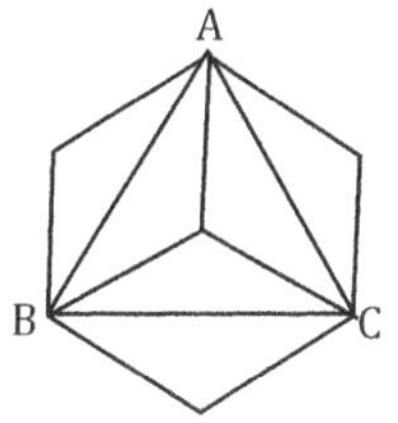


Each side of the triangle ABC $= \frac{x}{3}$

Thus, area of the triangle ABC $= \frac{\sqrt{3}}{4}\left(\frac{x}{3}\right)^2$

Area of each of six small isosceles triangles $= \frac{\sqrt{3}}{3 * 4}\left(\frac{x}{3}\right)^2$

Area of the hexagon = 6 * Area of small triangle $= 6 * \frac{\sqrt{3}}{3 * 4}\left(\frac{x}{3}\right)^2$

From the following diagram:

 

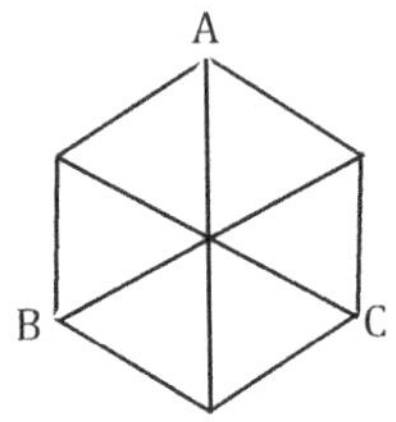


Let the side of the hexagon be $y$

Area of the hexagon = Area of six small equilateral triangles

$$=> 6 * \frac{\sqrt{3}}{4} y^2 = 6 * \frac{\sqrt{3}}{3 * 4}\left(\frac{x}{3}\right)^2 => y = \frac{x}{3\sqrt{3}}$$

$$=> \text{Perimeter of the hexagon} = 6y = 6 * \frac{x}{3\sqrt{3}} = \frac{2x}{\sqrt{3}}$$

(18) Six horses are tethered at six corners of a regular hexagonal plot of side 14m using equal length of rope so that the adjacent horses can just reach one another. Find the area of the plot that is not grazed.

The situation of the horses and their reaches is depicted in the diagram given below. We see information regarding a regular hexagon and six sectors of a circle.

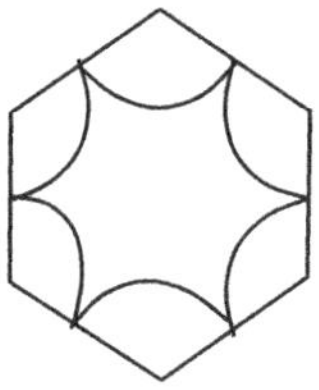

Thus, the main things we should focus on are:

- Find means of calculating the area of the hexagon, noting that a regular hexagon consists of six smaller equilateral triangles.
- What is the interior angle of a regular hexagon?
- Relation for the area of a sector of a circle.

Let us now solve the problem.

In a regular polygon of $n$ sides, measure of each interior angle = $\frac{(n-2) * 180^o}{n}$

Thus, in a regular hexagon, the measure of each interior angle

 

$$= \frac{(6-2) * 180^o}{6} = 120^o$$

Thus, the angle of each of the six sectors

$= 120^o$.

Since the horses are tethered using equal lengths of rope and the adjacent horses just reach each other, the length of rope = radius of the sector

$$= \frac{\text{(Side of hexagon)}}{2} = \frac{14}{2} = 7\text{m}.$$

Area of the sector of a circle having angle $\theta$ and radius $r$ is given by $\pi r^2 \left(\frac{\theta}{360}\right)$.

Thus, area not grazed = Area of hexagon - Area of six sectors

$$= 6 * \frac{\sqrt{3}}{4} * 14^2 - 6 * \frac{120}{360} * \pi * 7^2 = 499.80 - 307.7 = 192.1$$

 

### 2.9.4 Circles

(19) AB is tangent to the given circle. $\angle AED = 43^0$ and $\angle ACD = 70^0$. What is the measurement of $\angle ABC$?

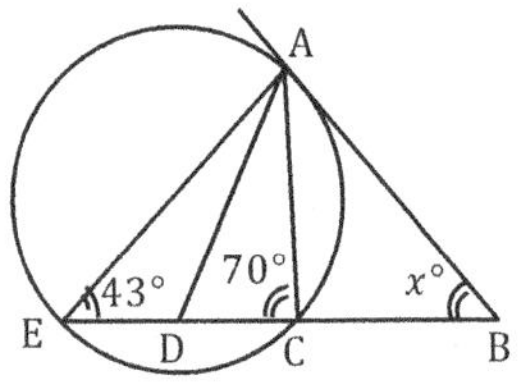


In the problem, we see information regarding a circle and a tangent.

We need to determine the measure of an angle.

Thus, the main thing we should focus on is:

- Angles in alternate segments between tangents and chords are equal.

Let us now solve the problem.

$\angle AED = \angle BAC = 43^0$
(Since $\angle AED$ is made on the alternate segment of $\angle CAB$ by chord AC with tangent AB)

$=> \angle ACB = 180^0 - 70^0 = 110^0$

$=> x = 1800 - (110^o + 43^o) = 27^o$

(20) O is the center of the semi-circle of radius 6 cm. Arc $AA_{10}$ is divided into 10 equal lengths. Find the area (in sq. cm.) bounded between $OA_1A_{10}O$.

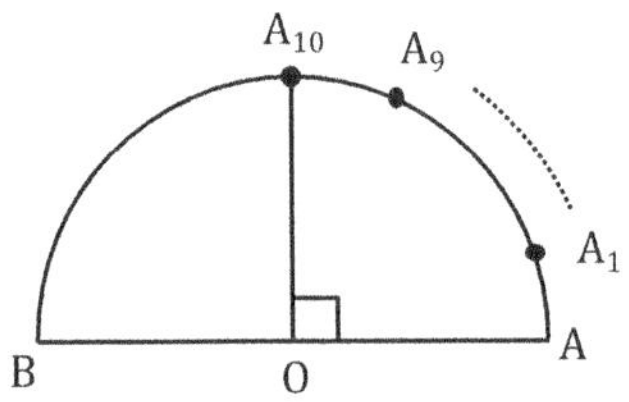


In the problem, we see information regarding a semi-circle.

We need to determine the area of a sector.

 

Thus, the main things we should focus on are:

- Angle subtended at the center of the sector.
- Relation for the area of a sector of a circle.

Let us now solve the problem.

$$\angle A_1OA = \angle A_2OA_1 = \angle A_3OA_2 = \angle A_{10}OA_9 = \frac{90^o}{10} = 9^o$$

$$=> \angle A_1OA_{10} = 9 * 9^o = 81^0$$

$$=> \text{Area bounded by } OA_1A_{10}O = \pi r^2 \left(\frac{\theta}{360}\right) = \pi \left(6^2\right) \left(\frac{81}{360}\right) = 8.1\pi$$

(21) Three equal circles having radius of 1 cm each, touch each other as shown in the figure. Find the area enclosed by the circles (approx. in sq. cm).

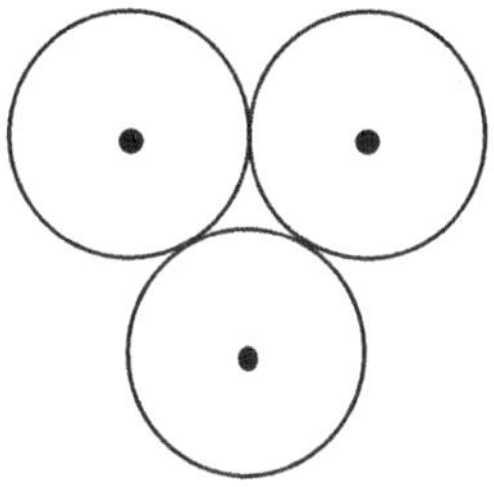

In the problem, we see information regarding three equal circles.

We need to determine the area enclosed by the circles.

Thus, the main things we should focus on are:

- Since the circles are equal, their centers form an equilateral triangle.
- Relation for the area of an equilateral triangle.
- Relation for the area of a sector of a circle.

Let us now solve the problem.

We join the centers X, Y, Z of the three circles to form an equilateral triangle of side 2cm.

 

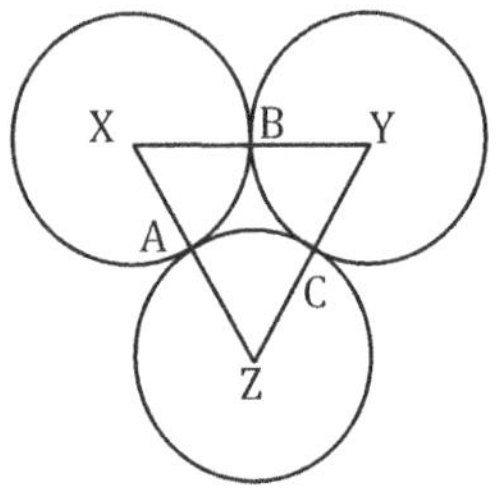


Let the points where the circles touch each other be A, B, C.

Area of each of the sectors XAB, YBC and ZAC $= \pi\,(1^2)\left(\frac{60^o}{360^o}\right) = \frac{\pi}{6}$

Thus, area of enclosed region

= Area of equilateral triangle XYZ - Area of the three sectors

$$= \frac{\sqrt{3}}{4}(2^2) - 3\left(\frac{\pi}{6}\right) = \sqrt{3} - \frac{\pi}{2} = 1.73 - \frac{3.14}{2} = 1.73 - 1.57 = 0.16$$

(22) Two circles with centers at P and Q and radii 5 cm and 3 cm, respectively touch each other externally, as given in the figure. What is the perimeter of triangle ABC (in cm)?

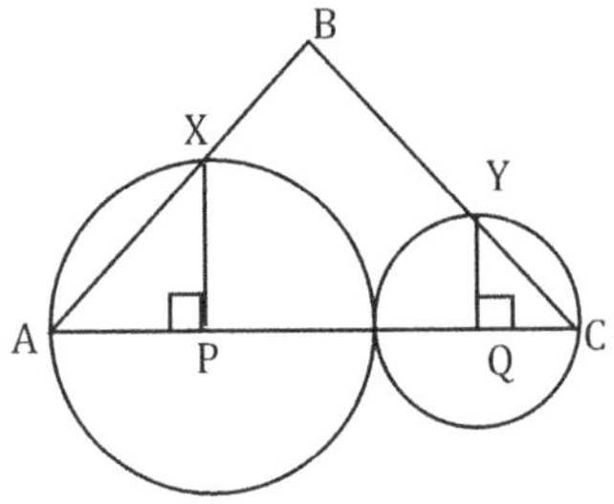


In the problem, we see information regarding circles and triangles.

We need to determine the perimeter of a triangle.

Thus, the main thing we should focus on is:

- Is the triangle equilateral, isosceles or right-angled?

Let us now solve the problem.

Since AX = PX, and triangle APX is right-angled, $\angle XAP = \frac{180^o - 90^o}{2} = 45^o$

 

Since QC = CY, and triangle CQY is right-angled, $\angle YCQ = \frac{180^\circ - 90^\circ}{2} = 45^\circ$

$=> \angle BAC = \angle BCA = 45^\circ => \angle ABC = 90^\circ$

In 45-45-90 triangle ABC: AC = AP + PQ + QC = 5 + 5 + 3 + 3 = 16

$=> AB = BC = \frac{16}{\sqrt{2}} = 8\sqrt{2}$

Thus, perimeter of triangle ABC = $16 + 8\sqrt{2} + 8\sqrt{2} = 16\left(1 + \sqrt{2}\right)$

(23) The outline of a tear-drop sign is made by placing $\frac{3}{4}$ of the circumference of a circle of radius 2 feet on top of an isosceles triangle of height 5 feet. What is the perimeter, in feet, of the sign?

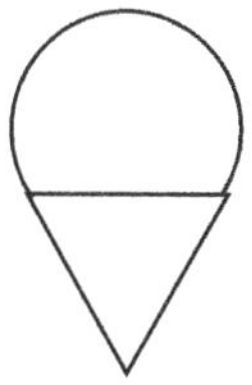

In the problem, we see information regarding a sector of a circle and an isosceles triangle.

Thus, the main things we should focus on are:

- Relation of the length of arc of a sector of a circle.

Let us now solve the problem.

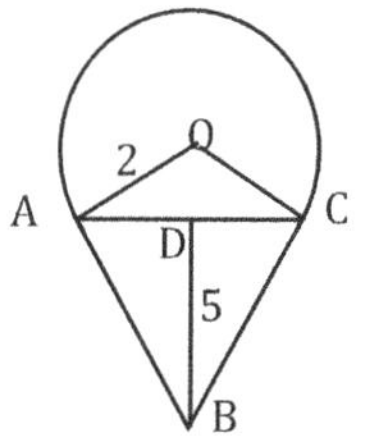


Reflex angle AOC = $\frac{3}{4} * 360^\circ = 270^\circ$

Thus, $\angle AOC = 90^\circ => AC = \sqrt{AO^2 + CO^2} = 2\sqrt{2} => AD = \sqrt{2}$

 

$$=> AB = BC = \sqrt{5^2 + \left(\sqrt{2}\right)^2} = \sqrt{27} = 3\sqrt{3}$$

$$\text{Perimeter of the sign} = \frac{3}{4} * (2\pi * 2) + 2 * 3\sqrt{3} = 3\pi + 6\sqrt{3}$$

(24) The triangle PAB is formed by three tangents to the circle with center at O. What is the measure of $\angle AOB$?

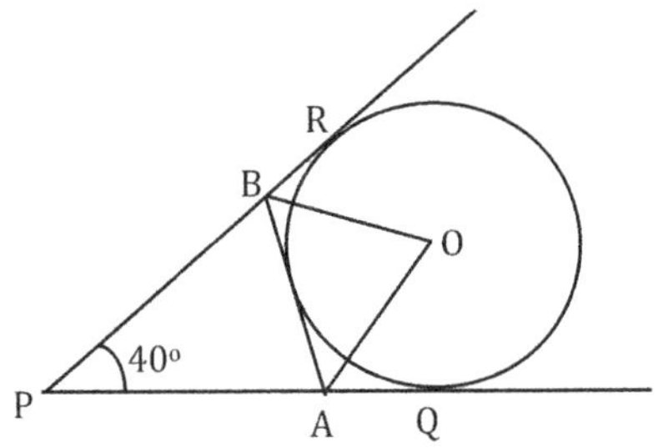


In the problem, we see information regarding a circle and tangents.

We need to determine an angle.

Thus, the main things we should focus on are:

- Radius $\perp$ Tangent.
- How to relate $\angle AOB$ to $\angle BPA$ using suitable constructions.

Let us now solve the problem.

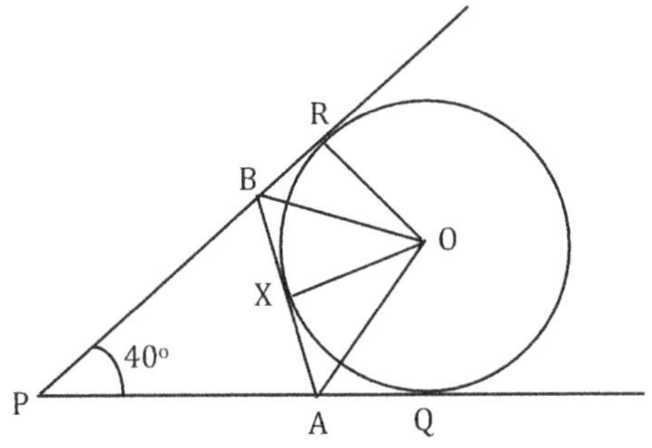


We drop perpendicular OX and join OR and OQ as shown.

$\angle ORB = \angle OQA = \angle OXA = 90^o$

Also: BOX =ROB

(Triangles ROB and BOX are congruent: BR = BX, $\angle ORB = \angle OXA$, OB is common)

 

Similarly, AOX =QOA

In PROQ, $\angle ROQ = 360^0 - 40^0 - 90 - 90^0 = 140^0$

$\Rightarrow 2\,(BOX + AOX) = 140^o \Rightarrow BOX + AOX = AOB = 70^o$

(25) In the figure, the straight lines $L_1$ and $L_2$ intersect each other at right angles. The circle touches the line $L_2$ at A and intersects the line $L_1$ at B and C. If OA = 6 and BC = 16, what is the radius of the circle?

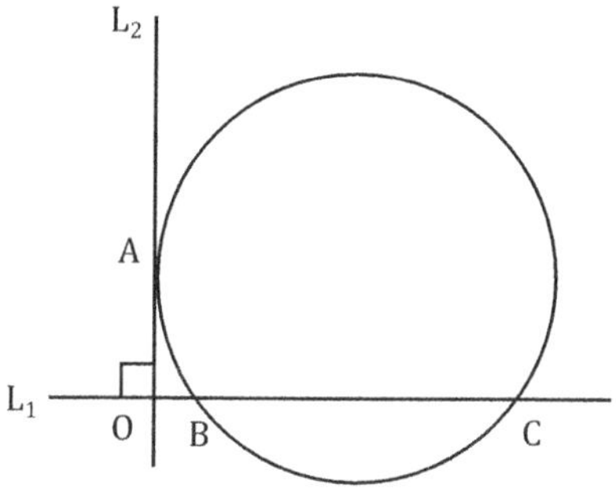


In the problem, we see information regarding a circle and a tangent.

We need to determine the radius of the circle.

Thus, the main things we should focus on are:

- Radius ⊥ Tangent.
- How to use the information of the lines being perpendicular?
- Since the length of a chord is given, do we use the property of a perpendicular on the chord bisects it? - Implying, do we need to construct a perpendicular on the chord?

Let us now solve the problem.

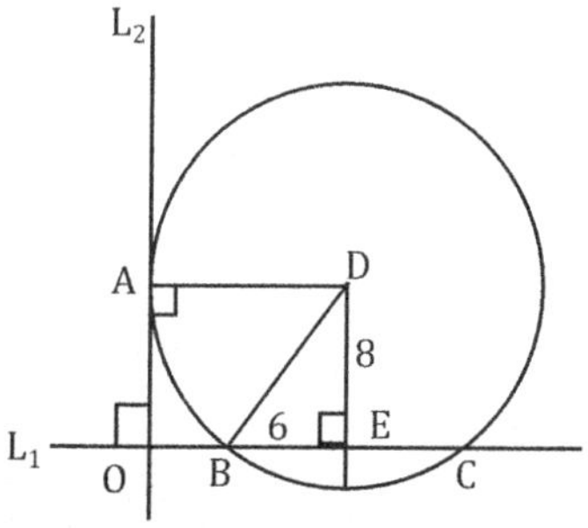

Let D be the center.

OADE is a square => AO = DE = 6

Also, $BE = \frac{1}{2}BC = 8$

=> $R = DB = \sqrt{8^2 + 6^2} = 10$

(26) CDE is a tangent to the circle at point D. O is the center of the circle. What is the measure of $\angle BCD$?

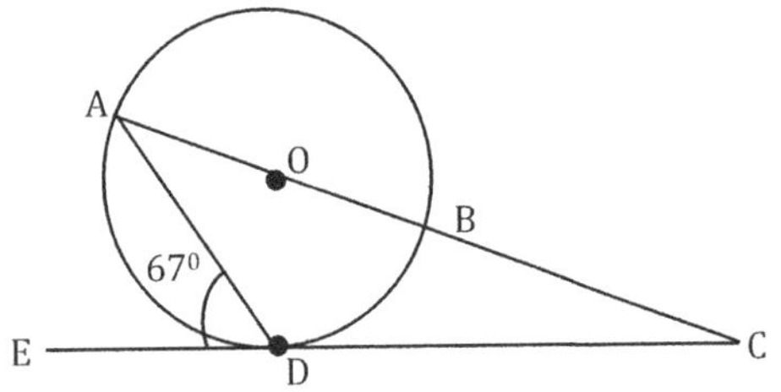


In the problem, we see information regarding a circle, a tangent and a diameter.

We need to determine an angle.

Thus, the main things we should focus on are:

- Radius ⊥ Tangent, so do we join OD?
- Angles in alternate segment are equal.
- Diameter subtends $90^\circ$ at the circumference, so do we join BD?

Let us now solve the problem.

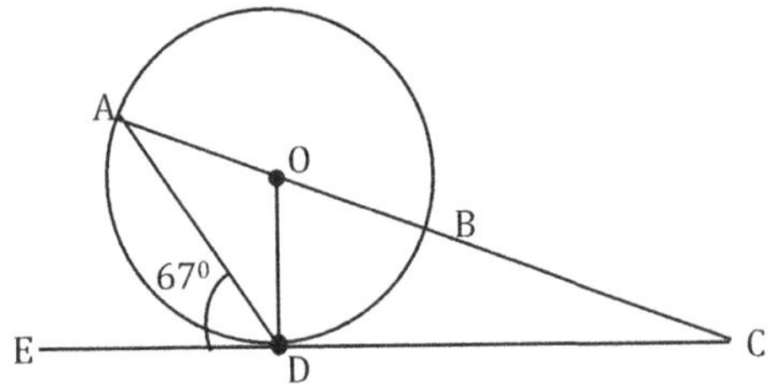


We join OD

$\angle ODE = 90^\circ$ (since radius ⊥ tangent)

 

$\angle ODA = 90^0 - 67^0 = 23^0 = \angle OAD$ (Since OD = OA = radius, triangle OAD is isosceles)

Exterior $\angle DOB$ for triangle AOD = $23^0 + 23^0 = 46^0$

$\angle BCD = 180^0 - 90^0 - 46^0 = 44^0$

**Alternate Approach:**

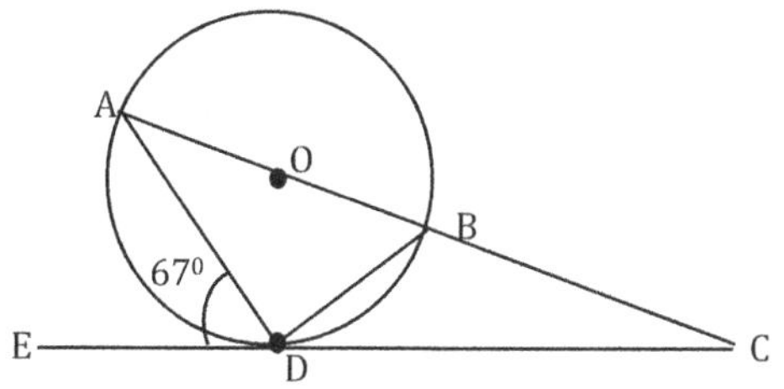


Let us join BD.

$\angle ADB = 90^o$ (Diameter subtends $90^o$ at the circumference)

=> $\angle BDC = 180^o - (67^o + 90^o) = 23^o$

Also, $\angle ABD = \angle ADE = 67^o$ (Angles in alternate segment are equal)

For triangle DBC, $\angle ABD = \angle BCD + \angle BDC$
(Since exterior angle equals the sum of opposite interior angles)

=> $\angle BCD = \angle ABD - \angle BDC = 67^o - 23^o = 44^o$

(27) In the figure given below, C is the center of the bigger semi-circle. AC and BC are the diameters of the other two identical smaller semi-circles. The full circle shown touches the two smaller semi-circles externally and the bigger semi-circle internally. If AC = 6, the radius of the full circle is

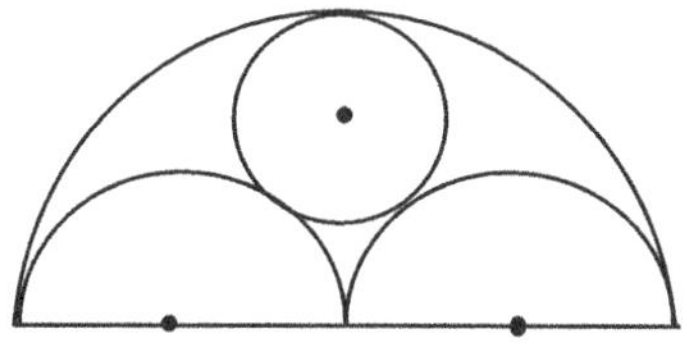

In the problem, we see information regarding a circle and three semi-circles.

We need to determine the radius of the circle.

 

Thus, the main things we should focus on are:

- How to determine the relation among the radii of the circle and the semi-circles?
- Since some construction is necessary, we must use the center of the circle as a part of the construction.

Let us now solve the problem.

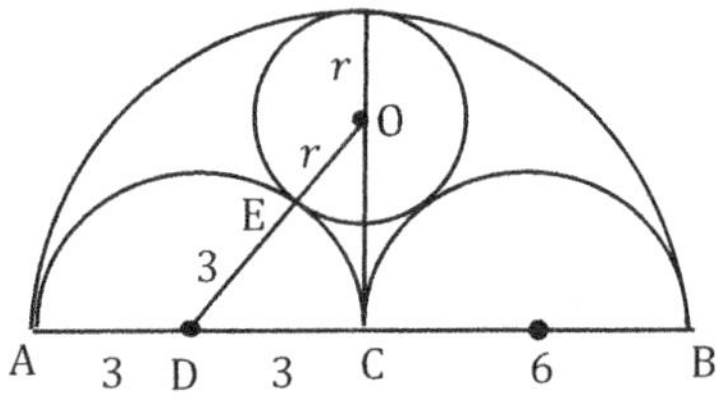


We join the lines as shown in the diagram.

AC = BC = 6 => AD = DC = DE = 3

OC = 6 − $r$

In right-angled triangle OCD:

$(6-r)^2 + 3^2 = (3+r)^2 \Rightarrow 36 - 12r + 9 = 9 + 6r \Rightarrow r = 2$

(28) A horse is tethered at one corner of a square pillar of width $L$. If the length of the rope is $2L$, what is the area that can be covered by the horse?

In the problem, we see information regarding sectors of a circle.

We need to determine the area of the region.

Thus, the main things we should focus on are:

- Understand that the radius of the circle keeps on changing.
- Determine the radii of each of the sectors.

Let us now solve the problem.

 

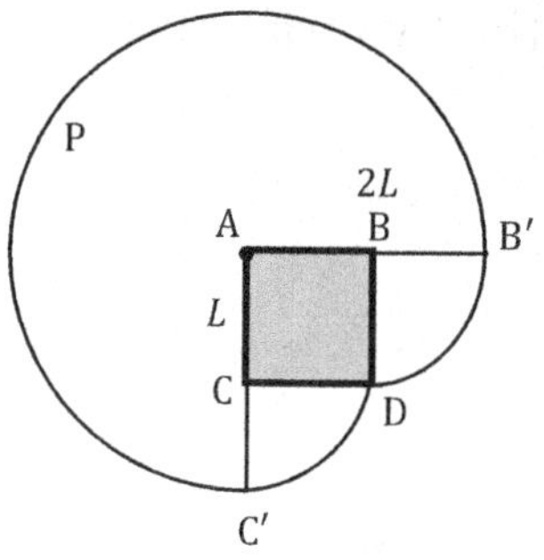


Let ABCD be the square pillar and the horse be tethered at A.

The horse first covers the area ABB'PCC'.

Once the horse is at B', it covers the area BB'D.

Similarly, once the horse is at C', it covers the area CC'D.

Thus, area covered by the horse

= Area of ABB'PCC' + Area of BB'D + Area of CC'D

= (Area of $\frac{3}{4}$ circle of radius $2L$ centered at A) + (Area of $\frac{1}{4}$ circle of radius $L$ centered at B) + (Area of $\frac{1}{4}$ circle of radius $L$ centered at C)

$$= \frac{3}{4}\pi(2L)^2 + \frac{1}{4}\pi(L)^2 + \frac{1}{4}\pi(L)^2 = \frac{7}{2}\pi L^2$$

(29) In the figure given below, both the triangles are equilateral. The circle shown is the in-circle to the outer triangle and is the circumcircle to the inner triangle. What is the ratio of the area of the outer triangle to the inner triangle?

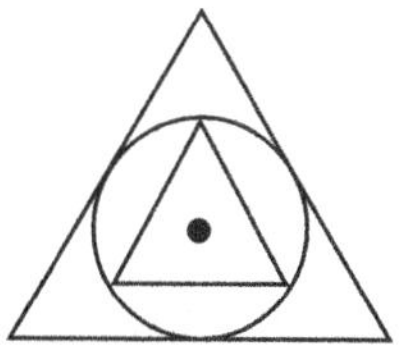

In the problem, we see information regarding a circle and two equilateral triangles.

We need to determine the ratio of the area of the triangles.

Thus, the main things we should focus on are:

- How to determine the relation between the sides of the two triangles?
- The relation for the area of an equilateral triangle.
- What is the use of the circle?

Let us now solve the problem.

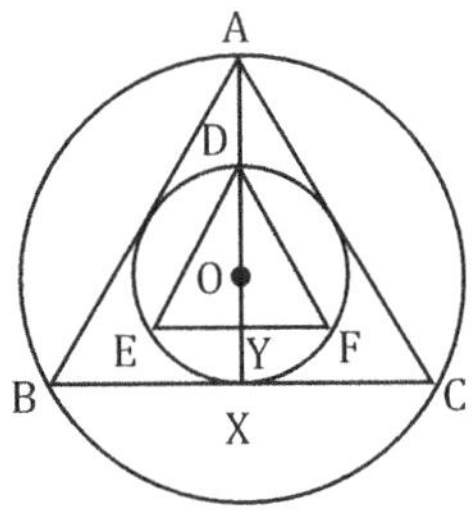


Let AX be drawn $\perp$ BC.

Let us draw a circum-circle of triangle ABC.

OX is the circum-radius of inner triangle and in-radius of outer triangle.

(Note: We do NOT need to use any relation for the in-circle or circum-circle)

OD = OX = radius of inner circle

O is the centroid of both triangles ABC and DEF.

Thus: $\frac{OD}{OY} = \frac{OA}{OX} = \frac{2}{1}$ (Since centroid divides a median in the ratio 2 : 1)

Triangles ABC and DEF are similar, since both are equilateral triangles having same angles.

Thus, we have: Ratio of area = Square of ratio of sides = Square of ratio of circum-radii

$$=> \frac{\text{Area of tringle ABC}}{\text{Area of triangle DEF}} = \left(\frac{OA}{OD}\right)^2 = \left(\frac{OA}{OX}\right)^2 = 2^2 = 4$$

**Alternate Approach 1:**

 

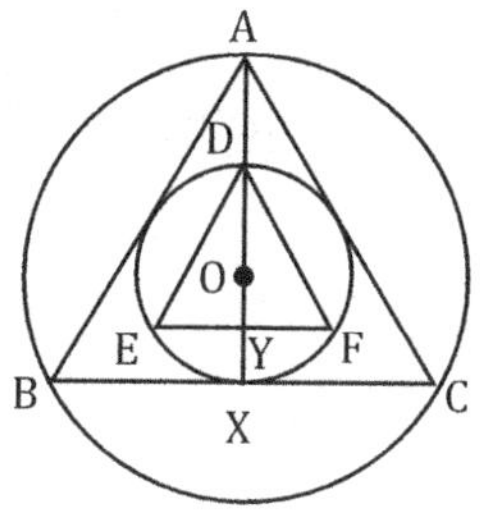


Let AX be perpendicular to BC.

OX is the circum-radius of inner triangle and in-radius of outer triangle.

OD = OX

O is the centroid of both triangles ABC and DEF.

Thus: $\frac{OD}{OY} = \frac{OA}{OX} = \frac{2}{1}$

Let OY = $x$ => OD = $2x$ = OX => OA = $4x$

Height of triangle ABC = AX = $6x$
Height of triangle DEF = DY = $3x$

Height of an equilateral triangle $h = \frac{\sqrt{3}}{2}$ (Side) => Side $= \frac{2h}{\sqrt{3}}$

Area of an equilateral triangle = $\frac{\sqrt{3}}{4}(\text{Side})^2 = \frac{\sqrt{3}}{4}\left(\frac{2h}{\sqrt{3}}\right)^2 = \frac{h^2}{\sqrt{3}}$

Thus, we have: $\frac{\text{Area of tringle ABC}}{\text{Area of triangle DEF}} = \frac{\left(\frac{(6x)^2}{\sqrt{3}}\right)}{\left(\frac{(3x)^2}{\sqrt{3}}\right)} = \frac{36x^2}{9x^2} = 4$

**Alternate Approach 2:**

Let us now see, how a simple modification of the diagram will give us the answer.

Let us rotate the inner triangle as shown:

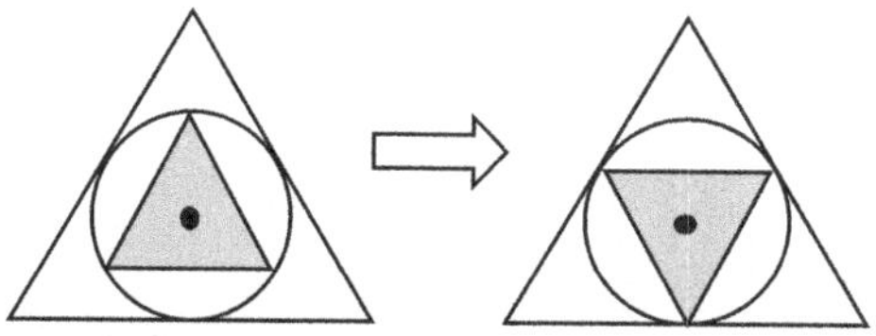

It can clearly be seen from the figure on the right, that the outer triangle has been divided into 4 equal parts.

Thus, the required ratio is 4.

Thus, the solution to the problem was actually just a one-diagram away!!

 

### 2.9.5 3-D geometry

(30) A cone is cut parallel to its base from a height equal to $\frac{1}{3}$ of the total height, $AS' = \frac{1}{3}AS$. Find the ratio of the volume of cone ADE to the frustum DECB.

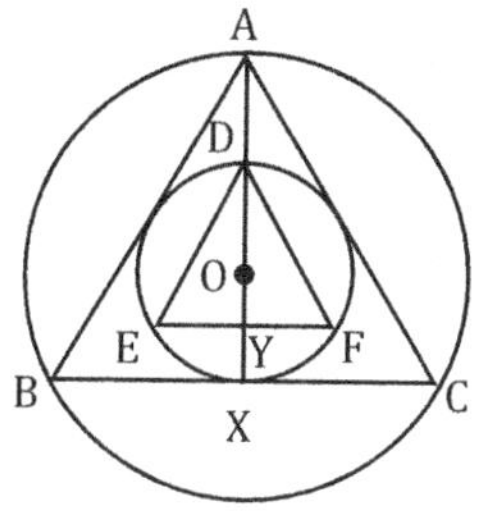


In the problem, we see information regarding a cone.

We need to determine the ratio of the volumes of two parts of the cone.

Thus, the main things we should focus on are:

- There are no dimensions given, so we do NOT need to calculate the exact volume.
- The smaller and larger cones seem similar; so do we use the property that the volume ratio of two similar solids equals the cube of the side ratio?

Let us now solve the problem.

The upper small cone and the entire cone (uncut) are similar solids.

Thus, ratio of their volume is cube of the ratio of their dimensions

$$=> \frac{\text{(Volume of cone ADE)}}{\text{(Volume of cone ABC)}} = \left(\frac{\text{(Height of come ADE)}}{\text{(Height of come ABC)}}\right)^3 = \left(\frac{1}{3}\right)^3 = \frac{1}{27}$$

$$=> \frac{\text{(Volume of cone ADE)}}{\text{(Volume of DECB)}} = \frac{1}{27-1} = \frac{1}{26}$$

(31) There is a wooden log of height 28 cm having a square base whose sides are 3 cm each. Find the minimum quantity of the log (in cubic cm.) that should be removed to make it cylindrical in shape.

In the problem, we see information regarding a cuboid and a cylinder.

 

We need to determine the volumes.

Thus, the main things we should focus on are:

- Relations for the volume of a cylinder and a cuboid.
- How to determine the largest cylinder that can be cut out from the cuboid.

Let us now solve the problem.

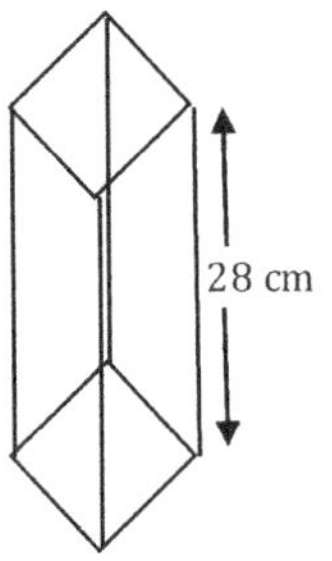


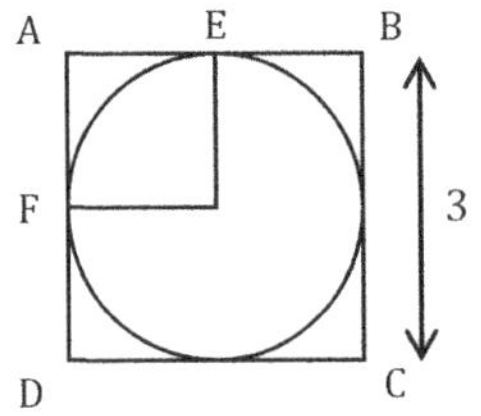


To make the log cylindrical in shape, the base needs to be made circular.

The radius of the circle would be half the side of the square = $\frac{3}{2}$ = 1.5 cm.

For this to happen 4 identical areas have to be removed from each corner, for example, AEF is shown in the diagram.

Thus, total volume that needs to be removed = 4 * (Area of AEF) * (Height of log)

= (Area of square base - Area of circle) * (Height of log)

$= (a^2 - \pi r^2)\, h = \left(3^2 - 3.14 * 1.5^2\right) * 28 = 54.18$ cc

(32) In a 21 × 14 × 11 (length × width × height) cuboid container containing water up to $\frac{1}{3}$ of its height, how many spherical marbles of diameter 1.4 cm, can be placed so that water just reaches the brink? Use the relation: Volume of a sphere of radius $r = \frac{4}{3}\pi r^3$.

In the problem, we see information regarding a cuboid and spheres.

We need to compare their volumes.

Thus, the main things we should focus on are:

- Relations for the volume of a sphere (already provided) and a cuboid.

 

- How to relate the volumes of the spheres and the cuboid?

Let us now solve the problem.

The cubical container was initially only $\frac{1}{3}$ full.

After the marbles were placed, it became completely full.

Thus, volume of the marbles is $\frac{2}{3}$ of the volume of the cuboid.

Let $n$ marbles are dropped.

Thus, we have:

$$\frac{2}{3} * 21 * 14 * 11 = n * \frac{4}{3} * \pi\left(\frac{1.4}{2}\right)^3 => n = 1500$$

(33) From a solid cone of height 6 cm and radius $6\sqrt{2}$ cm, the maximum possible cube is cut out. What is the volume of the remaining portion of the cone? Use the relation: Volume of a cone of radius $r$ and height $h = \frac{1}{3}\pi r^2 h$.

In the problem, we see information regarding a cube and a cone.

We need to determine the volume of the cube.

Thus, the main things we should focus on are:

- Since the volume of a cube depends only on its side (volume is the cube of its side), we need to determine the length of the side of the cube.
- Since the cone, represented in 2-D form, is basically a triangle, do we need to use similarity to determine the side of the cube?

Let us now solve the problem.

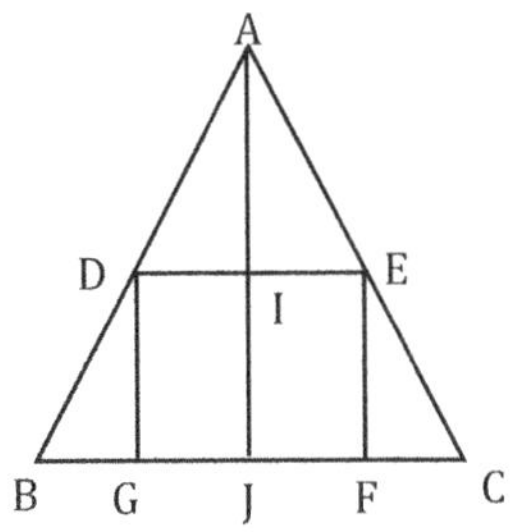


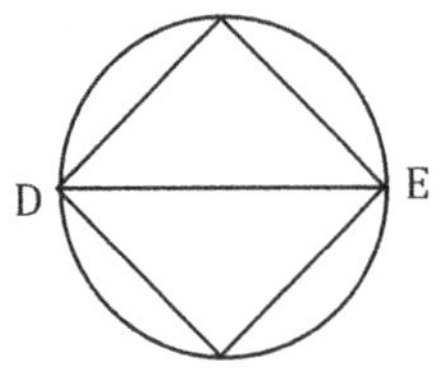


Let each side of the cube be $x$.

=> $AI = 6 - x$

DE is the diagonal of the top face of the cube = $x\sqrt{2}$

=> $IE = \frac{DE}{2} = \frac{x}{\sqrt{2}}$

Note: Do NOT, by mistake, assume that DE is the side of the cube.

Since the corners of the cube touch the surface of the cone, DE must be the diagonal of the square face on top of the cube, as shown beside:

$\Delta AIE$ is similar to $\Delta AJC$.

=> $\frac{6-x}{6} = \frac{\left(\frac{x}{\sqrt{2}}\right)}{6\sqrt{2}}$ => $12 - 2x = x$ => $x = 4$

Volume of remaining portion of cone

$= \frac{\pi}{3}\left(6\sqrt{2}\right)^2 * 6 - 4^3 = 144\pi - 64$

 

### 2.9.6 Co-ordinate geometry

(34) Find the equation of a line passing through (-2, 1) and parallel to the line $2x + 3y = 4$. Find the area of the triangle bounded by the new line and the X and Y axes.

In the problem, we see information regarding parallel lines.

We need to find the area of the triangle bounded by a line with the X and Y axes.

Thus, the main things we should focus on are:

- How to determine the equation of a line parallel to a given line? - Use the property that parallel lines have the same slope.
- How to determine the area of the triangle? - Find the X and Y intercepts and use the relation for the area equal to half times the product of base and height.

Let us now solve the problem.

The equation of a line parallel to the line $2x + 3y = 4$ is $2x + 3y = p$, where $p$ is a constant.

Since the line passes through (-2, 1), we have $2 * (-2) + 3 * 1 = p \Rightarrow p = -1$.

Hence, the equation of the required line is $2x + 3y = -1 \Rightarrow \frac{x}{\left(-\frac{1}{2}\right)} + \frac{y}{\left(-\frac{1}{3}\right)} = 1$.

Thus, the X and Y intercepts are $-\frac{1}{2}$ and $-\frac{1}{3}$.

For the area of the triangle, we ignore the signs and calculate the area.

Area of the required triangle $= \frac{1}{2} * \left(\frac{1}{2} * \frac{1}{3}\right) = \frac{1}{12}$ square units.

(35) Find the equation of a line which passes through the point (-2, 1) and is perpendicular to the line $2x + 3y = 4$.

In the problem, we see information regarding perpendicular lines.

Thus, the main thing we should focus on is:

- How to determine the equation of a line perpendicular to a given line? - Use the property that product of slopes of perpendicular lines equals '- 1'.

Let us now solve the problem.

The equation of any line perpendicular to the line $2x + 3y = 4$ is $3x - 2y = p$, where $p$ is a constant.

Since the line passes through the point (-2, 1), we have $(-2) * 3 - 2 * 1 = p \Rightarrow p = -8$.

Hence, the required equation: $3x - 2y = -8$

(36) What is the equation of the straight line passing through the point of X intercept and Y intercept for the equation $y = x^2 - 12x + 36$?

In the problem, we see information regarding the equation of a quadratic, i.e. a parabola.

Thus, the main things we should focus on are:

- How to determine the X intercept and Y intercept of a parabola?
- How to find the equation of a line given two points?

Let us now solve the problem.

We have: $y = x^2 - 12x + 36$

To find Y intercept:
On the Y-axis, we have $x = 0$
$\Rightarrow y = 0^2 - 12 * 0 + 36 = 36$
Thus, the coordinates of Y intercept is (0, 36)

To find X intercept:
On the X-axis, we have $y = 0$
Thus, we have:
$x^2 - 12x + 36 = 0 \Rightarrow (x - 6)^2 = 0 \Rightarrow x = 6$
Thus, the coordinates of X intercept is (6, 0)

Thus, the equation of the line passing through (0, 36) and (6, 0) is:

 

$$\frac{y - y_1}{x - x_1} = \frac{y_1 - y_2}{x_1 - x_2}$$

$$=> \frac{y - 36}{x - 0} = \frac{36 - 0}{0 - 6} => \frac{y - 36}{x} = -6 => y + 6x = 36$$

Chapter 3

# Practice Questions

## 3.1 Geometry

### 3.1.1 Problem Solving

1. In the figure below, ABCD is a rectangle with AB = 20, DA = 15. AE is the altitude on diagonal BD. What is the area of the $\triangle AEB$?

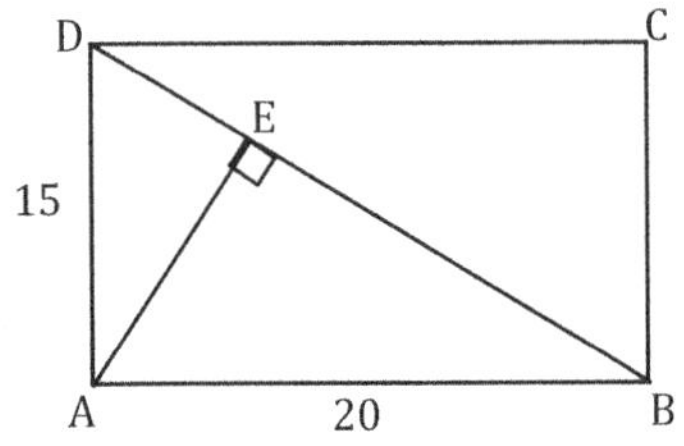


**(A)** 24
**(B)** 48
**(C)** 64
**(D)** 96
**(E)** 120

*Solve yourself:*

2. In a parallelogram ABCD, P is the midpoint of AB. Diagonal AC intersects PD at Q. What proportion of AC is AQ?

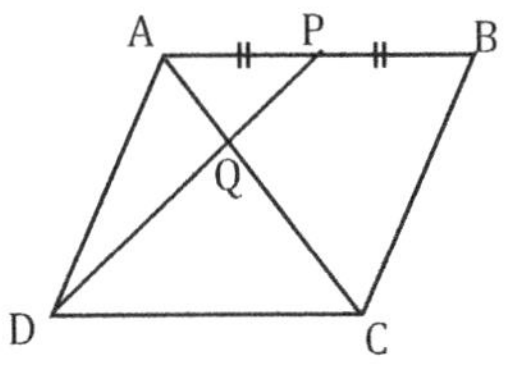


**(A)** $\frac{1}{2}$
**(B)** $\frac{1}{3}$
**(C)** $\frac{1}{4}$

 

**(D)** $\frac{1}{5}$

**(E)** $\frac{1}{6}$

*Solve yourself:*

**3.** PQRS is a rectangle in which PQ is twice as long as QR. T is a point such that the shortest distance of T from PQ is $\sqrt{3}$ times the length of QR and PT = QT. If M is the midpoint of QT, what is the measure of angle RMQ?

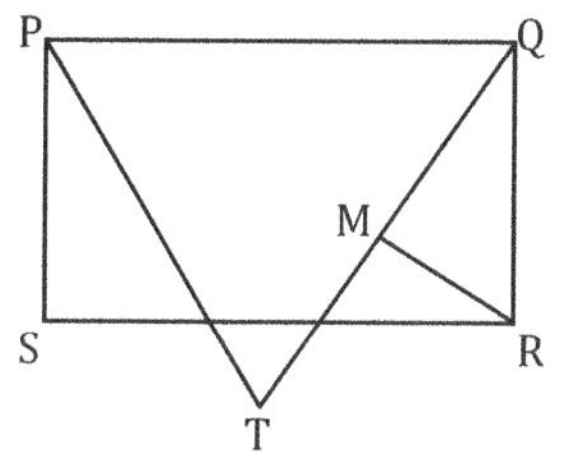


**(A)** $30^o$

**(B)** $45^o$

**(C)** $60^o$

**(D)** $75^o$

**(E)** $90^o$

*Solve yourself:*

**4.** PQRS is a square. T is a point on RS such that ST = 5. If the area of the triangle QRT is 42, what is the length of a side of the square PQRS?

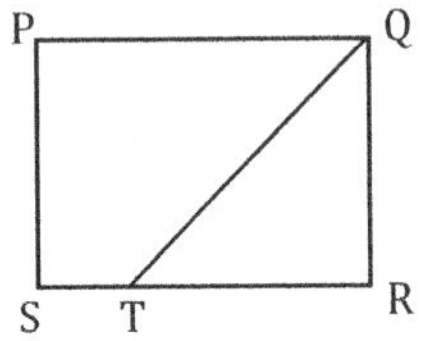


(A) 10
(B) 12
(C) 14
(D) 15
(E) 16

*Solve yourself:*

5. In a parallelogram, the ratio of the two adjacent sides is 3 : 2. If the area of the parallelogram is 243, and the angle between the two sides is $30^{o}$, what is the perimeter of the parallelogram?

(A) 60
(B) 75
(C) 90
(D) 100
(E) 120

*Solve yourself:*

6. A parallelogram has diagonals of lengths 12 and 8, which bisect each other making an angle of $45^{o}$. What is the area of the parallelogram?

(A) $24\sqrt{2}$
(B) $18\sqrt{2}$
(C) 25
(D) $16\sqrt{2}$
(E) 20

*Solve yourself:*

7. In a trapezium, the ratio of the length of the parallel sides is 2 : 3. The height of the trapezium is $\frac{3}{4}$ of the smaller side. If the area of trapezium is 60, what is the length of the smaller of the two parallel sides?

(A) 3
(B) 6
(C) 8
(D) 10
(E) 12

*Solve yourself:*

8. PQRS is a quadrilateral drawn in a circle with RS as the diameter, such that PS = QR = $\frac{1}{2}$ RS. What is the ratio of the lengths of the sides PQ and RS?

(A) 1 : 2
(B) 2 : 3
(C) 3 : 4
(D) 4 : 3

**(E)** 3 : 2

*Solve yourself:*

**9.** ABCD and CDEF are two trapeziums, such that the sides AB, CD and EF are parallel and measure 12, 27 and 72, respectively. If ED = 3, the points B, C and F are collinear and A, D and E are also collinear, what is the length of AD?

**(A)** 1
**(B)** 1.5
**(C)** 2
**(D)** 2.5
**(E)** 4

*Solve yourself:*

**10.** The sides of a square ABCD are each produced in the same order by its own length to form another square PQRS, as shown is the diagram below. What is the ratio of the areas of ABCD and PQRS?

**(A)** 1 : 3
**(B)** 1 : 4
**(C)** 1 : 5
**(D)** 1 : 6
**(E)** 1 : 8

*Solve yourself:*

**11.** The radius of a circle is 13 and the length of one of its chords is 10. What is the shortest distance of the chord from the center of the circle?

**(A)** 5
**(B)** 6
**(C)** 8
**(D)** 10
**(E)** 12

*Solve yourself:*

**12.** In the diagram below, O is the center of the circle. What is the measure of $\angle AOC$?

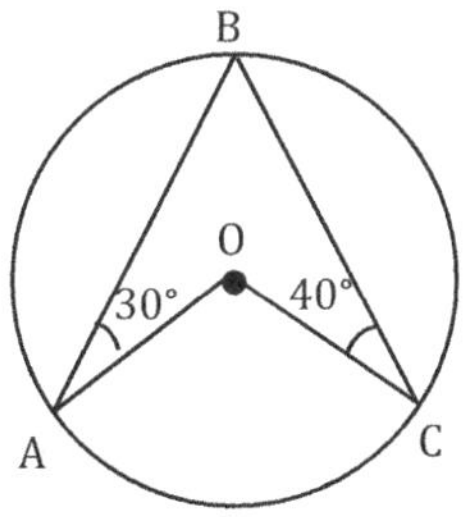


**(A)** $70^o$
**(B)** $100^o$
**(C)** $120^o$
**(D)** $140^o$
**(E)** $150^o$

*Solve yourself:*

**13.** In the diagram below, O is the center of the circle. What is the measure of $\angle PQB$?

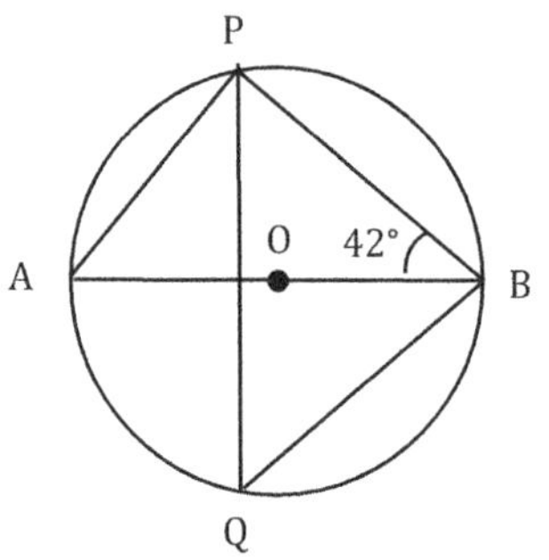


**(A)** $30^0$
**(B)** $48^0$
**(C)** $50^0$
**(D)** $60^0$
**(E)** $75^0$

*Solve yourself:*

**14.** In the diagram below, PQRS is a quadrilateral such that sum of the angles at P and Q is $180^0$. What is the value of $\angle Q$?

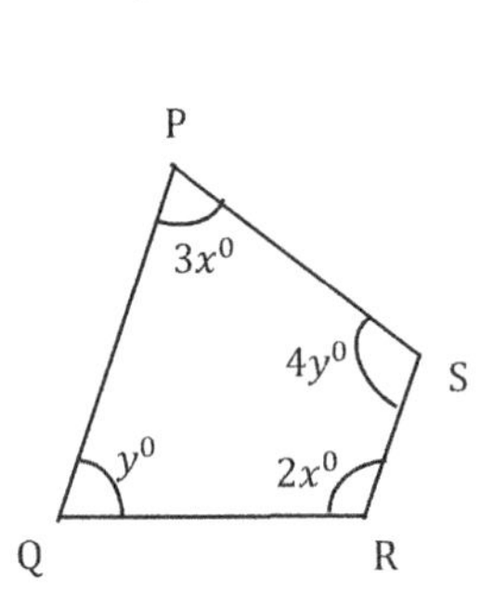


 

(A) 18
(B) 36
(C) 54
(D) 72
(E) 108

*Solve yourself:*

**15.** Two circles of radii 20 and 13 intersect at two points and the length of the line joining the two points is 24. What is the distance between their centers of the two circles?

(A) 5
(B) 12
(C) 15
(D) 16
(E) 21

*Solve yourself:*

**16.** In the diagram below, O is the center of the circle. Chord ED is parallel to the diameter AC of the circle. If $\angle CBE = 65^\circ$, what is the measure of $\angle DEC$?

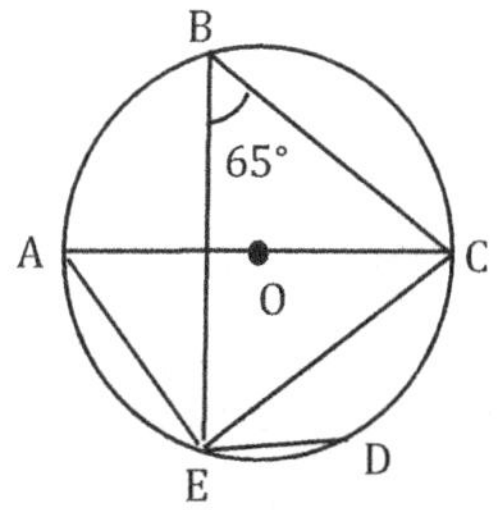

**(A)** 20°
**(B)** 25°
**(C)** 30°
**(D)** 32°
**(E)** 45°

**17.** In the diagram shown below, if AB = BC, what is the measure of ∠DCA?

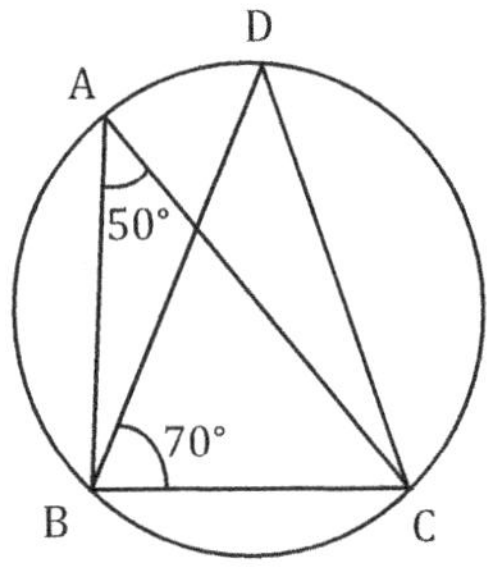


**(A)** 10°
**(B)** 16°
**(C)** 35°
**(D)** 50°
**(E)** 60°

*Solve yourself:*

**18.** In the diagram below, O is the center of the circle and AC and BD are diameters. What is the value of $x$?

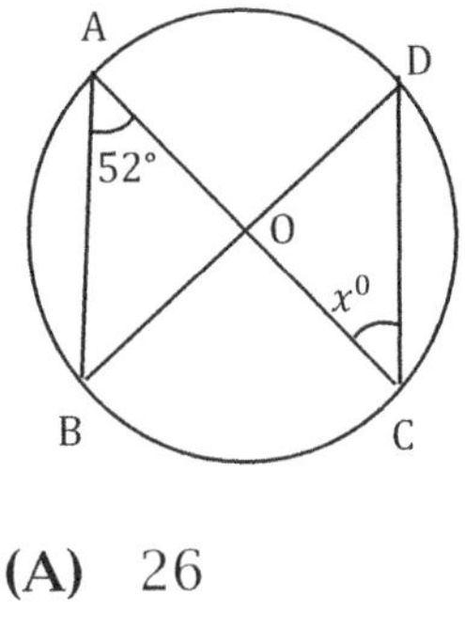


**(A)** 26

(B) 35
(C) 52
(D) 76
(E) 104

*Solve yourself:*

**19.** ABCD is a quadrilateral such that $\angle D = 90^{\circ}$. A circle drawn inside the quadrilateral touches the sides AB, BC, CD and DA at P, Q, R and S, respectively. If BC = 38, CD = 25 and BP = 27, what is the radius of the circle?

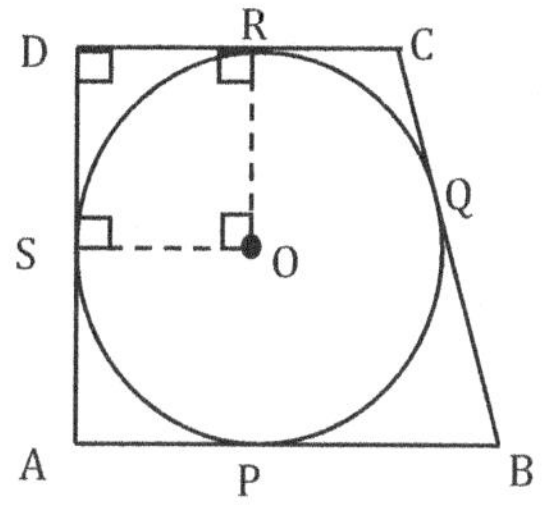


(A) 11
(B) 12
(C) 13
(D) 14
(E) 16

*Solve yourself:*

**20.** In the diagram below, PQ is a tangent to circle. If $\angle ABC = 80^{\circ}$, what is the value of $x$?

 

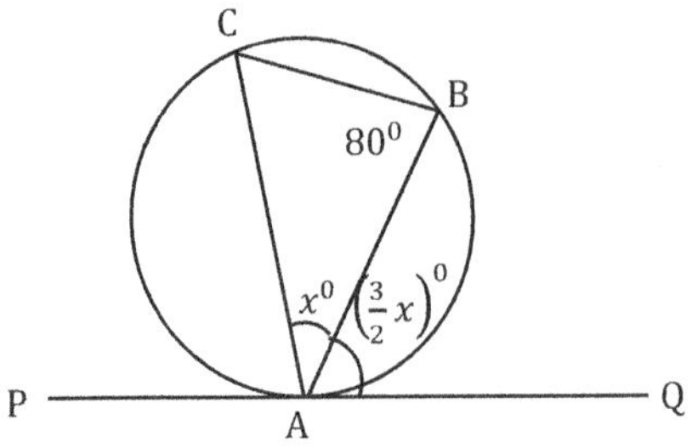


**(A)** 40

**(B)** 45

**(C)** 50

**(D)** 60

**(E)** 80

*Solve yourself:*

**21.** In the diagram below, P is the center of the circle. What is the area of the shaded region? Assume $\pi = 3$.

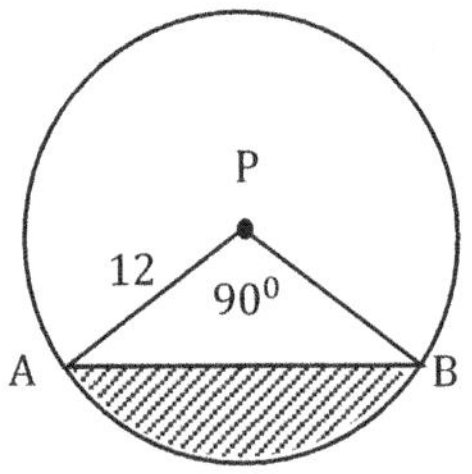


**(A)** 18

**(B)** 36

**(C)** 54

**(D)** 72

**(E)** 108

*Solve yourself:*

**22.** In $\triangle ABC$, $AB = AC = 12$ and $\angle BAC = 45^{\circ}$. What is the area of $\triangle ABC$?

**(A)** 18
**(B)** 24
**(C)** $36\sqrt{2}$
**(D)** $54\sqrt{2}$
**(E)** 80

*Solve yourself:*

**23.** Two ants start crawling at a speed of 2 meters per minute from point A to point B, the two points being the ends of a diameter of a circle. One ant moves along the diameter while the other along circumference of the circle. If the first ant beats the second one by 45 seconds, what is the diameter of the circle? Assume $\pi = 3$.

**(A)** 1.5 meters
**(B)** 3 meters
**(C)** 4.5 meters
**(D)** 6 meters
**(E)** 7.5 meters

*Solve yourself:*

 

**24.** In the diagram below, two smaller identical semicircles are drawn inside a larger semicircle having diameter 14. What is the area of the shaded region?

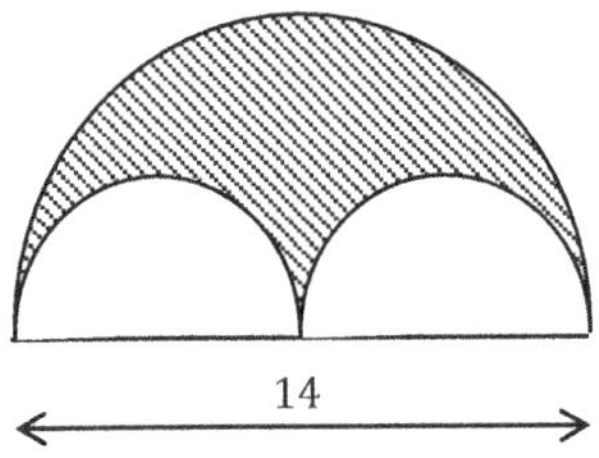


**(A)** 28.7

**(B)** 38.5

**(C)** 77

**(D)** 91

**(E)** 154

*Solve yourself:*

**25.** In the diagram below, AC = BD = 25 and OC = 7. If $AB = \frac{CD}{2}$, what is the length of CD?

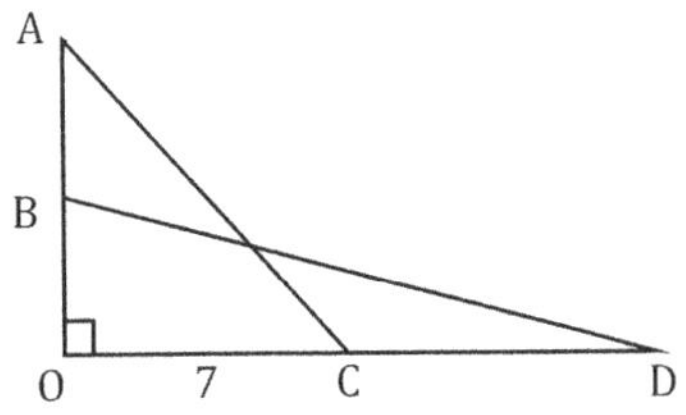


**(A)** 4

**(B)** 6

**(C)** 8

**(D)** 12

**(E)** 16

*Solve yourself:*

**26.** $\triangle$ABC and $\triangle$DBC are equal in area and the points A and D lie on the same side of BC. Which of the following options is definitely correct?

**(A)** AD is perpendicular to AB

**(B)** AD is perpendicular to DC

**(C)** AD is parallel to BC

**(D)** AD is equal to BC

**(E)** AC is equal to BD

*Solve yourself:*

**27.** In the diagram below, RST is a right-angled triangle, right angled at S. X and Y are mid points of RS and ST, respectively. What is the value of $\left(\frac{RY^2+XT^2}{XY^2}\right)$?

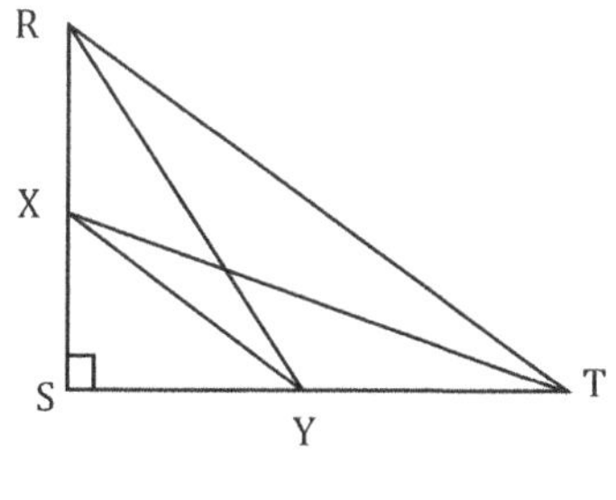


**(A)** 2.5

**(B)** 3

**(C)** 4.5

**(D)** 5

**(E)** 7.5

*Solve yourself:*

**28.** In the diagram below, D is the midpoint of side BC of triangle ABC. The straight lines drawn through the point D parallel to CA and BA intersect CA and BA at the points F and E, respectively. If the area of $\triangle$FBD is 12, what is the area of $\triangle$ECD?

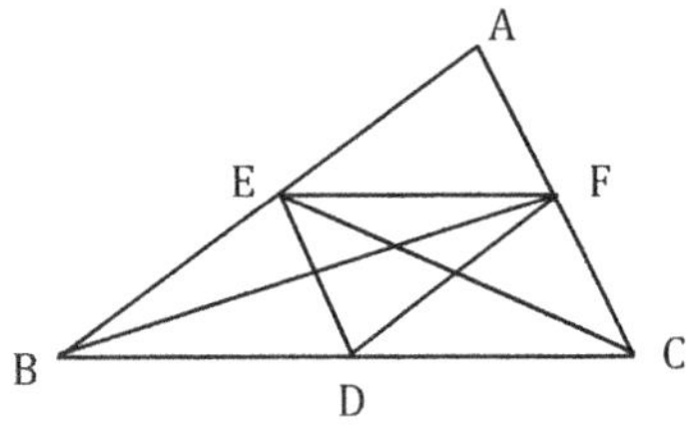


**(A)** 6
**(B)** 9
**(C)** 12
**(D)** 18
**(E)** 24

*Solve yourself:*

**29.** The perimeter of an isosceles triangle is $A$ and each of the two equal sides is $B$ longer than the third side. Which of the following represents the length of one of the equal sides?

**(A)** $\frac{A-B}{3}$

**(B)** $A+\frac{B}{3}$

**(C)** $\frac{A+B}{3}$

**(D)** $\frac{A}{3} + B$

**(E)** $A - \frac{B}{3}$

*Solve yourself:*

**30.** The sides of an isosceles triangle are $(5p + 20)$, $(p + 196)$ and $(3p + 76)$. If $p$ is a positive integer, what is the greatest possible perimeter of the triangle?

**(A)** 431

**(B)** 544

**(C)** 688

**(D)** 715

**(E)** 832

*Solve yourself:*

**31.** In the diagram shown below, area of △ABE is 24. Also, AB = ED = 6 and AC is parallel to DE. What is the length of CE?

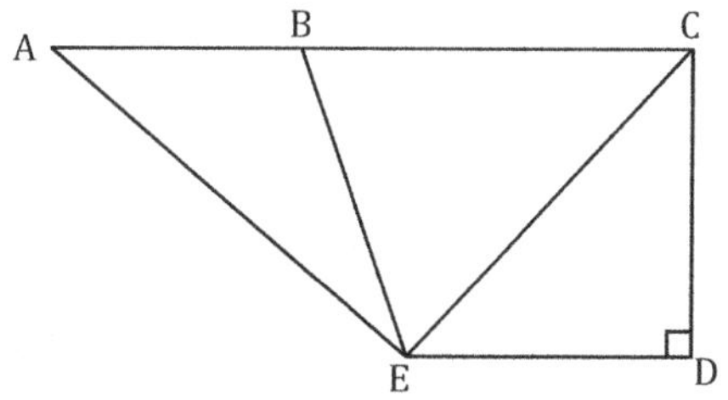


**(A)** 4

**(B)** 6

**(C)** 8

**(D)** 10

**(E)** 11

*Solve yourself:*

**32.** In the diagram below, AB = BC and CE is parallel to AB. If CE bisects ∠ACD, what is the measure of ∠ABC?

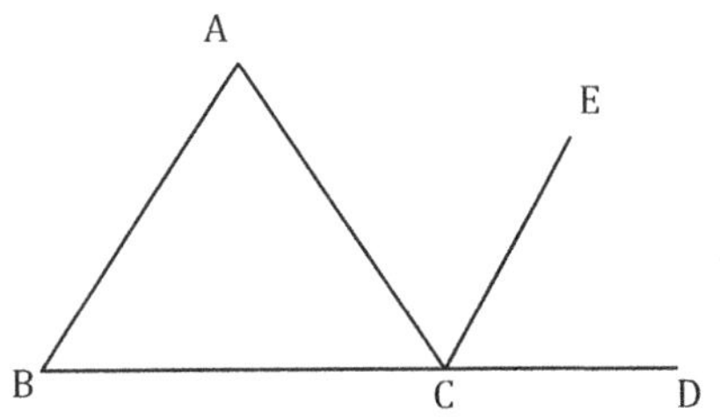


**(A)** $30^o$

**(B)** $45^o$

**(C)** $60^o$

**(D)** $75^o$

**(E)** $90^o$

*Solve yourself:*

**33.** In the diagram below, what is the value of $x + y + z + w$?

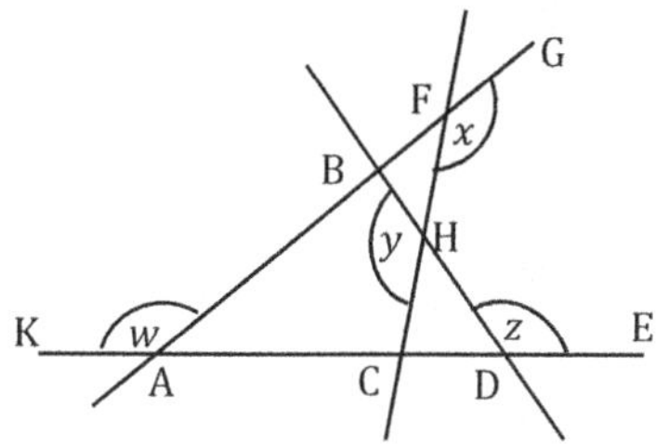


**(A)** 270°

**(B)** 360°

**(C)** 450°

**(D)** 540°

**(E)** 630°

*Solve yourself:*

**34.** In the diagram below, what is the correct expression for $x$ in terms of $y$?

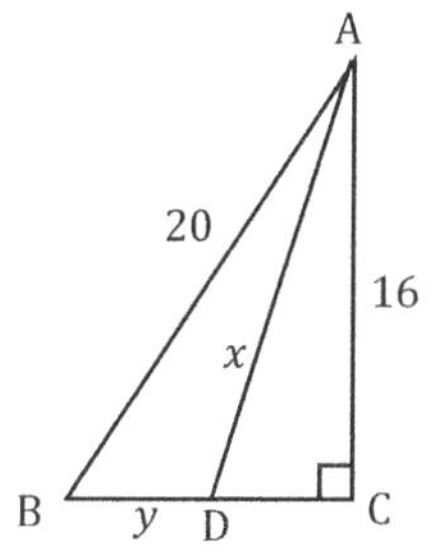


**(A)** $12 - y$

**(B)** $16 - y$

**(C)** $20 - y$

**(D)** $\sqrt{144 + y^2 - 40y}$

**(E)** $\sqrt{400 + y^2 - 24y}$

*Solve yourself:*

**35.** In the diagram below, each side of $\triangle ABC$ is of length 24. Point D is the foot of the perpendicular drawn from A to side BC. Point E is the midpoint of segment AD. What is the length of BE?

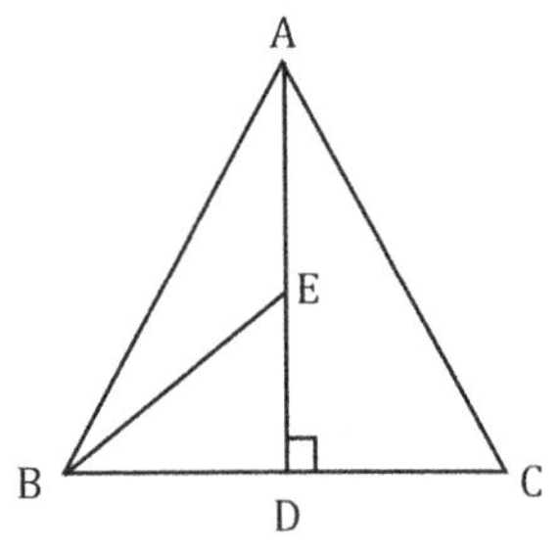


**(A)** $3\sqrt{7}$
**(B)** $6\sqrt{3}$
**(C)** 12
**(D)** $6\sqrt{7}$
**(E)** $12\sqrt{2}$

*Solve yourself:*

**36.** In a $\triangle ABC$, point D is on side AB and point E is on side AC, such that BCED is a trapezium. If DE : BC = 3 : 5, what is the ratio of the areas of $\triangle ADE$ and trapezium BCED?

**(A)** 3 : 4
**(B)** 3 : 5
**(C)** 9 : 16
**(D)** 9 : 25

 

**(E)** 1 : 3

*Solve yourself:*

**37.** An equilateral triangle BPC is drawn inside a square ABCD. What is the measure of $\angle$APD?

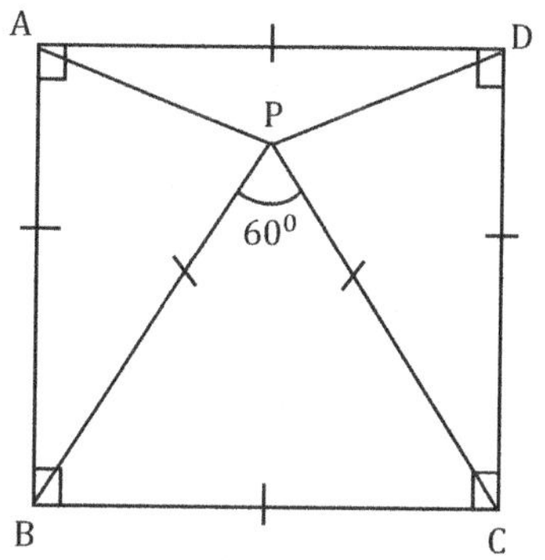


**(A)** 30°

**(B)** 60°

**(C)** 90°

**(D)** 120°

**(E)** 150°

*Solve yourself:*

**38.** In the diagram below, AB = AF and BC = CD. What is the measure of $\angle$DBF?

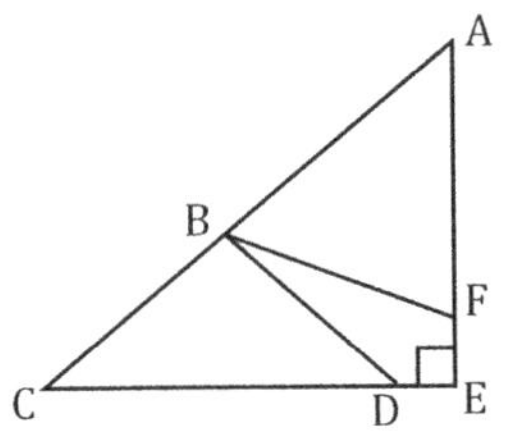


**(A)** $22.5^{\circ}$

**(B)** $30^{\circ}$

**(C)** $45^{\circ}$

**(D)** $60^{\circ}$

**(E)** $67.5^{\circ}$

*Solve yourself:*

**39.** In the diagram shown below, if AB is parallel to EF, what is the measure of $\angle$CDE?

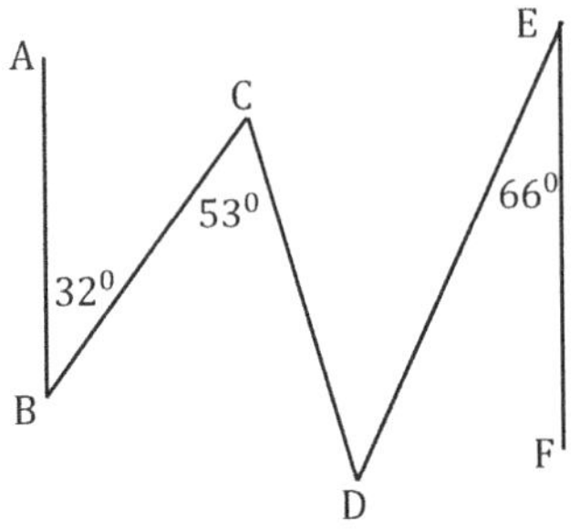


**(A)** $35^{\circ}$

**(B)** $55^{\circ}$

**(C)** $66^{\circ}$

**(D)** $87^{\circ}$

**(E)** $93^{\circ}$

*Solve yourself:*

 

**40.** In the diagram below, AQ = QD = DB = PD = DC = CR. If $\angle BAC = 40^o$, what is the measure of $\angle PRQ$?

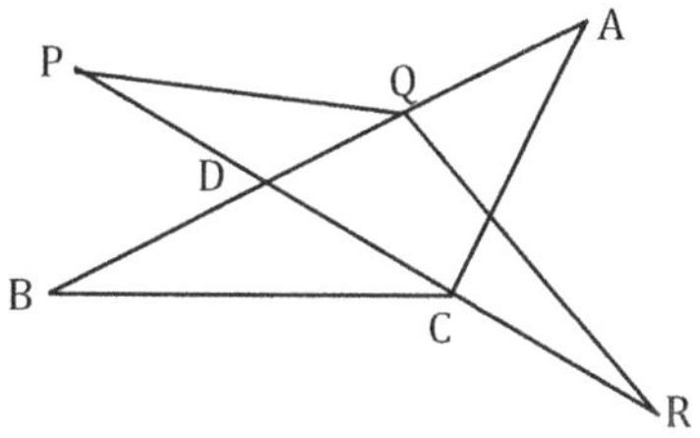


**(A)** $20^o$

**(B)** $30^o$

**(C)** $40^o$

**(D)** $45^o$

**(E)** $60^o$

*Solve yourself:*

**41.** In $\triangle ABC$, AB = 6, BC = 8 and AC = 10. A perpendicular dropped from B, meets the side AC at D. A circle with center B and radius BD is drawn which intersects AB and BC at P and Q, respectively. What is the ratio of the lengths AP and CQ?

**(A)** 1 : 1

**(B)** 3 : 8

**(C)** 2 : 3

**(D)** 3 : 4

**(E)** 3 : 2

 

*Solve yourself:*

**42.** In a trapezium ABCD, AB and CD are the parallel sides. The diagonals AC and BD meet at point O. If AB = 3DC and area of $\triangle$OCD is 6, what is the area of the trapezium ABCD?

**(A)** 18
**(B)** 36
**(C)** 72
**(D)** 96
**(E)** 108

*Solve yourself:*

**43.** In a quadrilateral, the longer diagonal is 16. The perpendiculars dropped from the opposite vertices on the longer diagonal are 10 and 12. What is the area of the quadrilateral?

**(A)** 88
**(B)** 176
**(C)** 252
**(D)** 320
**(E)** 352

*Solve yourself:*

**44.** In the diagram below, ABCD is a parallelogram and E is the midpoint of AB. DE bisects ∠ADC and CE bisects ∠BCD. What is the measure of ∠DEC?

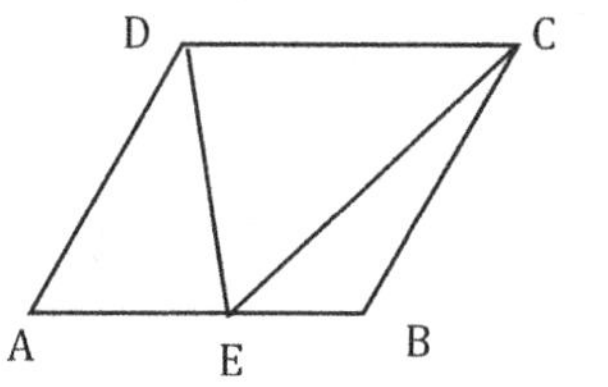


**(A)** 30°

**(B)** 45°

**(C)** 66°

**(D)** 90°

**(E)** 120°

*Solve yourself:*

**45.** In the diagram below, PQRS is a rectangle which has been divided in three congruent rectangles. What is the ratio of the sides PQ and QR?

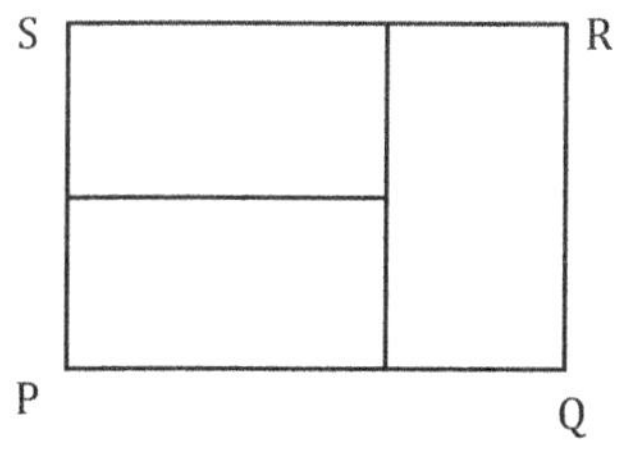


**(A)** 2 : 1

**(B)** 3 : 2

**(C)** 4 : 3

**(D)** 3 : 1

**(E)** 1 : 1

 

*Solve yourself:*

**46.** In the diagram below, ABCD is a trapezium with AB parallel to CD. What is the area of the trapezium ABCD?

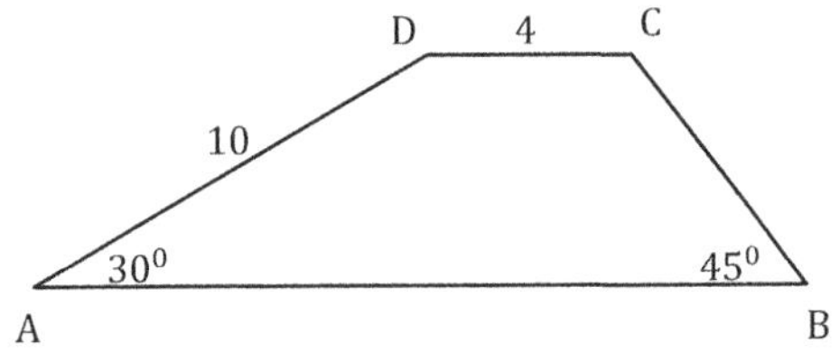


**(A)** $45\sqrt{3}$

**(B)** $\frac{5}{2}(13 + 5\sqrt{3})$

**(C)** $\frac{5\sqrt{3}}{2}(4 + 5\sqrt{3})$

**(D)** $\frac{5}{2}(9 + 5\sqrt{3})$

**(E)** 35

*Solve yourself:*

**47.** In the diagram below, ABCD is a rectangle with AD = $\sqrt{2}$ and AB = 1. AE is an arc of a circle with center D and radius AD. What is the length of BE?

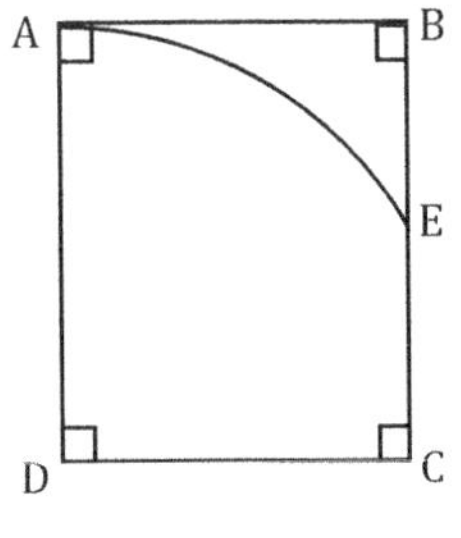


 

(A) $\sqrt{2} - 1$

(B) $\frac{1}{\sqrt{2}}$

(C) $2\sqrt{2} - 2$

(D) 1

(E) $1 + \frac{1}{\sqrt{2}}$

*Solve yourself:*

**48.** In a pentagon, each of the interior angles is a distinct integer. What is the largest possible value of an interior angle of the pentagon?

(A) $179^{o}$

(B) $359^{o}$

(C) $360^{o}$

(D) $530^{o}$

(E) $536^{o}$

*Solve yourself:*

**49.** In the diagram below, ABCD is a square. The two circles touch each other and also touch two sides of the square. The centers of the circles, P and Q, lie along the diagonal AC. What is the length of a side of square ABCD if the radius of each circle is 1?

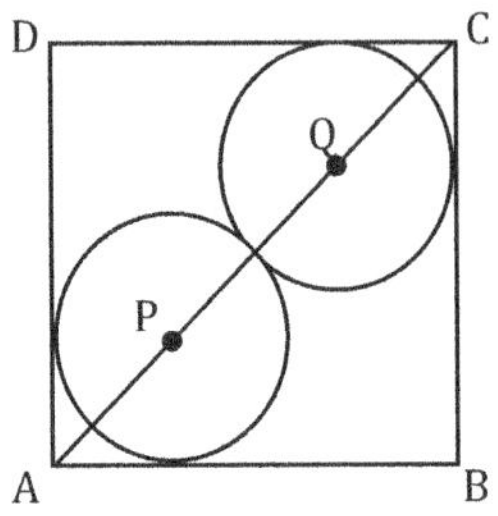


**(A)** $2\left(1+\sqrt{2}\right)$

**(B)** $2+\sqrt{2}$

**(C)** $2\sqrt{2}$

**(D)** $1+\sqrt{2}$

**(E)** $\sqrt{2}$

*Solve yourself:*

**50.** In the diagram below, OABC is a rectangle. The arc OXBY is drawn with radius OX and center O. If $OC = \frac{3}{5}OY$ and $AX = 2$, what is the length OB?

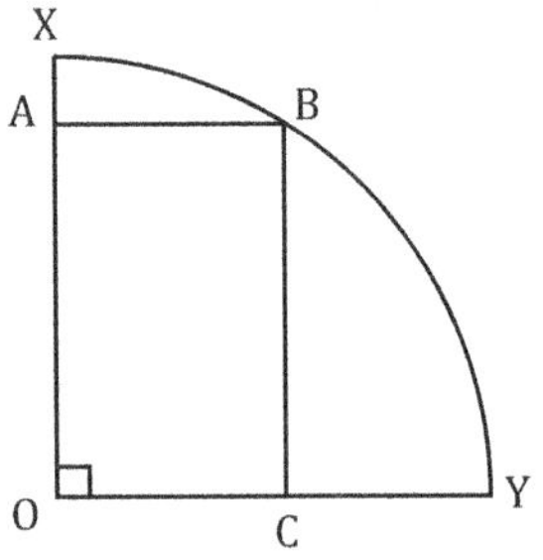


**(A)** 8

**(B)** $6\sqrt{2}$

**(C)** 10

**(D)** $8\sqrt{2}$

**(E)** 12

*Solve yourself:*

**51.** The perimeter of $\triangle$PQR is 36. A circle inscribed in this triangle touches PR at C such that PC = 6 and CR = 9. What is the area of $\triangle$PQR?

**(A)** 36

**(B)** 48

**(C)** 54

**(D)** 60

**(E)** 96

*Solve yourself:*

**52.** In the diagram below, AB = BD = DC = CE = EA. What is the measure of $\angle$DAC?

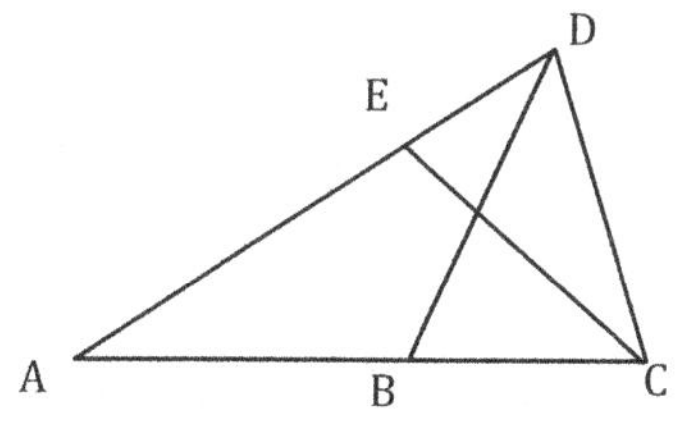


**(A)** $30^{\circ}$

**(B)** $36^{\circ}$

**(C)** $45^{\circ}$

**(D)** $54^{\circ}$

**(E)** $60^{\circ}$

*Solve yourself:*

**53.** In the diagram below, ABFE is a rectangle with AB = 20 and AE = 10. C is any point on CityAB. If DE = DF and EG = GC, what is the area of the shaded region?

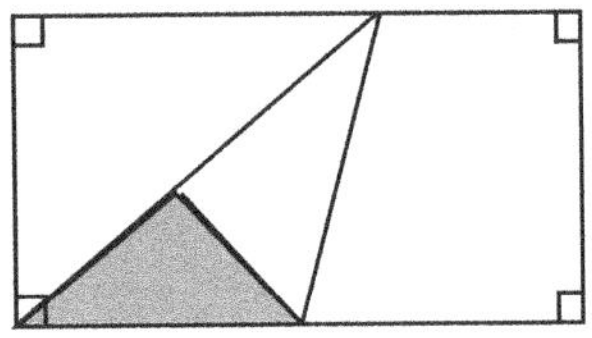

**(A)** 16

**(B)** 20

**(C)** 25

**(D)** 30

**(E)** 45

*Solve yourself:*

**54.** A cube of edge 6 cm is immersed completely in a rectangular vessel containing water. If the dimensions of the base of the vessel are 15 cm by 12 cm, what is the rise in the water level of the vessel?

**(A)** 1 cm

**(B)** 1.2 cm

**(C)** 2.5 cm

**(D)** 3 cm

**(E)** 3.2 cm

 

*Solve yourself:*

**55.** What is the radius of the largest sphere that can be placed inside a hollow cone having height 4 and radius 3?

**(A)** $\frac{1}{2}$
**(B)** 1
**(C)** $\frac{3}{2}$
**(D)** $\frac{5}{3}$
**(E)** 2

*Solve yourself:*

**56.** What is the volume of the largest cube that can be placed inside a cylinder having height 3 and radius 2?

**(A)** $16\sqrt{2}$
**(B)** 24
**(C)** 27
**(D)** $32\sqrt{2}$
**(E)** 64

*Solve yourself:*

57. A rectangular box of 3 cm by 2.5 cm by 2 cm is made up of glass plates held together with tapes. If the box is to be kept open on one side, what is the minimum total length of tape required to hold the plates together (ignore the length of overlapping tapes)?

(A) 16
(B) 18
(C) 19
(D) 20
(E) 21

*Solve yourself:*

58. A rectangular reservoir is 120 m long and 60 m wide. At what speed, in meters per hour, must water flow into it through a square pipe 2 m wide, so that the water rises by 3 m in 18 hours?

(A) 150
(B) 200
(C) 250
(D) 300
(E) 360

*Solve yourself:*

59. If a cube is cut thrice parallel to any of its faces, what is the percent increase in surface area as a result?

 

(A) 33.3%
(B) 50%
(C) 100%
(D) 150%
(E) 200%

*Solve yourself:*

**60.** A cylinder and a cube have the same volume. If the radius and height of the cylinder are equal, what is the ratio of the curved surface area of the cylinder and the total surface area of the cube?

(A) $\frac{\pi}{3}$
(B) $\frac{\sqrt[3]{\pi}}{2}$
(C) $\frac{\sqrt{\pi}}{3}$
(D) $\frac{\sqrt[3]{\pi}}{3}$
(E) $\frac{\sqrt{\pi}}{9}$

*Solve yourself:*

### 3.1.2 Data Sufficiency

Standard options for Data Sufficiency questions are as follows.

A. Statement (1) ALONE is sufficient, but statement (2) ALONE is not sufficient to answer the question asked.

B. Statement (2) ALONE is sufficient, but statement (1) ALONE is not sufficient to answer the question asked.

C. BOTH statements (1) and (2) TOGETHER are sufficient to answer the question asked, but NEITHER statement ALONE is sufficient to answer the question asked.

D. EACH statement ALONE is sufficient to answer the question asked.

E. Statements (1) and (2) TOGETHER are NOT sufficient to answer the question asked, and additional data specific to the problem are needed.

**61.** In $\triangle ABC$, is the measure of one of the angles $60^\circ$?

(1) The difference between exactly two pairs of angles of $\triangle ABC$ is $20^\circ$.

(2) $AB = \sqrt{3}AC$.

*Solve yourself:*

**62.** What is the area of the rhombus?

(1) A side of the rhombus is 13.

(2) The length of one diagonal of the rhombus is 10.

*Solve yourself:*

 

**63.** In the diagram below, ABCD is a rectangle and P is a point inside it. What is the length of AP?

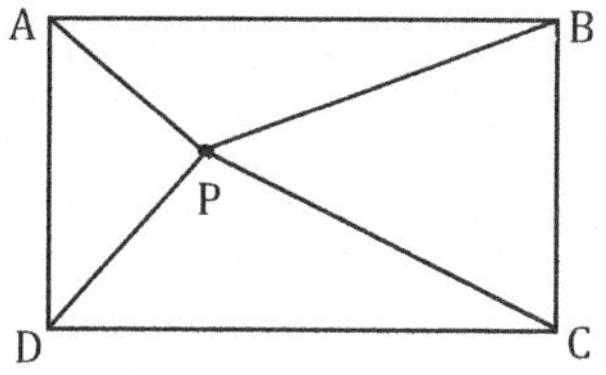


(1) BP = 8 and DP = 6.

(2) CP = 5.

*Solve yourself:*

**64.** △ABC is right-angled at B. What is the length of AB?

(1) The perpendicular distances of a point M on AC from AB and BC are 3 and 4, respectively.

(2) BM is perpendicular to AC.

*Solve yourself:*

**65.** In the diagram below, ABCD is a rectangle. What is the area of ABCD?

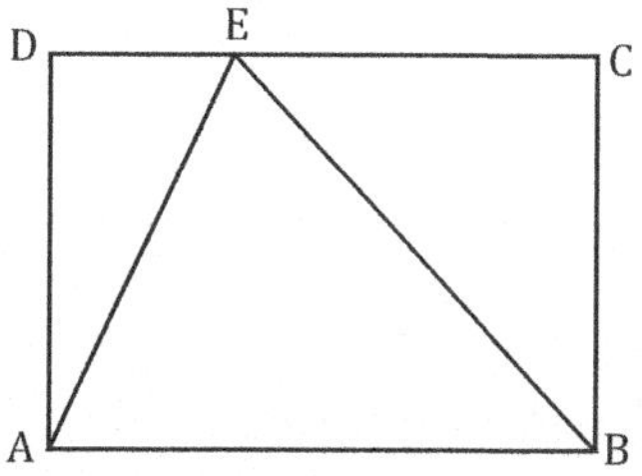

(1) Area of $\triangle BCE$ is 30.

(2) Area of $\triangle ADE$ is 20.

*Solve yourself:*

**66.** In the diagram below, is M the center of the circle?

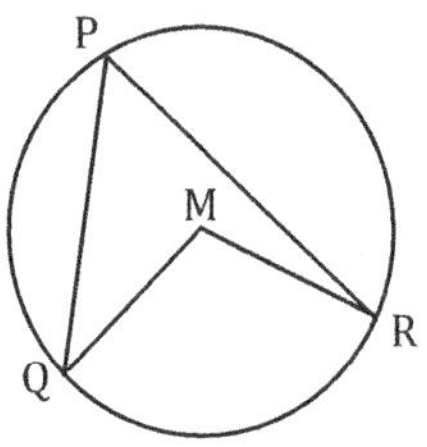


(1) Measure of $\angle QMR$ is $150^o$.

(2) Measure of $\angle QPR$ is $75^o$.

*Solve yourself:*

**67.** A cylindrical vessel with its top open is completely filled with water. Then it is tilted and some of the water is drained out. The remaining water in the cylinder is poured in a cubical vessel, filling it completely. What is the length of a side of the cubical vessel?

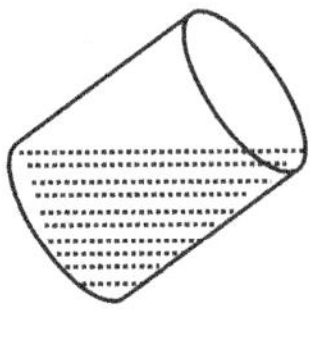

(1) The cylinder has radius 3 and height 16.

(2) After the water was drained out, the water level formed a straight line joining the upper and lower rims as shown below:

 

*Solve yourself:*

**68.** In the diagram below, the arc PQ is drawn with X as center. What is the measure of $\angle PXQ$?

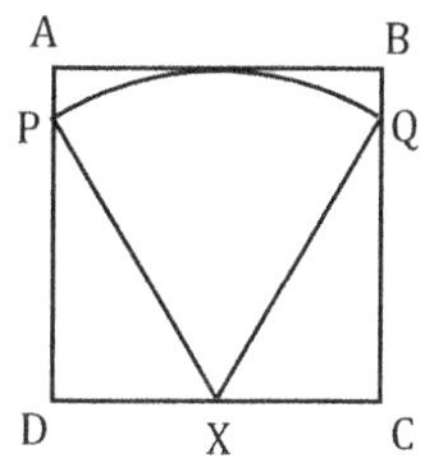


(1) ABCD is a square.

(2) $\angle PXD = 60^\circ$.

*Solve yourself:*

**69.** In the diagram below, ABCD is a rectangle. What is the length of BE?

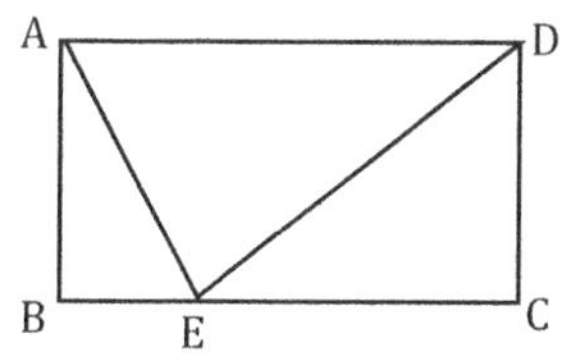


(1) AD = 5 and DE = 4.

(2) AB = 2.4

*Solve yourself:*

 

**70.** In the diagram below, what is the ratio of the areas of $\triangle ABE$ and $\triangle BDC$?

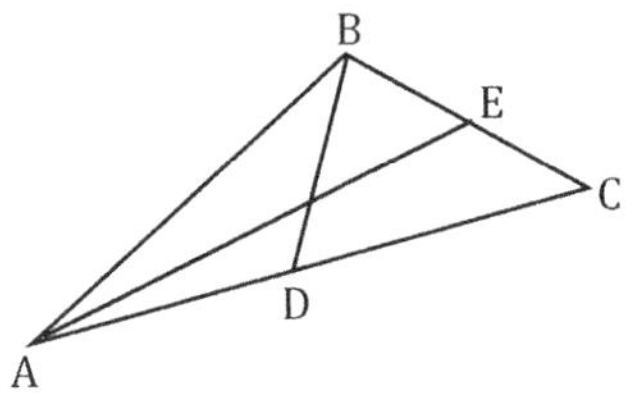


(1) AD = CD

(2) BE = CE

*Solve yourself:*

**71.** In the diagram below, ABCD is a square. A, B, C, D, E, F, G and H are the centers of the circles. Each of the larger circles is identical and each of the smaller circles is also identical. What is the radius of the smaller circles?

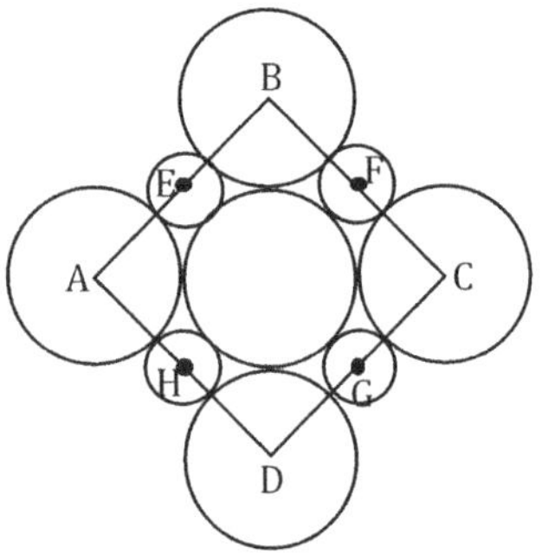


(1) Each of the larger circles has radius 2.

(2) AC = 8.

*Solve yourself:*

**72.** In the diagram below, each of the larger circles is identical. A, B, C, and D are the centers of the circles. What is the area of the shaded region?

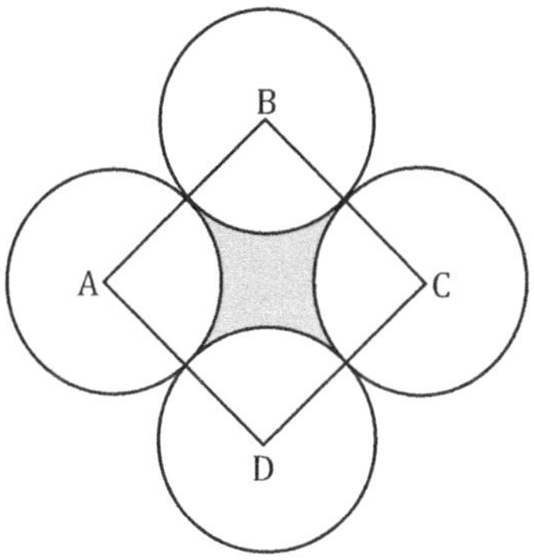


(1) Each of the larger circles has radius 2.

(2) ABCD is a square.

*Solve yourself:*

**73.** What is the area of the isosceles triangle?

(1) The perimeter of the isosceles triangle is 110.

(2) The ratio of the lateral side to the base is 3 : 4.

*Solve yourself:*

 

**74.** In an isosceles triangle, the unequal side and the altitude to the unequal side are equal. What is the length of the equal sides?

(1) The perimeter of the triangle is $6\left(\sqrt{5}+1\right)$.

(2) The area of the triangle is 18.

*Solve yourself:*

**75.** In the diagram below, M, N and P are the midpoints of the sides of the rectangle ABCD. What is the area of the shaded region?

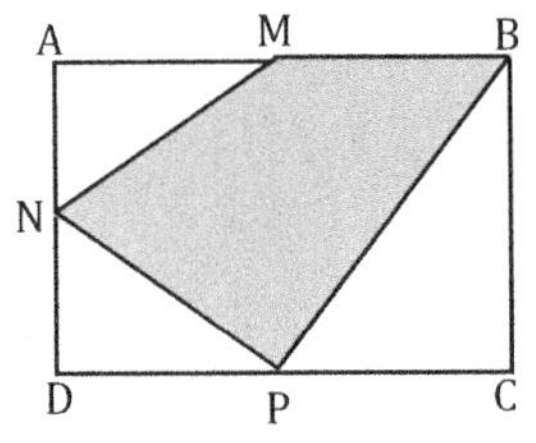


(1) The sides of the rectangle are 14 and 8.

(2) The area of the rectangle is 112.

*Solve yourself:*

**76.** What is the area of the quadrilateral ABCD as shown in the diagram below?

 

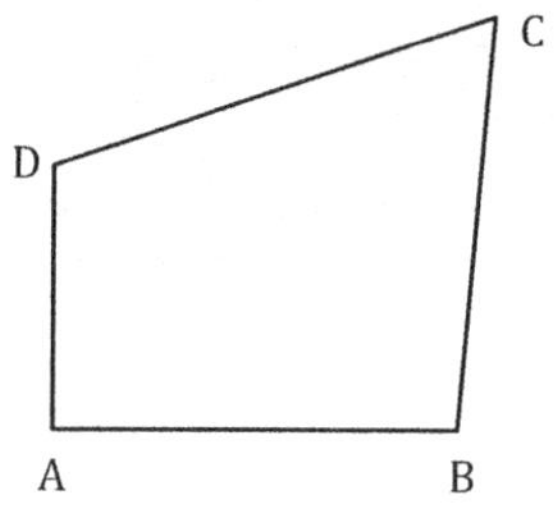


(1) AB = 24, AD = 18 and $\angle$DAB = 90°.

(2) CD = CB = 30.

*Solve yourself:*

**77.** In the diagram below, what is the area of $\triangle$ABC?

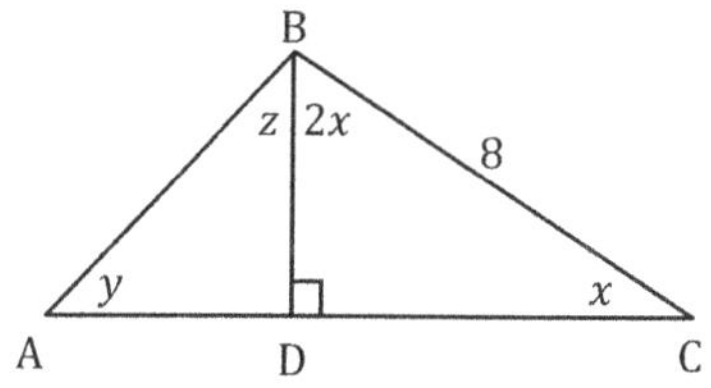


(1) $y = z$

(2) $x + y = 75^\circ$

*Solve yourself:*

**78.** In the diagram below, ABCD is a rectangle. What is the area of $\triangle$AED?

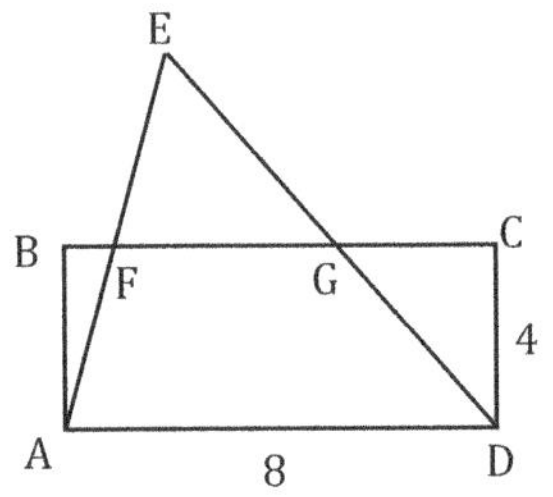


(1) FG = 4

(2) BF = 1

*Solve yourself:*

**79.** In the diagram below, A, B and C are three corners of a rectangular solid. What is the measure of $\angle ABC$?

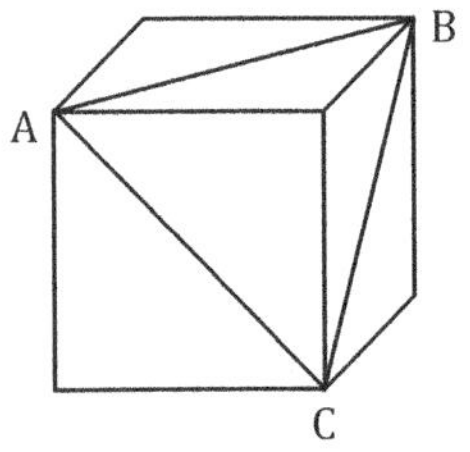


(1) All edges of the rectangular solid are equal.

(2) The sum of the lengths of all the edges of the solid is 24.

*Solve yourself:*

**80.** In the diagram below five equal circles are drawn with the vertices of the pentagon as their centers. What is the area of shaded region?

 

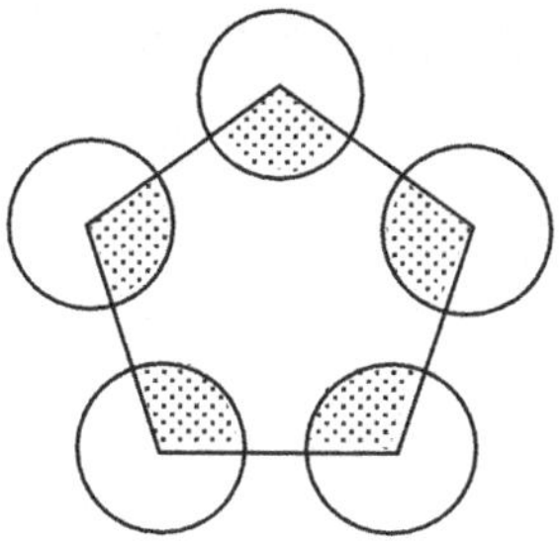

(1) The radius of each of the circles is 1.

(2) The pentagon is regular.

*Solve yourself:*

**81.** In the diagram below, ABCD is a rectangle. What is the length of EG?

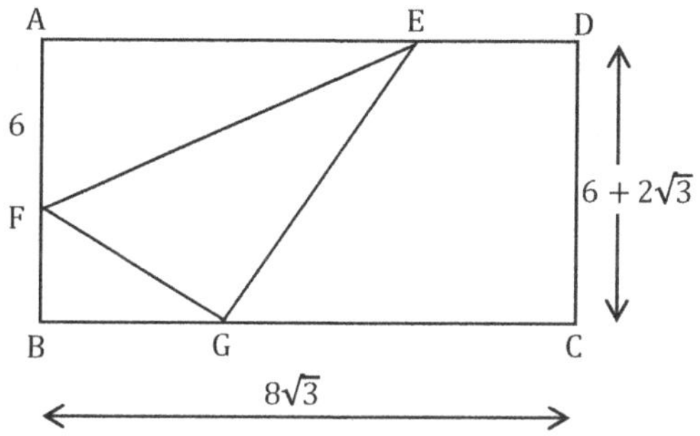


(1) ED = $2\sqrt{3}$, BG = 2.

(2) $\angle EFG = 90^\circ$.

*Solve yourself:*

**82.** In the diagram below, the intersection of diagonals of squares ABCD and EFGH shares the same point O. What is the perimeter of the trapezium ABFE?

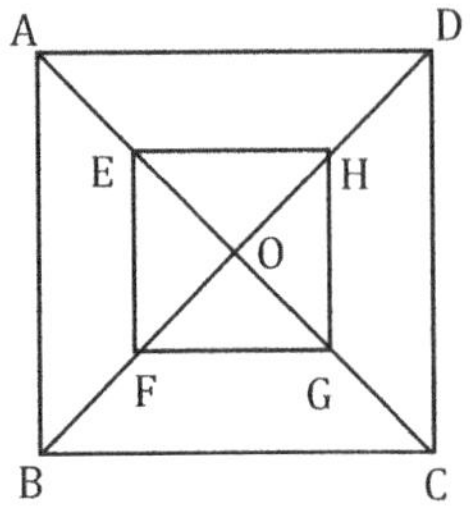


(1) Perimeter of ABCD is 120.

(2) Perimeter of EFGH is 40.

*Solve yourself:*

**83.** Two isosceles triangles △ABE and △CFD, with AB = BE and CF = CD, respectively, are cut off from an isosceles trapezium ABCD having BC parallel to AD, to form another isosceles trapezium BCFE, as shown in the diagram below. What is the length of AD?

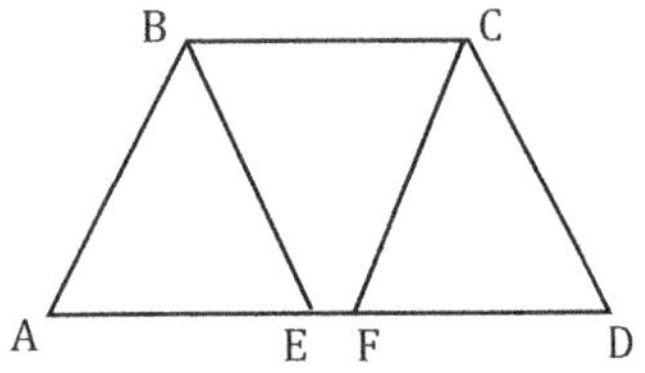


(1) The perimeter of the new trapezium is 20 less than the perimeter of the original trapezium.

(2) BC : EF = 5 : 3.

*Solve yourself:*

 

**84.** In the diagram below, is area of $\triangle ABC$ greater than the area of $\triangle XYZ$?

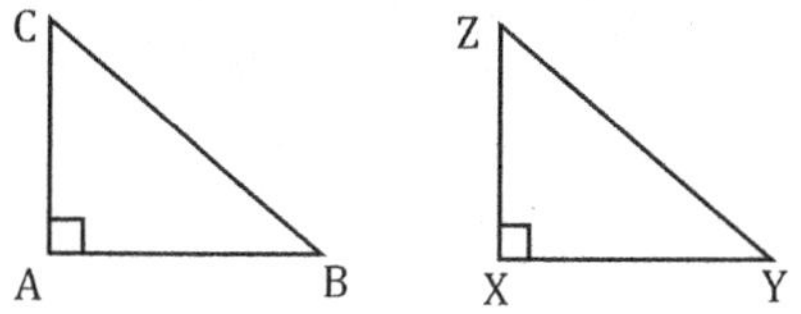


(1) $AB = 4$ and $XZ = 5$.

(2) $\frac{AC}{BC} = \frac{XY}{ZY}$.

*Solve yourself:*

**85.** Is $\triangle ABC$ an acute angled triangle?

(1) The three altitudes of $\triangle ABC$ are of equal length.

(2) The altitude drawn from vertex A on BC is equal to the median drawn through A.

*Solve yourself:*

**86.** In the diagram below, $AB = 6$. What is the length of CD?

 

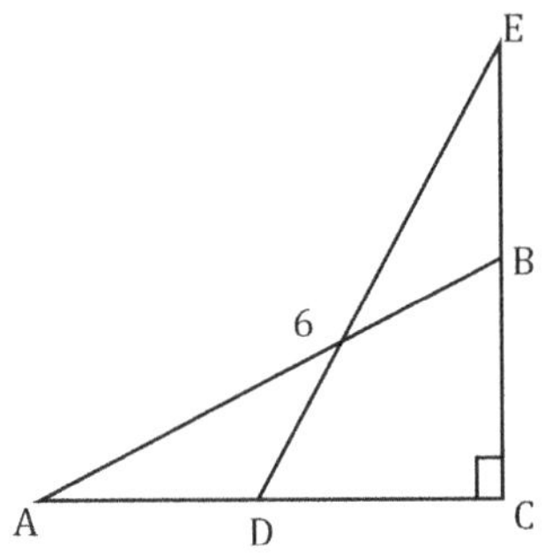


(1) BC = BE = 3.
(2) ∠BAC = 90° - ∠EDC.

*Solve yourself:*

**87.** In the diagram below, TP is a tangent to the circle. Is TP = TS?

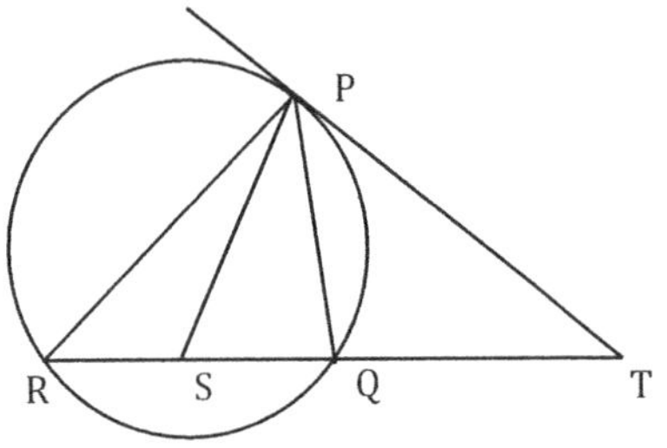


(1) PS bisects ∠QPR.
(2) Length of PR is greater than that of PQ.

*Solve yourself:*

**88.** In the diagram below, C is a point inside the circle. What is the length of AC?

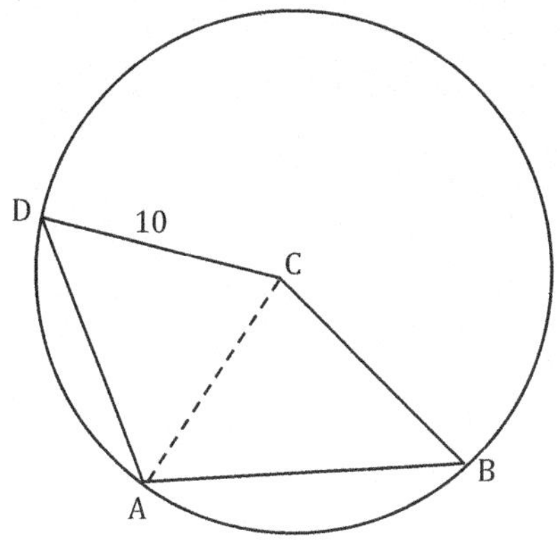


(1) $\angle DAB = 105^\circ$.

(2) $\angle DCB = 150^\circ$.

*Solve yourself:*

**89.** In the diagram below, ABCD is a rectangle. Is the area of ABCD greater than 22?

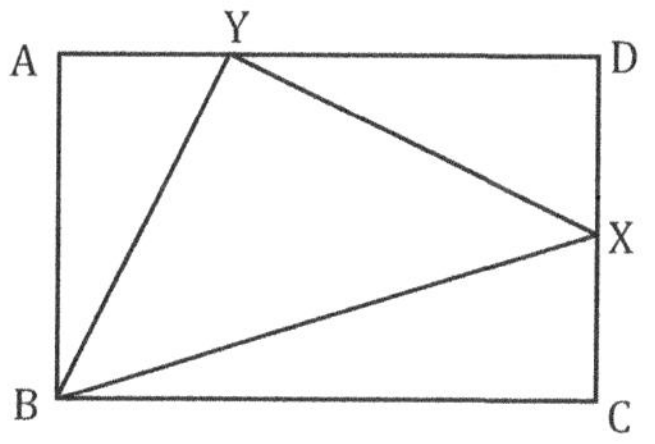


(1) Area $\triangle ABY = 4$.

(2) Area $\triangle BXC = 9$ and area $\triangle DXY = 2$.

*Solve yourself:*

**90.** In the pentagon ABCDE shown in the diagram below, AB = 5. What is the length of EA?

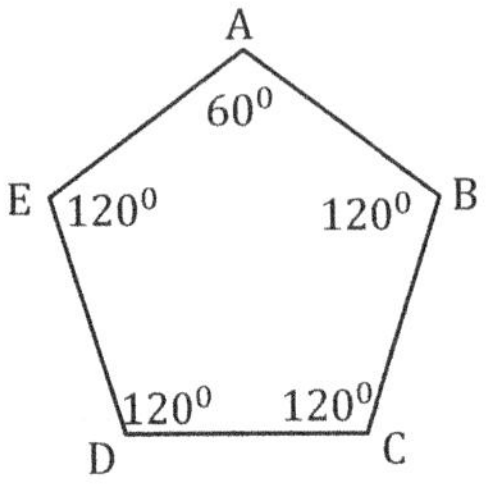


(1) BC = 6.
(2) CD = 2.

*Solve yourself:*

**91.** What is the area of the right-angled triangle?

(1) The perimeter of the triangle is 90.
(2) The length of the hypotenuse is 39.

*Solve yourself:*

**92.** In the diagram below, what is the measure of ∠DBC?

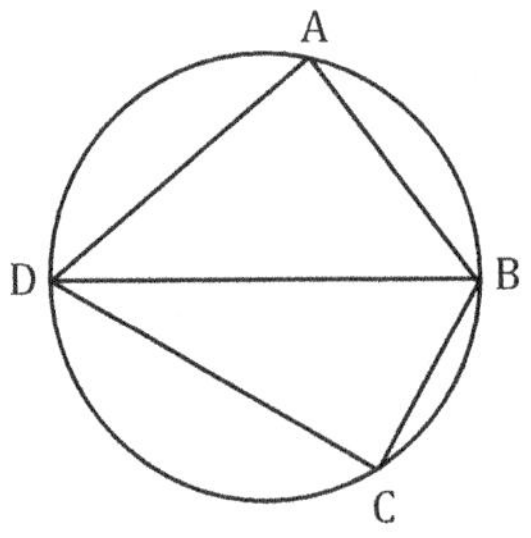


(1) ∠DAB = $90^0$.

 

(2) $\angle BDC = 20^o$.

*Solve yourself:*

**93.** In the diagram below, what is the measure of $\angle QRS$?

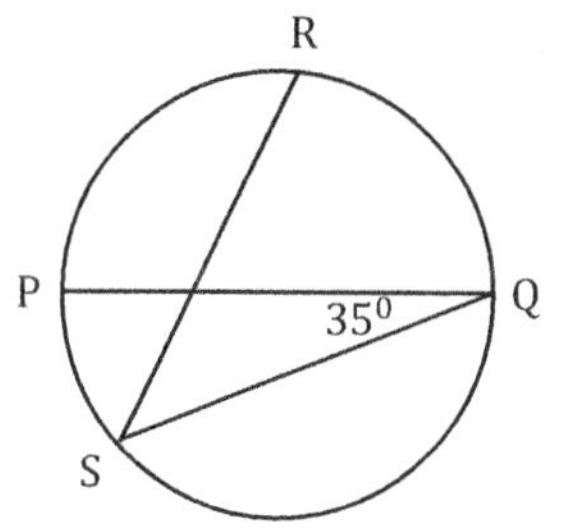


(1) PQ is the diameter of the circle.

(2) $\angle PQR = 55^o$.

*Solve yourself:*

**94.** In the diagram below, PQ is the diameter. What is the measure of $\angle QPR$?

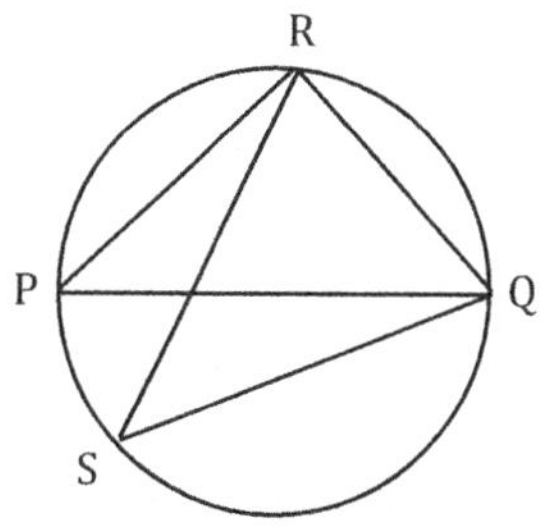


(1) $\angle PQS = 22^o$.

(2) $\angle SQR = 90^o$.

*Solve yourself:*

**95.** In the diagram below, the circles touch each other at P. XY and PQ are common tangents to both circles. What is the measure of ∠PQX?

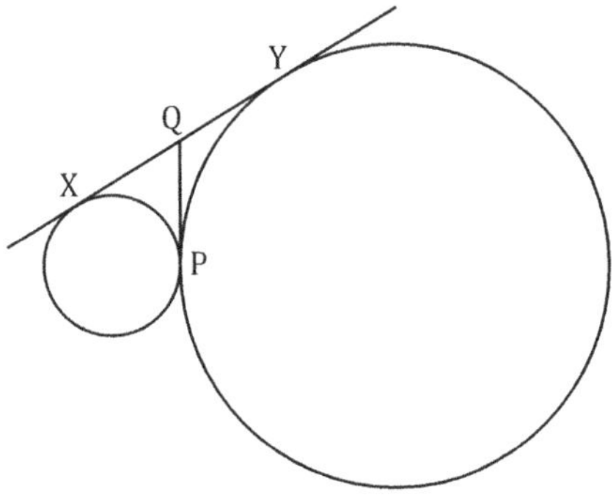


(1) The ratio of the two circles is 1 : 3.
(2) PQ = QX = QY.

*Solve yourself:*

**96.** What is the value of $x$?

(1) The volume of a cube is $x^3$ cubic inches.
(2) The surface area of the cube is $x^3$ square inches.

*Solve yourself:*

**97.** In the diagram below, ADEF is a rectangle. EB and FC are the bisectors of ∠DEF and ∠AFE, respectively. What is the area of △GBC?

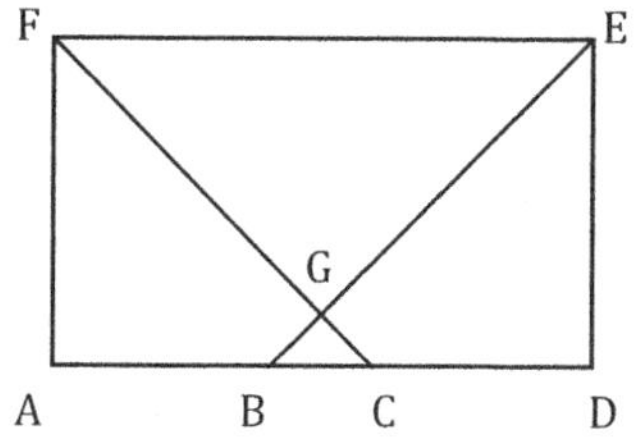


(1) AF = 4.

(2) AD = 6.

*Solve yourself:*

**98.** In the diagram below, DE is parallel to BC. If the length of BC is 2, what is the length of DE?

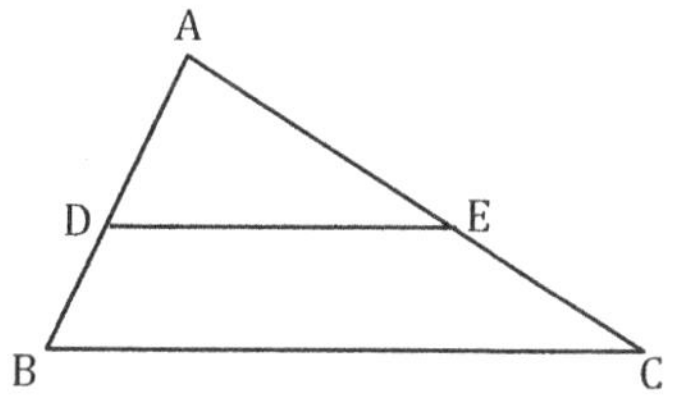


(1) Ratio of areas of △ABC and △ADE is 2.

(2) Area of △ABC = 16.

*Solve yourself:*

**99.** In triangles △ABC and △DEF, ∠ABC = ∠DEF and ∠ACB = ∠DFE. What is the numerical value of the length of DF?

(1) The lengths of AB and AC are $(10x - 2)$ and $6x$.

(2) The lengths of DE and DF are $(2x + 2)$ and $(x + 2)$.

*Solve yourself:*

**100.** The perimeter of a rectangle is 24. What is its area?

(1) The difference between the area of the rectangle and a quadrilateral with perimeter 24 having the maximum area is 4.

(2) The rectangle can be divided into exactly two identical squares by drawing a line joining the midpoints of two opposite sides.

*Solve yourself:*

**101.** In the diagram below, $\angle BCD = \angle BAC$. What is the length of AB?

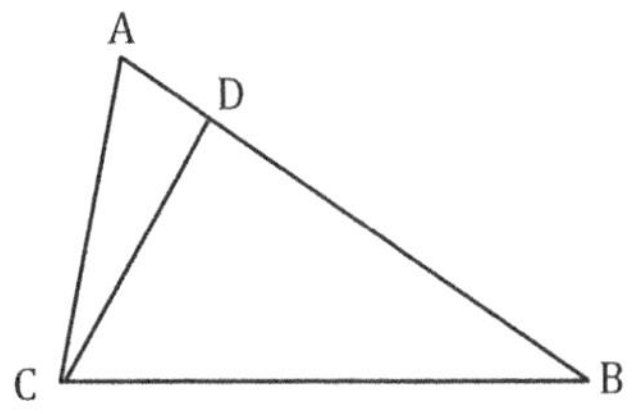


(1) BC = 12 and BD = 9.

(2) CD = 6.

*Solve yourself:*

 

**102.** In the diagram below, is CD = BF?

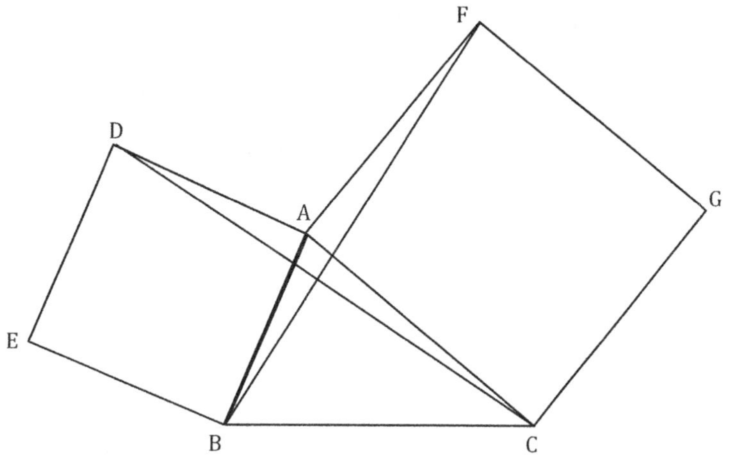


(1) ABED and ACGF are squares.

(2) $\triangle$ABC is an isosceles triangle.

*Solve yourself:*

**103.** In the diagram below, ABCD is a square. The area of $\triangle$DEF forms what fraction of the area of the square ABCD?

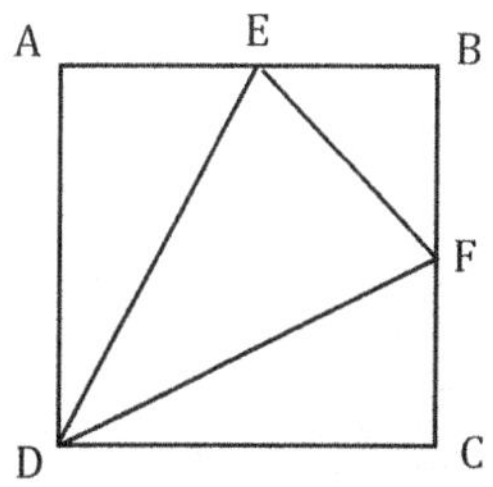

(1) DE = DF.

(2) E and F are the midpoints of AB and CB, respectively.

*Solve yourself:*

**104.** In the diagram below, PQ and PR are tangents to the circle. What is the measure of ∠QSR?

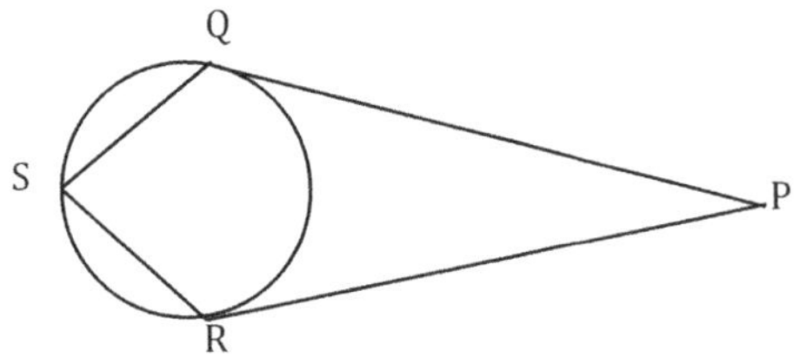


(1) ∠QPR = $60^{\circ}$.

(2) SQ = SP.

*Solve yourself:*

**105.** In the diagram below, what is the measure of ∠ACP?

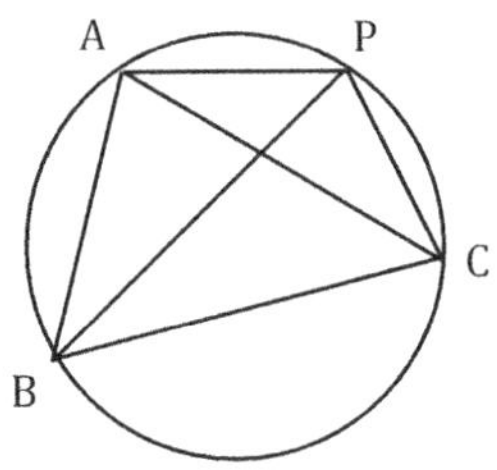


(1) ∠ABC = $60^{\circ}$.

(2) Arc AB = Arc APC = Arc BC = 2 * (Arc AP).

 

*Solve yourself:*

**106.** In the diagram below, what is the measure of the sum of ∠BAC and ∠ABD?

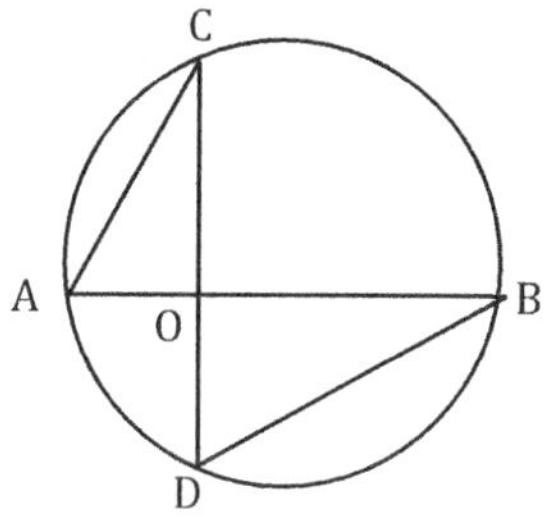


(1) ∠COB = 90°.

(2) AB is the diameter of the circle.

*Solve yourself:*

**107.** In the diagram below, AE is the diameter of the circle. What is the length of AE?

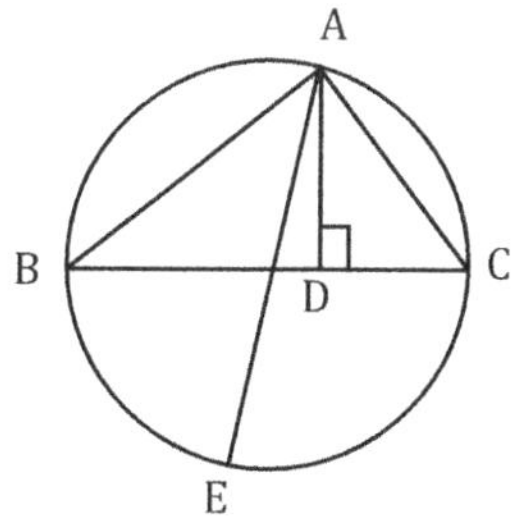


(1) AB = 40 and AC = 30.

(2) AD = 24.

*Solve yourself:*

 

**108.** In the diagram below, the circles with centers at P and Q touch each other externally at R. A straight line drawn through the point of contact of the circles meets them at A and B, respectively. What is the measure of ∠PAR?

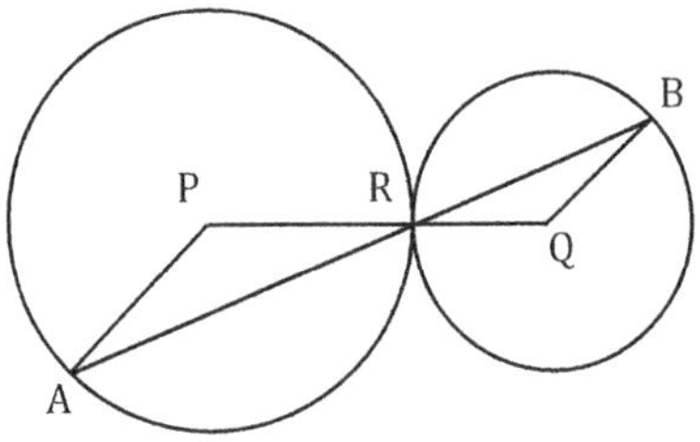


(1) ∠QBR = 30°.

(2) ∠BQR = 120°.

*Solve yourself:*

**109.** What is the value of $x$?

(1) The sum of the interior angles of a polygon is $9x^2$ degrees.

(2) The number of sides of the polygon is 3 less than $x$.

*Solve yourself:*

 

**110.** What is the number of sides of the polygon?

(1) The sum of interior angles of the polygon is '4' times the sum of exterior angles.

(2) The number of diagonals in the polygon is 25 greater than its number of sides.

*Solve yourself:*

## 3.2 Co-ordinate geometry

### 3.2.1 Problem Solving

**111.** If the points (1, 1), ($a$, 0) and (0, $b$) are collinear, which of the following is equivalent to ($a + b$)?

**(A)** $\frac{a}{b}$
**(B)** $\frac{b}{a}$
**(C)** $(a + 1)(b + 1)$
**(D)** $ab$
**(E)** $\sqrt{(a + 1)(b + 1)}$

*Solve yourself:*

**112.** If the vertices of a triangle have the co-ordinates (0, 0), (3, 2) and (0, 5), what is the area of the triangle?

**(A)** 3
**(B)** 4
**(C)** 4.5
**(D)** 6
**(E)** 7.5

*Solve yourself:*

**113.** If the points A (7, 9), B (3, 7) and C (3, 3) are the vertices of a triangle, what is the measure of $\angle$C?

 

(A) $0^o$
(B) $30^o$
(C) $45^o$
(D) $60^o$
(E) $90^o$

*Solve yourself:*

**114.** If the vertices of triangle ABC are A (0, 0), B (5, 1) and C (7, 3), what is the length of the median through vertex A?

(A) 3
(B) 5
(C) $\sqrt{27}$
(D) $\sqrt{40}$
(E) 8

*Solve yourself:*

**115.** What is the ratio in which the Y axis intersects the line joining the points (4, 5) and (10, 2)?

(A) 1 : 3
(B) 5 : 2
(C) 1 : 1
(D) 3 : 2
(E) 5 : 3

 

*Solve yourself:*

**116.** What is the X intercept of the line parallel to $2x - 3y + 5 = 0$, and passing through $(1,\ 1)$?

**(A)** $-1$
**(B)** $-\frac{1}{2}$
**(C)** $\frac{1}{2}$
**(D)** $2$
**(E)** $3$

*Solve yourself:*

**117.** Three vertices of a parallelogram, taken in order, are $(a + b,\ a - b)$, $(2a + b,\ 2a - b)$ and $(a - b,\ a + b)$. What are the coordinates of the fourth vertex?

**(A)** $(-b, b)$
**(B)** $(a, -a)$
**(C)** $(b, b)$
**(D)** $(a, a)$
**(E)** $(a, -b)$

*Solve yourself:*

**118.** For what integer value of $m$ are the points A $(m+1,\ 1)$, B $(2m+1,\ 3)$ and C $(2m+2,\ 2m)$ collinear?

**(A)** $-2$
**(B)** $-1$
**(C)** 0
**(D)** 1
**(E)** 2

*Solve yourself:*

**119.** The points A $(5,\ 3)$, B $(8,\ 8)$, C $(3,\ 5)$ and D $(0,\ 0)$ are the vertices of a quadrilateral ABCD. Which of the following options are correct?

**I.** ABCD is a rectangle with unequal adjacent sides
**II.** ABCD is a square
**III.** ABCD is a rhombus with unequal diagonals

**(A)** Only I
**(B)** Only II
**(C)** Only III
**(D)** Both I and II
**(E)** Both II and III

*Solve yourself:*

 

**120.** What is the equation of a line passing through $(-4, 1)$, making equal intercepts on the coordinate axis?

**(A)** $x + 2y + 3 = 0$
**(B)** $x + y - 7 = 0$
**(C)** $2x - y + 8 = 0$
**(D)** $x + y + 3 = 0$
**(E)** $2x - y - 5 = 0$

*Solve yourself:*

**121.** If the lines $3y + 4x = 1$, $y = x + 5$ and $5y + bx = 3$ are concurrent, what is the value of $b$?

**(A)** 0
**(B)** 1
**(C)** 2
**(D)** 3
**(E)** 6

*Solve yourself:*

**122.** Which of the following is correct if the lines $\frac{x}{a} + \frac{y}{b} = 1$ and $\frac{x}{p} + \frac{y}{q} = 1$ are perpendicular to one another?

**(A)** $ap - bq = 0$
**(B)** $ap + bq = 0$
**(C)** $ap + bq = 1$

 

**(D)** $ap - bq = 1$

**(E)** $bq - ap = 1$

*Solve yourself:*

**123.** A function $f(x)$ is defined on the interval $0 \le x \le 2$ as:

- $f(x)$ = Integer closest to $x$; $x \neq 0.5$ or $1.5$
- $f(0.5) = 0$
- $f(1.5) = 1$

What is the area under the graph of this function above the X axis?

**(A)** 5

**(B)** 4

**(C)** 3

**(D)** 2

**(E)** 1

*Solve yourself:*

**124.** What are the point(s) on the X axis whose perpendicular distance from the straight line $\frac{x}{3} + \frac{y}{4} = 1$ is 3?

**I.** $\left(\frac{27}{4}, 0\right)$

**II.** $\left(-\frac{3}{4}, 0\right)$

**III.** $\left(\frac{3}{4}, 0\right)$

**(A)** Only I
**(B)** Only II
**(C)** Only III
**(D)** Both I and II
**(E)** Both II and III

*Solve yourself:*

**125.** P and Q are two points on the line $3x + 4y + 15 = 0$ such that OP and OQ are both 5 units, where O is the origin. What is the area of triangle POQ?

**(A)** $18\sqrt{2}$
**(B)** 15
**(C)** 12
**(D)** $6\sqrt{2}$
**(E)** 3

*Solve yourself:*

**126.** Lattice points are those points whose coordinates can take integral values. What is the number of lattice points on the boundary and inside the region bounded by a circle having the equation $x^2 + y^2 = 9$?

**(A)** 35
**(B)** 29
**(C)** 21

 

**(D)** 20

**(E)** 16

*Solve yourself:*

**127.** The graph of the quadratic $y = x^2 + ax + b$ intersects the X axis at two points to the right of the origin and also has a positive Y intercept. Which of the following is correct about the straight line $y = bx + a$?

**(A)** The line has a positive slope and a positive Y intercept

**(B)** The line has a positive slope and a negative Y intercept

**(C)** The line has a negative slope and a positive Y intercept

**(D)** The line has a negative slope and a negative Y intercept

**(E)** The line has zero slope and a positive Y intercept

*Solve yourself:*

**128.** A and B are two points with the co-ordinates $(-3, 0)$ and $(0, 4)$, respectively. What is the length of the diagonal AC if AB forms one of the sides of the square ABCD?

**(A)** 5

**(B)** 6

**(C)** $5\sqrt{2}$

**(D)** $6\sqrt{2}$

**(E)** 10

 

*Solve yourself:*

**129.** There is a grass field represented in the XY coordinate plane as $x > 0$, $y > 0$ and $3x + 4y \leq 60$. A cow is tied with a cord to a pole situated exactly at the point having coordinates (0, 0). If the length of the cord is 12 units, what is the area of the grass field which cannot be grazed by the cow? Assume $\pi = 3$.

(A) 42
(B) 66
(C) 108
(D) 120
(E) 150

*Solve yourself:*

**130.** What is the area of the region bounded by the lines $y = 2x$, $x + y = 6$ and the X axis?

(A) 4
(B) 8
(C) 12
(D) 16
(E) 24

*Solve yourself:*

### 3.2.2 Data Sufficiency

**131.** What is the Y intercept of the straight line?

(1) The line is at a perpendicular distance of 3 from the origin.

(2) The line has a slope '$-1$'.

*Solve yourself:*

**132.** What is the value of $k$?

(1) The line $2x+3y+6+k(9x-y+12)=0$ is perpendicular to $7x+5y-4=0$.

(2) The Y intercept of the line $x+ky=4$ is '$-8$'.

*Solve yourself:*

**133.** For a straight line, what is the value of $(a-b)$?

(1) The line passes through the points $(3, -6)$ and $(a, b)$.

(2) The line is parallel to $3x-3y+5=0$.

*Solve yourself:*

**134.** What is the area of the circle?

(1) The end-points of a diameter of the circle have coordinates $(-3, -2)$ and $(5, 2)$.
(2) The center of the circle is at $(1, 0)$.

*Solve yourself:*

**135.** What is the area of the circle?

(1) The circle passes through the points having coordinates $(0, 6)$ and $(6, 0)$.
(2) The circle passes through the point $(0, 0)$.

*Solve yourself:*

**136.** What are the coordinates of the center of the circle?

(1) The circle passes through the points having coordinates $(1, 2)$ and $(5, 4)$.
(2) The center of the circle lies on the line $y = 2x + 7$.

*Solve yourself:*

**137.** What is the value of $k$?

 

(1) The lines $2y + kx = 16$, $y = x + 5$ and $ky + x = 9$ are concurrent.

(2) $k$ is an integer.

*Solve yourself:*

**138.** What is the value of $a$?

(1) A line passing through the points $(a, 2a)$ and $(-2, 3)$ is perpendicular to the line $4x + 3y + 5 = 0$.

(2) $a$ is a positive number.

*Solve yourself:*

**139.** What is the value of the Y coordinate of a point?

(1) The point is at a perpendicular distance of 3 units from the line $4x - 3y = 12$.

(2) The point lies on the Y axis.

*Solve yourself:*

**140.** The coordinates of A, B, C and D are (2, 0), (9, 0), $(11, p)$ and $(q, 6)$ respectively. What is the length of BC?

(1) The slope of AD is 2.

(2) The slope of CD is $\frac{1}{2}$.

*Solve yourself:*

**141.** In a co-ordinate plane, if triangle APB is right-angled at P, what is the value of the Y coordinate of the point P?

(1) The coordinates of the points A and B are (3, 4) and (5, 2), respectively.

(2) The area of triangle APB is 2.

*Solve yourself:*

**142.** In the equation $y = ax + b$, what is the value of $(a + b)$?

(1) The segment of the line intercepted between the axes is bisected at (2, 3).

(2) The line passes through the point $\left(1, \frac{9}{2}\right)$.

*Solve yourself:*

**143.** What is the slope of the line $l$?

(1) The line $l$ cuts off an intercept 4 on the positive direction of X axis and an intercept 3 on the positive direction of Y axis.

(2) The area of the triangle bounded by the line $l$ with the X and Y axes is 6.

*Solve yourself:*

**144.** What is the slope of the line $l$?

(1) The line $l$ passes through the point $(3, 4)$.

(2) The sum of the intercepts of the line on the X and Y axes is 14.

*Solve yourself:*

**145.** What is the value of $k$?

(1) The line passing through $(3, k)$ and $(4, 7)$ has a slope of $k$.

(2) The line passing through $(1, k)$ and $(k, 6)$ is parallel to the line $y = x$.

*Solve yourself:*

**146.** What is the slope of the line $l$?

(1) The line $l$ is formed by reflection of the line $2x + y = 8$ about the Y axis.

(2) The line $l$ is formed by reflection of the line $2x + y + 8 = 0$ about the X axis.

*Solve yourself:*

**147.** What is the sum of the coordinates of point P?

(1) The point P is obtained by reflecting the point $(2, -5)$ about the line $y = x$.
(2) The point P is obtained by reflecting the point $(-2, 5)$ about the line $y+x = 0$.

*Solve yourself:*

**148.** If $k$ is positive, what is the value of $k$?

(1) The area of the triangle bounded by the lines $y = x$, $y = 4x - k$ and X axis is 6.
(2) $y = 4x - k$ makes a positive intercept with the X axis.

*Solve yourself:*

**149.** If the coordinates of A and B are $(1, 1)$ and $(4, 4)$, respectively, what is the sum of the coordinates of M?

(1) M is a point on the line AB.

(2) AM = BM.

*Solve yourself:*

**150.** If the slope of the line $l$ is $m$, does $m$ satisfy the equation $m^2 - 5m + 6 = 0$?

(1) The line $l$ makes equal intercepts of equal magnitude on the X and Y axes.
(2) The line $l$ passes through the point $(1, 1)$.

*Solve yourself:*

 

# Chapter 4

# Answer-key

(1) D

(2) B

(3) D

(4) B

(5) C

(6) A

(7) C

(8) A

(9) A

(10) C

(11) E

(12) D

(13) B

(14) A

(15) E

(16) B

(17) A

(18) C

(19) D

(20) A

(21) B

(22) C

(23) B

(24) B

(25) C

(26) C

(27) D

(28) C

(29) C

(30) E

(31) D

(32) C

(33) D

(34) E

(35) D

(36) C

(37) E

(38) C

(39) D

(40) C

(41) B

(42) D

(43) B

(44) D

(45) B

(46) B

(47) A

(48) B

(49) B

(50) C

(51) C

(52) B

(53) C

(54) B

(55) C

(56) A

(57) C

(58) D

(59) C

(60) D

(61) E

(62) C

(63) C

(64) C

(65) C

(66) E

(67) C

(68) C

(69) C

(70) C

(71) D

(72) C

(73) E

(74) D

(75) D

(76) C

(77) D

(78) A

(79) A

(80) A

(81) A

(82) C

(83) C

(84) C

(85) A

(86) C

(87) A

(88) E

(89) B

(90) C

(91) C

(92) C

(93) A

(94) C

(95) A

(96) C

(97) C

(98) A

(99) E

(100) D

(101) A

(102) E

(103) B

(104) A

(105) B

(106) A

(107) C

(108) D

(109) C

(110) D

(111) D

(112) E

(113) E

(114) D

(115) B

(116) B

(117) A

(118) D

(119) C

(120) D

(121) E

(122) B

(123) D

(124) D

(125) C

(126) B

(127) B

(128) C

(129) A

(130) C

(131) E

(132) D

(133) C

(134) A

(135) C

(136) C

(137) C

(138) A

(139) E

(140) C

(141) E

(142) D

(143) A

(144) E

(145) D

(146) D

(147) D

(148) A

(149) B

(150) A

# Chapter 5

# Solutions

## 5.1 Geometry

### 5.1.1 Problem Solving

**1.**

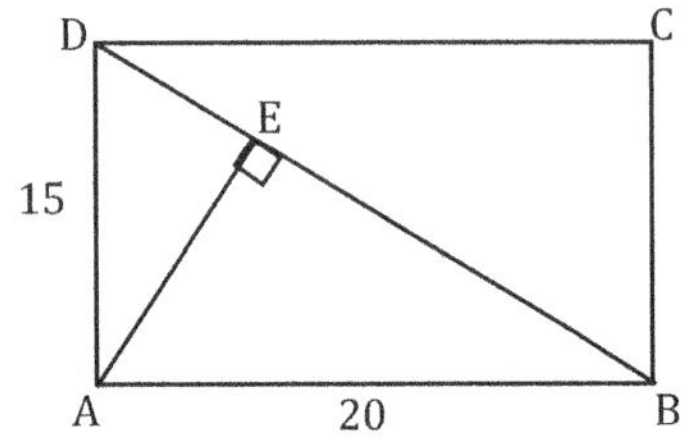


In triangles DAB and AEB:

$\angle DAB = \angle AEB = 90°$

$\angle DBA$ is the common angle

Since the two angles are equal, their respective third angle will also be equal.

Thus, $\Delta DAB$ is similar to $\Delta AEB$

By Pythagoras, theorem,

$DB^2 = AD^2 + AB^2$

$DB^2 = 15^2 + 20^2$

$DB^2 = 625 \Rightarrow DB = 25$

$\Rightarrow \dfrac{\text{Area of DAB}}{\text{Area of AEB}} = \left(\dfrac{DB}{AB}\right)^2 = \left(\dfrac{25}{20}\right)^2 = \dfrac{25}{16}$

=> Area of AEB

$= \dfrac{16}{25} * \left(\dfrac{1}{2} * 20 * 15\right) = 96$

The correct answer is option D.

**Alternate approach**:

We know that area of $\Delta ABD = \dfrac{1}{2} * 20 * 15 = 150$.

Again, area of $\Delta ABD = \dfrac{1}{2} * DB * AE = 150$

$\dfrac{1}{2} * 25 * AE = 150 \Rightarrow AE = 12$

By Pythagoras theorem,

$EB^2 = AB^2 - AE^2$

$EB^2 = 20^2 - 12^2$

$EB^2 = 256 \Rightarrow EB = 16$

Area of AEB $= \frac{1}{2} * AE * EB$

$\frac{1}{2} * 12 * 16 = 96.$

**2.**

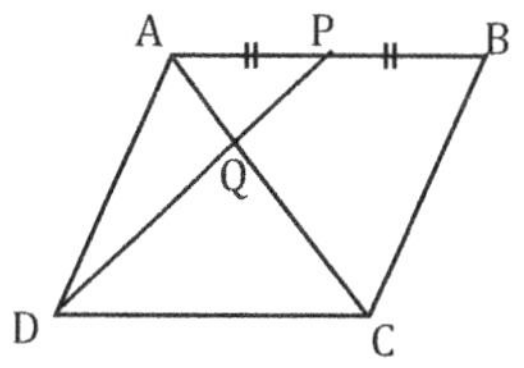


Since P is the midpoint of AB, we have:

$PA = \frac{1}{2} AB = \frac{1}{2} DC$

Also: $\angle AQP = \angle CQD$ (vertically opposite angles)

$\angle PAQ = \angle DCQ$ (alternate angles since ABCD is a parallelogram, i.e. AB is parallel to CD)

Hence, $\Delta APQ$ and $\Delta CDQ$ are similar

$\Rightarrow \frac{AQ}{CQ} = \frac{AP}{CD} = \frac{1}{2}$

$\Rightarrow \frac{AQ}{AQ + CQ} = \frac{1}{2+1} = \frac{1}{3}$

$\Rightarrow \frac{AQ}{AC} = \frac{1}{3}$

The correct answer is option B.

**3.**

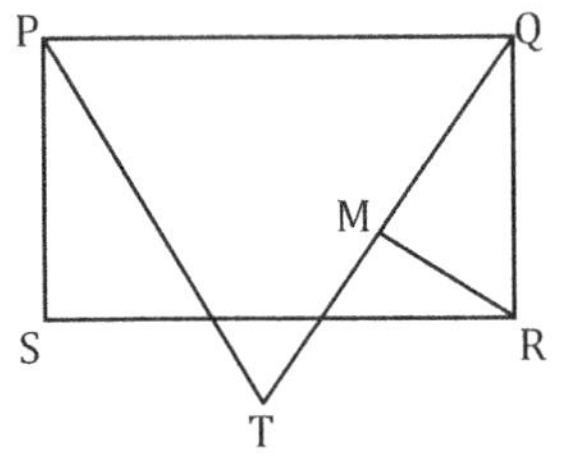


Let QR = $x$

=> PQ = $2x$

We know that PT = QT

=> $\triangle$PTQ is an isosceles triangle.

The perpendicular distance of T from PQ is $x\sqrt{3} = \frac{\sqrt{3}}{2}(2x) = \frac{\sqrt{3}}{2} * \text{Side}$

We know that, in an equilateral triangle, the height is given by $\frac{\sqrt{3}}{2} * \text{Side}$

Thus, $\triangle$PQT is equilateral

=> $\angle PQT = 60^\circ$ and PQ = QT = PT = $2x$

Since PQRS is a rectangle, $\angle PQR = 90^\circ$

=> $\angle MQR = 90^\circ - 60^\circ = 30^\circ$

Also, we have M to be the midpoint of QT

=> TM = MQ = $x$

Thus, in $\triangle$MQR, QM = QR = $x$

=> $\triangle$MQR is an isosceles triangle

=> $\angle RMQ = \frac{180^\circ - MQR}{2} = \frac{180^\circ - 30^\circ}{2} = 75^\circ$

The correct answer is option D.

**Alternate Approach**:

Let QR = 1

=> PQ = 2

We can do the following construction: We draw TU $\perp$ PQ.

From the given condition, we know that: $TU = \sqrt{3} * QR = \sqrt{3}$

Also, since PT = QT, $\triangle PTU$ is isosceles.

Thus, UT is a perpendicular from the vertex to the unequal side

$\Rightarrow PU = UQ = \frac{1}{2} * PQ = 1$

By Pythagoras theorem,

$TQ^2 = TU^2 + UQ^2$

$\Rightarrow TQ^2 = (\sqrt{3})^2 + 1^2 = 4$

$\Rightarrow TQ = 2$

$\Rightarrow MQ = \frac{1}{2} * TQ = 1$

Since in $\triangle UQT$, $UQ : UT : TQ :: 1 : \sqrt{3} : 2$, we can conclude that it is a 30-60-90 triangle, where $\angle UQT = 60^\circ$

Thus, $\angle MQR = \angle PQR - \angle UQT = 90^\circ - 60^\circ = 30^\circ$

Since in $\triangle MQR$, $MQ = QR$, $\angle QRM = \angle RMQ = \frac{1}{2} * (180^\circ - 30^\circ) = 75^\circ$

**4.**

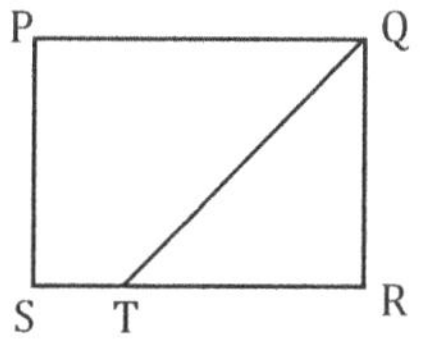


Area of $\Delta QRT = 42$

Let each side of the square $= x$

Thus, $TR = SR - ST = x - 5$

Thus, we have:

$\frac{1}{2}(x)(x-5) = 42$

$\Rightarrow x^2 - 5x = 84$

$\Rightarrow (x - 12)(x + 7) = 84$

 

$=> x = 12$ OR $-7$

Since $x$ is the length of aside, the value of $x$ must be positive

$=> x = 12$

The correct answer is option B.

**5.**

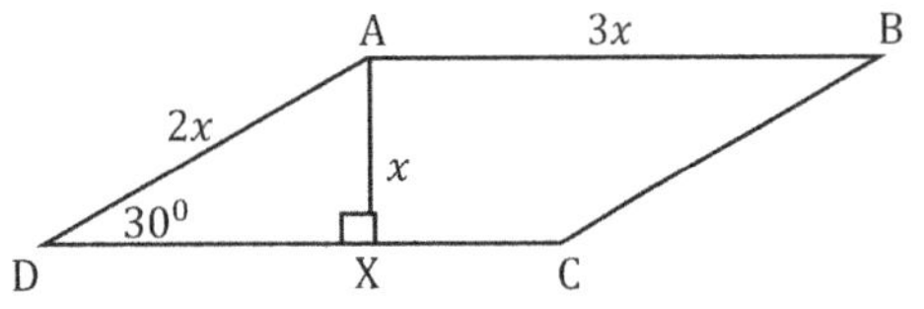


Let the parallelogram be ABCD, with AB : BC = 3 : 2.

Area of the parallelogram = (AX) (CD).

Let AB = CD = $3x$ and AD = BC = $2x$, where $x$ is a constant of proportionality.

Since $\triangle$ADX is a 60-30-90 triangle, we have:

$$AX = \frac{AD}{2} = x$$

Since area of ABCD is 243, we have:

$x * 3x = 243 => x^2 = 81 => x = 9$

Thus, AB = CD = $3x = 27$ and AD = BC = $2x = 18$

Thus, perimeter of ABCD = $2\,(27 + 18) = 90$

The correct answer is option C.

**6.**

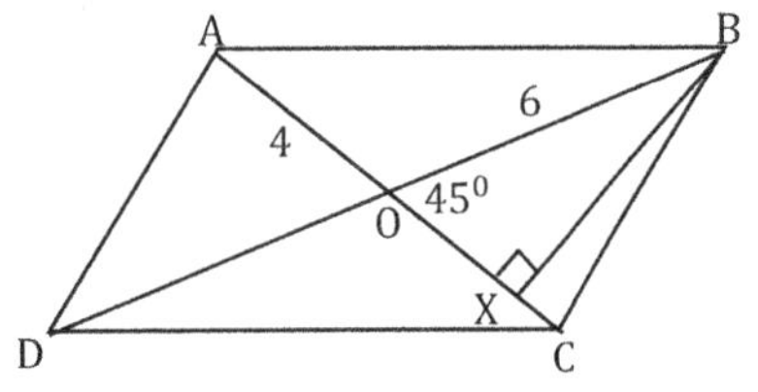


Let ABCD be the parallelogram.

Since the diagonals are of length 12 and 8, and they bisect each other, we have:

AO = OC = 4 and BO = OD = 6

Also, $\angle$BOC = 45°.

Let us draw BX $\perp$ AC.

In right-angled $\triangle$BOX, we have:

$\angle XBO = 90^\circ - 45^\circ = 45^\circ$

Thus, $\triangle$BOX is a 45-45-90 triangle

$=> BX = \frac{BO}{\sqrt{2}} = \frac{6}{\sqrt{2}} = 3\sqrt{2}$

Thus, area of $\triangle BOC = \frac{1}{2}(BX)(OC) = \frac{1}{2} * 3\sqrt{2} * 4 = 6\sqrt{2}$

Considering $\triangle$ABC, BO is a line drawn from the vertex dividing the base AC equally.

Thus, area of $\triangle$AOB = area of $\triangle BOC = 6\sqrt{2}$

Also, area of $\triangle$AOD = area of $\triangle$BOC (both are congruent triangles) and area of $\triangle$AOB = area of $\triangle$DOC (both are congruent triangles)

Thus, we have:

Area of $\triangle$AOD = Area of $\triangle$BOC = Area of $\triangle$AOB = area of $\triangle DOC = 6\sqrt{2}$

$=>$ Area of $ABCD = 4 * 6\sqrt{2} = 24\sqrt{2}$

The correct answer is option A.

7. Let the parallel sides be of length $2k$ and $3k$, where $k$ is a constant of proportionality.

Height of the trapezium $= \frac{3}{4} * 2k = \frac{3}{2}k$.

Thus, area of the trapezium

$= \frac{1}{2}$ * (Sum of parallel sides) * height

$= \frac{1}{2}(2k + 3k) * \left(\frac{3}{2}k\right)$

Since the area of the trapezium is 60, we have:

$\frac{1}{2}(2k + 3k) * \left(\frac{3}{2}k\right) = 60$

$=> 15k^2 = 240$

$=> k = 4$

Thus, the length of the smaller of the two parallel sides of the trapezium

$= 2k = 8$

The correct answer is option C.

**8.**

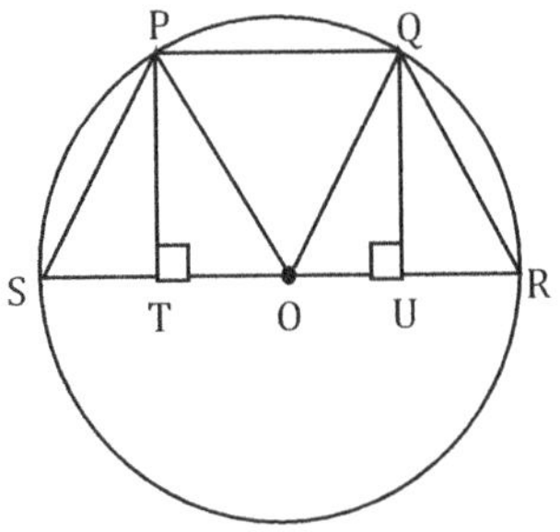


Let O be the center of the circle.

Let the perpendiculars drawn from P and from Q on SR intersect it and T and U respectively.

Let the radius of the circle be $r$.

Since RS is the diameter, we have: RS = $2r$.

Also, PS = QR = $\frac{1}{2}$ RS = $r$.

Let ST = $x$.

=> OT = OS - TS = $r - x$

Also, OP = OQ = OS = OR = $r$.

From Pythagoras' theorem in $\triangle$PST:

$PT^2 = PS^2 - ST^2 = r^2 - x^2$

From Pythagoras' theorem in $\triangle$POT:

$PT^2 = OP^2 - OT^2 = r^2 - (r - x)^2$

 

Thus, we have:

$r^2 - x^2 = r^2 - (r - x)^2$

$=> x = \frac{r}{2}$

Thus, we have:

PQ : RS = TU : RS

= 2 * OT : 2 * OS

= OT : OS

$= (r - x) : r = \left(r - \frac{r}{2}\right) : r = \frac{r}{2} : r$

= 1 : 2

The correct answer is option A.

**9.** The diagram representing the above scenario is shown below:

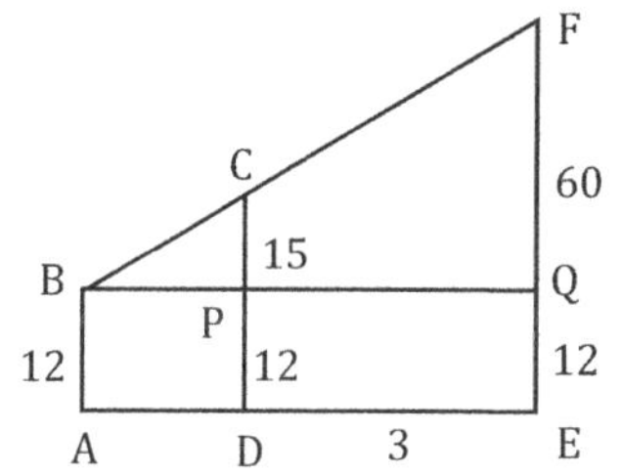


AB = 12, CD = 27 and EF = 72

=> CP = CD - PD = CD - AB

= 27 - 12

= 15

Also, FQ = EF - QE = EF - AB

= 72 - 12

= 60

Also, DE = PQ = 3

We know that CP is parallel to FQ

=> $\angle BCP = \angle BFQ$ and $\angle BPC = \angle BQF$ (corresponding angles)

=> $\Delta BPC$ and $\Delta$ BQF are similar

=> $\frac{CP}{FQ} = \frac{BP}{BQ}$ => $\frac{15}{60} = \frac{BP}{BP + 3}$

=> $4 * BP = BP + 3$

=> $BP = 1 = AD$

The correct answer is option A.

**10.**

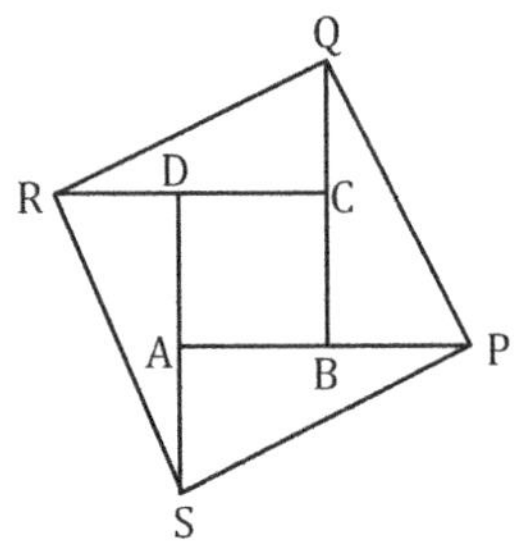


Since we need the ratio of the areas of two squares, we can assume any suitable dimension for any one of the two squares.

Let AB = BC = CD = DA = 1

Since the sides of the square ABCD are produced by its own length, we have:

=> SD = RC = QB = PA = 2

From Pythagoras' theorem in triangle QRC:

$QR = \sqrt{QC^2 + RC^2} = \sqrt{1 + 4} = \sqrt{5}$

Similarly, we have: $PQ = RS = SP = \sqrt{5}$

Thus, we have:

Area of ABCD : Area of PQRS = $1^2 : (\sqrt{5})^2 = 1 : 5$

The correct answer is option C.

 

**11.**

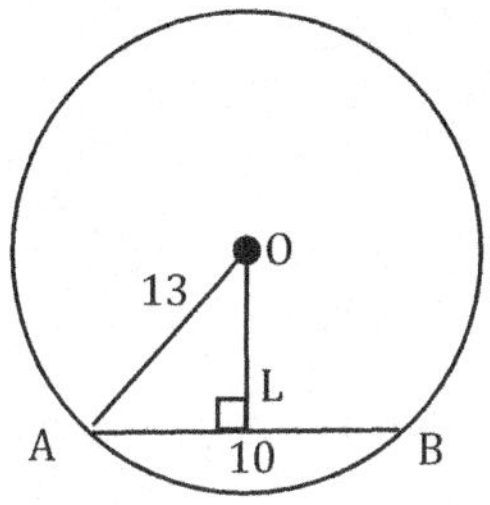


Let AB be the chord of a circle with center O and radius 13 such that AB = 10.

From O, we draw OL ⊥ AB and also, we join OA.

We know that: The perpendicular from the center of a circle to a chord bisects the chord.

=> $AL = LB = \frac{1}{2} AB = 5$.

In right-angled △OLA, we have:

$OA^2 = OL^2 + AL^2$

=> $OL = \sqrt{13^2 - 5^2} = 12$

Hence, the shortest distance (perpendicular distance) of the chord from the center is 12.

The correct answer is option E.

**12.**

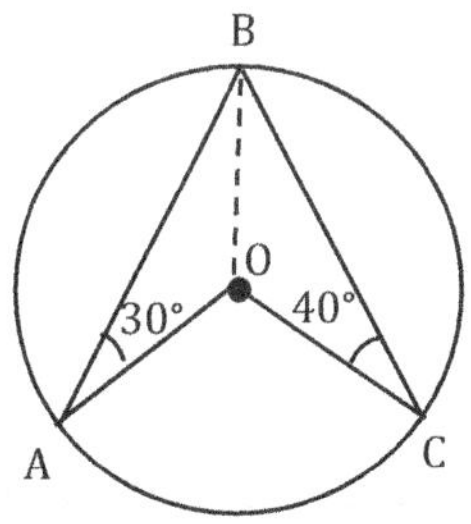


Let us join OB.

In ΔAOB, we have:

OA = OB (Each being the radius)

=> ∠OBA = ∠OAB (Since the angles opposite to equal sides of a triangle are equal)

=> $\angle OBA = 30^o$

In $\Delta BOC$, we have

OB = OC (Each being the radius)

=> $\angle OCB = \angle OBC$ (Since the angles opposite to equal sides of a triangle are equal)

=> $\angle OBC = 40^o$

=> $\angle ABC = \angle OBA + \angle OBC = 30^o + 40^o = 70^o$

We know that the angle subtended by an arc of a circle at the center of the circle is double the angle subtended by the same arc on the circumference.

Thus, we have:

$\angle AOC = 2 * \angle ABC$

$= 2 \times 70^o$

$= 140^o$

The correct answer is option D.

**13.**

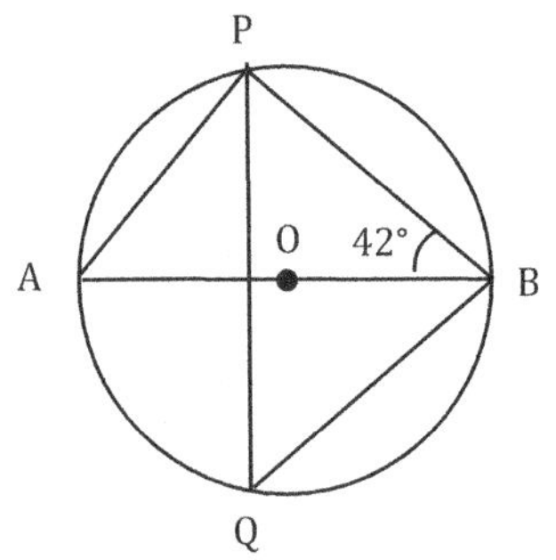


We know that the angle subtended at the circumference by the diameter is a right angle.

=> $\angle APB = 90^\circ$

In $\Delta APB$, we have

$\angle PAB = 180^o - 90^o - 42^o = 48^o$

 

Considering arc BP, we find that $\angle$PAB and $\angle$PQB are angles in the same segment of a circle.

Since angles in the same segment are equal, we have:

=> $\angle PQB = \angle PAB = 48^0$

The correct answer is option B.

**14.**

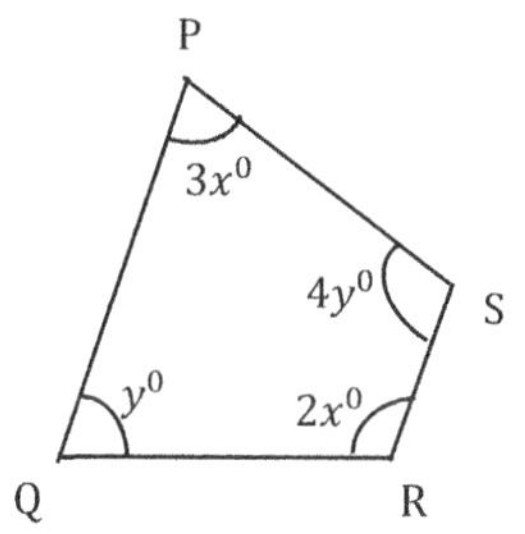


Since in a quadrilateral, sum of all interior angles is $360^0$, and we know that $\angle P + \angle Q = 180^0$, we have:

$3x + y = 180 \ldots$(i)

$\angle R + \angle S = 360^0 - 180^0 = 180^0$

Thus, we have,

$4y + 2x = 180$

$2y + x = 90 \ldots$(ii)

Solving equations (i) and (ii), we get: $y = 18^0$ or $\angle Q = 18^0$

The correct answer is option A.

**15.**

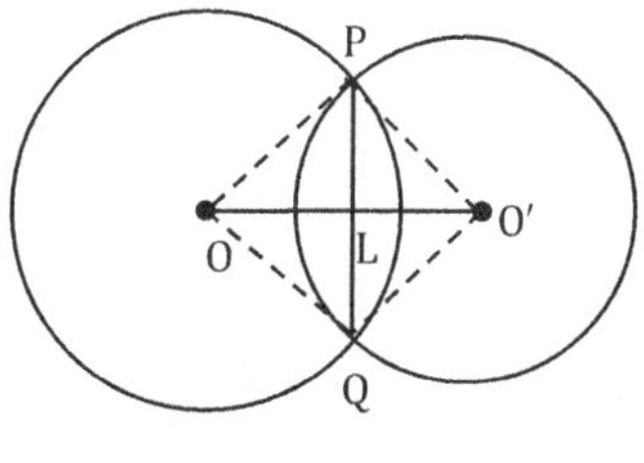

Let O and O′ be the centers of the circles of radii 20 and 13, respectively and let PQ be the line joining their points of intersection.

We have OP = OQ = 20, O′P = O′Q = 13 and PQ = 24.

Triangles POO′ and QOO′ are congruent triangles

(Since OP = OQ, O′P = O′Q, OO′ is common side)

=> $PL = QL = \frac{PQ}{2} = 12$

In right-angled △OLP, we have:

$OL = \sqrt{OP^2 - PL^2} = \sqrt{20^2 - 12^2} = 16$

Again, in right-angled △O′LP, we have:

$OL = \sqrt{OP^2 - PL^2} = \sqrt{13^2 - 12^2} = 5$

Thus, we have:

OO′ = OL + O′L

= 16 + 5

= 21

The correct answer is option E.

**16.**

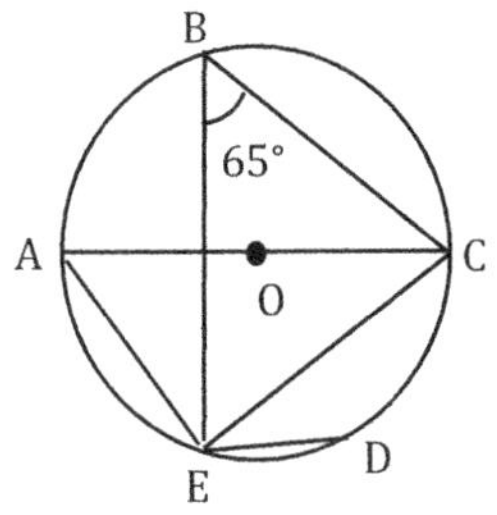


Consider the arc CDE. We find that ∠CBE and ∠CAE are angles in the same segment of arc CDE

=> $\angle CAE = \angle CBE = 65^o$

Since AC is the diameter of the circle and the angle subtended by a diameter on the circumference is a right angle, we have:

 

$\angle AEC = 90^o$.

In $\Delta ACE$: $\angle ACE = 180^o - 90^o - 65^o = 25^o$

Since $\angle DEC$ and $\angle ACE$ are alternate angles (since AC is parallel to DE), we have:

$\angle DEC = \angle ACE = 25^o$

The correct answer is option B.

**17.**

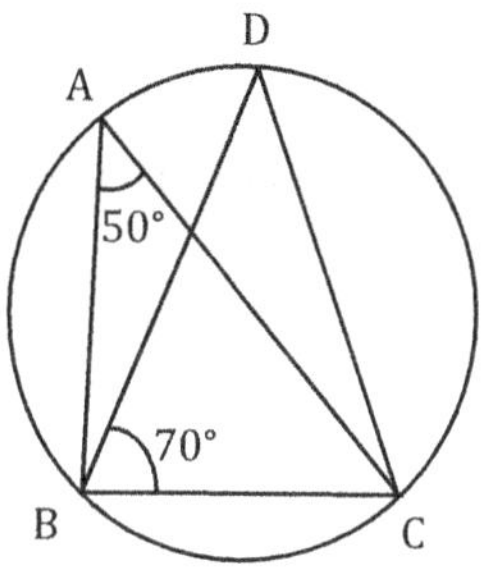


We know that angles in the same segment of a circle arc equal.

=> $\angle BAC = \angle BDC = 50^o$

Also, in the $\triangle BDC$:

$\angle BCD = 180^o - \angle DBC + \angle BDC = 180^o - 70^o - 50^o = 60^o$

Since in $\triangle ABC$, AB = BC, we have:

$\angle BCA = \angle BAC = 50^o$ (angles opposite equal sides in a triangle are equal)

Thus, we have:

$\angle DCA = \angle BCD - \angle BCA$

$= 60^o - 50^o$

$= 10^o$

The correct answer is option A.

**18.**

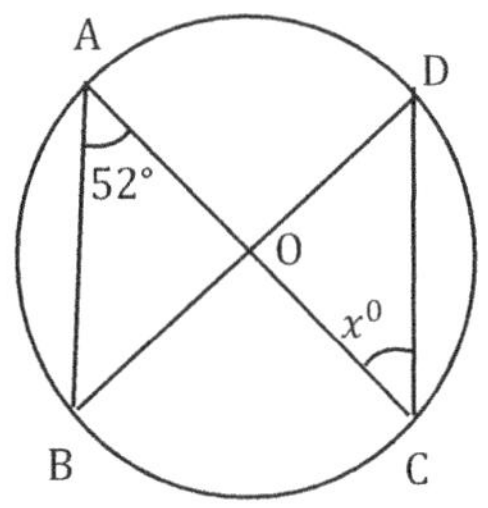


We know that angles in the same segment of a circle are equal.

Thus, we have:

$\angle BAC = \angle BDC = 52^0$

Also, the angle subtended by an arc at the center is twice the angle subtended by the same arc at the circumference.

Thus, for arc BC, we have:

$\angle BOC = 2 * \angle BDC = 2 * 52^0 = 104^0$

Since BD is a straight line, we have:

$\angle DOC = 180^0 - \angle BOC = 180^0 - 104^0 = 76^0$

In triangle DOC, we have:

$x = 180^0 - \angle DOC - \angle ODC$

$= 180^0 - 76^0 - 52^0$

$= 52^0$

The correct answer is option C.

**Alternate Approach 1:**

In $\triangle AOB$, OA = OB (radius)

=> $\angle ABO = \angle BAO = 52^0$

=> $\angle AOB = 180^0 - 52^0 - 52^0 = 76^0$

Thus, $\angle COD = \angle AOB = 76^0$ (vertically opposite angles)

In $\triangle COD$, OD = OC (radius)

 

=> $\angle ODC = \angle OCD = x = \frac{180^o - 76^o}{2} = 52^o$ (angles opposite to equals sides are also equal)

**Alternate Approach 2:**

$\triangle AOB$ and $\triangle COD$ are isosceles triangles since AO = BO = CO = DO (radius)

Also, $\angle COD = \angle AOB$ = (vertically opposite angles)

Thus, $\triangle AOB$ and $\triangle COD$ are congruent isosceles triangles.

Thus, $x = 52^o$

**Alternate Approach 3:**

We know that angles in the same segment of a circle are equal.

Thus, we have:

$\angle BAC = \angle BDC = 52^o$

In $\triangle COD$, OD = OC (radius)

$\angle BDC = \angle OCD = x^o = 52^o$ (angles opposite to equals sides are also equal)

**19.** The diagram for the above scenario is shown below:

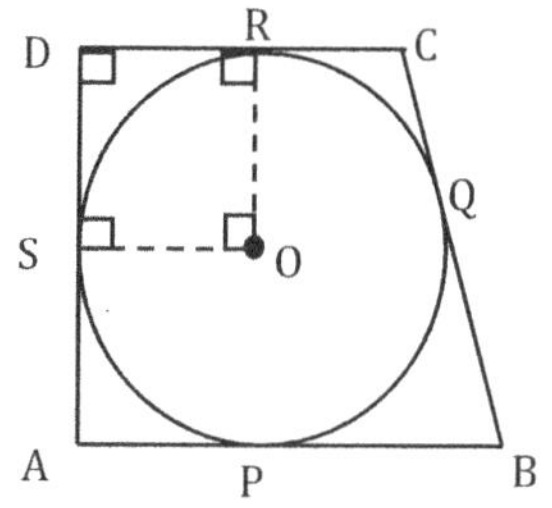


We know that tangent to a circle is perpendicular to the radius drawn at that point.

Thus, we have:

$OS \perp AD$, and $OR \perp CD$

Let the radius of the circle be $r$.

Thus, OS = OR = $r$

Thus, OSDR is a rectangle with adjacent sides equal, i.e. it is a square

=> SD = DR = $r$

We know that tangents from an exterior point to a circle are equal in length.

Thus, we have:

CR = CQ, BQ = BP and AS = AP

Since CD = 25 and DR = $r$, we have: CR = 25 − $r$ = CQ

Since BC = 38 and CQ = 25 − $r$, we have: BQ = 38 − (25 − $r$) = 13 + $r$ = BP

Since BP = 27, we have:

$13 + r = 27$

=> $r = 14$

The correct answer is option D.

**20.**

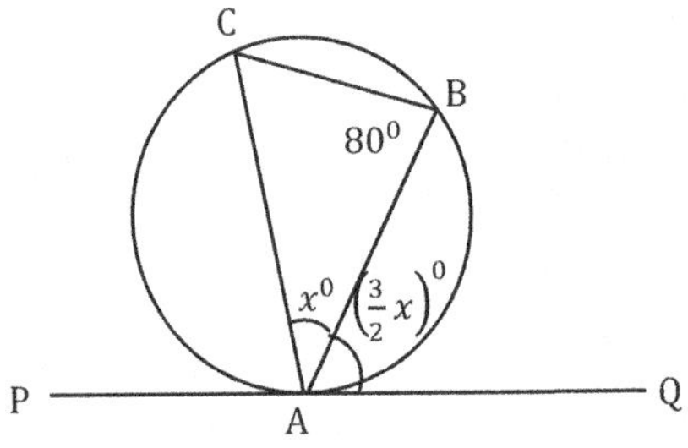


Here, ∠BAQ is the angle between the tangent QA and the chord AB and ∠ACB is the angle subtended by the same chord AB on the circumference.

Since angles in alternate segments are equal, we have:

$\angle ACB = \angle BAQ = \left(\frac{3}{2}x\right)^{o}$

In ΔABC, we have:

$\angle ABC = 180^{o} - x^{o} - \left(\frac{3}{2}x\right)^{o} = 80^{o}$

=> $x^{o} + \left(\frac{3}{2}x\right)^{o} = 100^{o}$

=> $\left(\frac{5}{2}x\right)^{o} = 100^{o}$

=> $x = 100 * \frac{2}{5} = 40$

 

The correct answer is option A.

**21.**

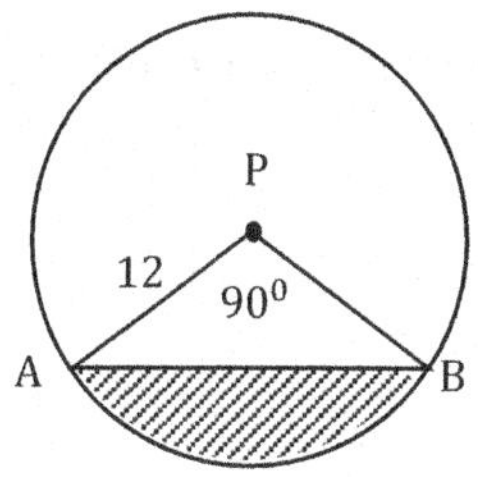


The area of the sector PAB = $\pi\left(12^2\right)\left(\frac{90}{360}\right) = 3\,(36) = 108$

The area of $\triangle$PAB = $\frac{1}{2}$ (PA) (PB) = $\frac{1}{2}$ (12) (12) = 72

Thus, the area of the shaded region

= Area of sector PAB – Area of $\triangle$PAB

= 108 – 72 = 36

The correct answer is option B.

**22.** The diagram for $\triangle$ABC is shown below.

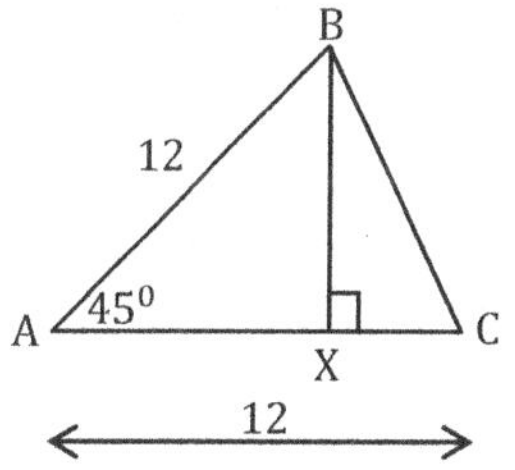


We draw a perpendicular BX on AC.

Thus, right-angled $\triangle$ABX is a 45-45-90 triangle

=> AX = BX = $\frac{AB}{\sqrt{2}} = \frac{12}{\sqrt{2}} = 6\sqrt{2}$

Thus, area of $\triangle$ABC = $\frac{1}{2}$ (AC) (BX) = $\frac{1}{2}$ (12) $\left(6\sqrt{2}\right)$ = $36\sqrt{2}$

The correct answer is option C.

**23.** Let the radius of the circle be $r$ meters.

Speed of each ant = 2 meters per minute.

Distance travelled by the first ant = $2r$ meters.

Thus, time taken by the first ant = $\frac{2r}{2} = r$ minutes.

Distance travelled by the second ant is half the circumference of the circle = $\pi r$ meters.

Thus, time taken by the second ant = $\frac{\pi r}{2} = \frac{3r}{2}$ minutes.

Since the first ant beats the second one by 45 seconds, i.e. $\frac{45}{60} = \frac{3}{4}$ minutes, we have:

$\frac{3r}{2} - r = \frac{3}{4} \Rightarrow \frac{r}{2} = \frac{3}{4} \Rightarrow r = \frac{3}{2}$ meters

Thus, the diameter of the circle = $2r$ = 3 meters.

The correct answer is option B.

**24.**

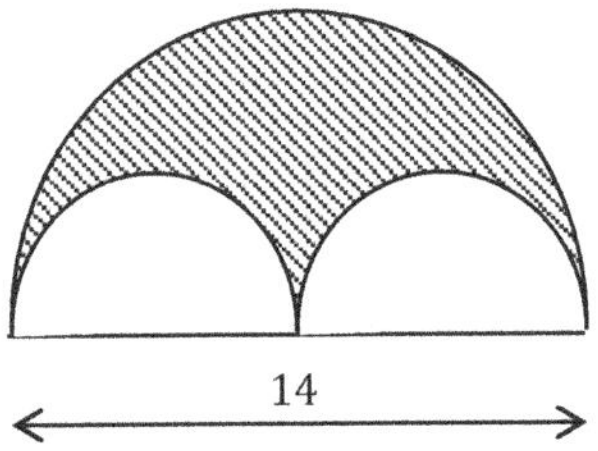


Radius of the larger semicircle = $\frac{14}{2} = 7$

=> Area of the larger semicircle = $\frac{\pi (7^2)}{2} = \frac{22}{7}\left(\frac{7^2}{2}\right) = 77.$

Radius of each smaller semicircle = $\left(\frac{7}{2}\right)$

=> Total area of both the smaller semicircle = $2 * \frac{\pi\left(\frac{7}{2}\right)^2}{2} = \frac{22}{7}\left(\frac{7^2}{2^2}\right) = \frac{77}{2} = 38.5$

Thus, the shaded area

= Area of the larger semicircle – Total area of both the smaller semicircles

= 77 - 38.5 = 38.5

The correct answer is option B.

 

Note: You would notice that a circle equals four smaller circles whose radius is equal to half the radius of the larger circle.

**25.**

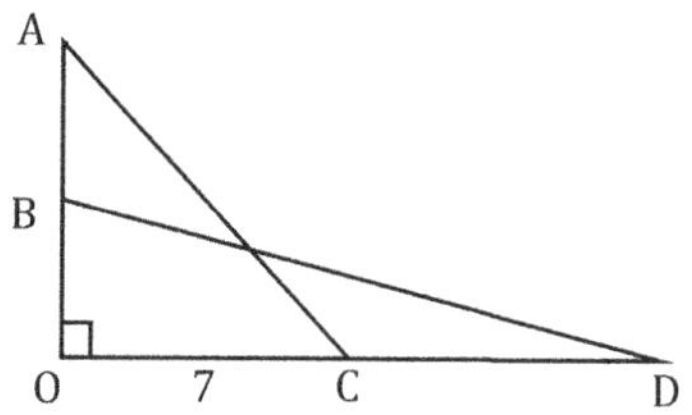


Let AB = $x$.

Thus, CD = $2x$.

AC = BD = 25.

From right-angled △AOC:

AO = $\sqrt{AC^2 - OC^2} = \sqrt{25^2 - 7^2} = 24$

Thus, BO = AO - AB = $(24 - x)$.

OD = OC + CD = $(7 + 2x)$.

Thus, from right-angled △BOD:

$BO^2 + OD^2 = BD^2$

=> $(24 - x)^2 + (7 + 2x)^2 = 25^2$

=> $576 + x^2 - 48x + 49 + 4x^2 + 28x = 625$

=> $5x^2 - 20x = 0$

=> $x(x - 4) = 0$

=> $x = 0$ OR 4

Since $x$ cannot be '0', we have: $x = 4$

=> CD = $2x = 8$

The correct answer is option C.

**26.** The diagram for the above scenario is shown below:

Let us drop perpendiculars from D and A on BC, which intersect at point X and Y, respectively.

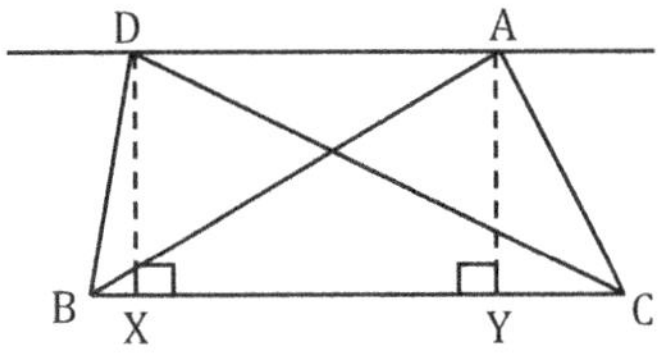


Area of $\triangle ABC = \frac{1}{2}(AY)(BC)$.

Area of $\triangle DBC = \frac{1}{2}(DX)(BC)$.

Since the areas of the above two triangles are equal, we have:

$\frac{1}{2}(AY)(BC) = \frac{1}{2}(DX)(BC)$

=> AY = DX

Also, AY and DX are parallel since both are perpendicular to the same line BC.

Thus, ADXY is a rectangle

=> AD is parallel to XY, i.e. BC

The correct answer is option C.

**27.**

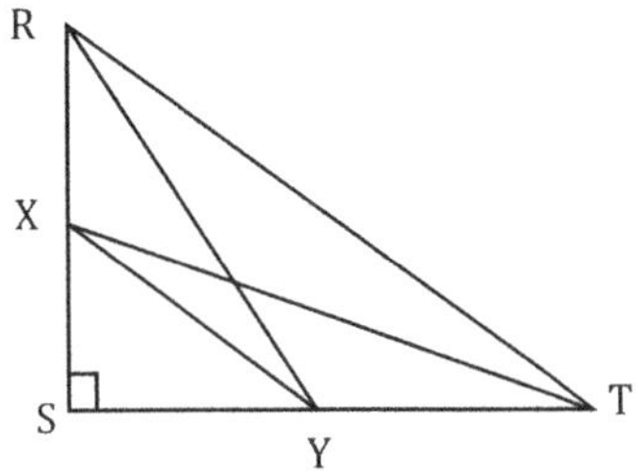


$\triangle RSY$, $\triangle XST$, $\triangle XSY$, and $\triangle RST$ are right-angled triangles.

Thus, we have:

$$\frac{RY^2+XT^2}{XY^2} = \frac{\left(RS^2+SY^2\right)+\left(SX^2+ST^2\right)}{SX^2+SY^2}$$

$$= \frac{(2SX)^2+SY^2+SX^2+(2SY)^2}{SX^2+SY^2}$$

 

$= 5$

The correct answer is option D.

**28.** D is the midpoint of BC.

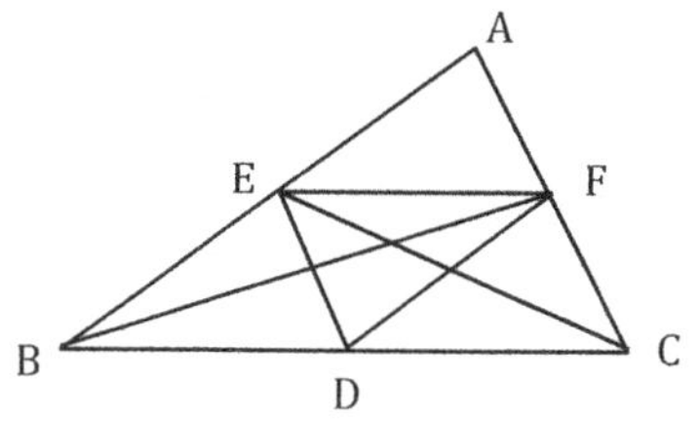


Since DE is parallel to AC, E is also the midpoint of AB.

Similarly, since DF is parallel to AB, F is also the midpoint of AC.

Thus, EF, the line joining the midpoints of the sides BA and CA, is parallel to BC.

Thus, $\triangle$FBD and $\triangle$ECD line between the same parallel lines, implying both triangles have the same height.

Thus, we have:

$$\frac{\text{Area of } \triangle FBD}{\text{Area of } \triangle ECD} = \frac{\frac{1}{2} * BD * \text{Height}}{\frac{1}{2} * CD * \text{Height}} = \frac{BD}{CD} = 1$$

=> Area of $\triangle$ECD = Area of $\triangle$FBD = 12.

The correct answer is option C.

**Alternate Approach:**

D, E and F are midpoints of sides BC, AB, and AC respectively in $\triangle$ABC.

By applying Basic Proportionality Theorem, we can conclude that EF is parallel to BC.

Thus, here $\triangle$FBD and $\triangle$ECD are triangles with same base and height so their area will be equal that is 12.

**29.** Let the length of the side not equal to any other side be $x$.

Thus, the length of the equal sides = $(x + B)$.

Thus, the perimeter of the triangle = $\{x + 2(x + B)\}$.

Thus, we have:

$x + 2(x + B) = A$

$=> x = \dfrac{A - 2B}{3}$

Thus, length of one of the equal sides

$= x + B$

$= \dfrac{A - 2B}{3} + B$

$= \dfrac{A + B}{3}$

The correct answer is option C.

**30.** Perimeter of the triangle = $(5p + 20) + (p + 196) + (3p + 76)$

$= 9p + 292$

Since we need to maximize the perimeter, we need to maximize the value of $p$.

Since two sides are equal, we have:

**Case I**: If $5p + 20 = p + 196 => p = 44$

=> The three sides are: $(5p + 20)$, $(p + 196)$, $(3p + 76)$ = 240, 240 and 208, which satisfy the condition that sum of two sides should be greater than the third side.

**Case II**: If $5p + 20 = 3p + 76 => p = 28$

Since this value of $p$ is LESS than the previous value, we need not verify whether the sum of two sides is greater than the third side.

**Case III**: If $3p + 76 = p + 196 => p = 60$

Since this value of $p$ is GREATER than the first value of $p$, we need to verify whether the sum of two sides is greater than the third side:

=> The three sides are: $(5p + 20)$, $(p + 196)$, $(3p + 76)$ = 320, 256 and 256, which satisfy the condition that sum of two sides should be greater than the third side.

Thus, the maximum possible perimeter of the triangle

$= 9p + 292$

$= 9 * 60 + 292$

$= 832$

The correct answer is option E.

**31.**

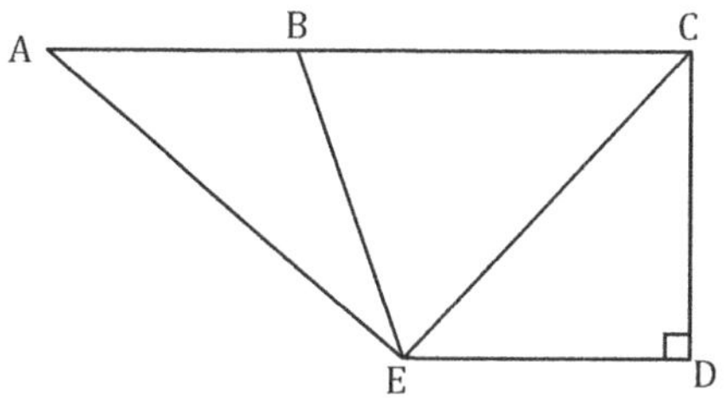


AB = ED = 6

Also, area of $\triangle$ABE = 24

=> $\frac{1}{2}$ (CD) (AB) = 24

=> $\frac{1}{2}$ (CD) (6) = 24

=> CD = 8

Thus, in right-angled $\triangle$CED:

$CE = \sqrt{CD^2 + DE^2} = \sqrt{8^2 + 6^2} = 10$

The correct answer is option D.

**32.**

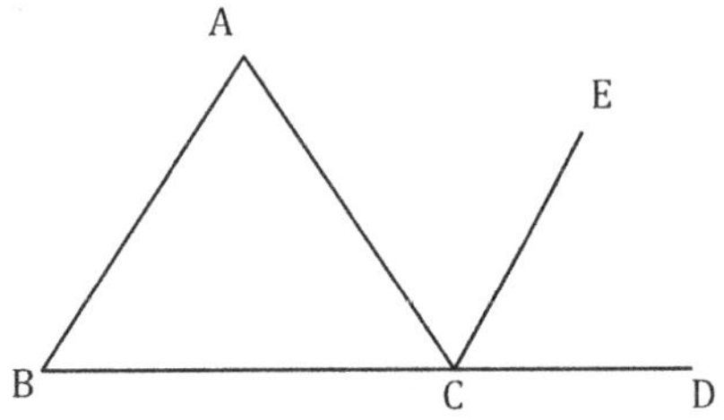


In $\triangle ABC$, AB = BC

=> $\angle BAC = \angle BCA$

Let $\angle BAC = \angle BCA = x$

=> $\angle ACD = 180^o - x$

Since CE bisects $\angle ACD$, we have:

$\angle ACE = \angle DCE = \dfrac{180^o - x}{2}$

Since CE is parallel to AB, we have:

$\angle BAC = \angle ACE$ (alternate angles)

=> $x = \dfrac{180^o - x}{2}$

=> $x = 60^o$

Thus, in $\triangle ABC$:

$\angle ABC = 180^o - \angle BAC - \angle BCA = 180^o - 2x$

$= 60^o$

The correct answer is option C.

**33.**

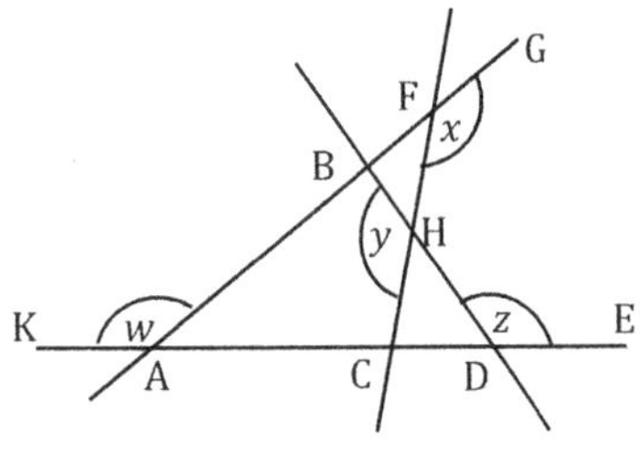


We have:

 

In $\triangle$CHD:

$\angle HDC = 180^o - z$

$\angle CHD = 180^o - y$

Thus, exterior $\angle HCA = (180^o - z) + (180^o - y) = 360^o - (y + z)$

In $\triangle$FAC:

$\angle FAC = 180^o - w$

$\angle AFC = 180^o - x$

$\angle FCA = \angle HCA = 360^o - (y + z)$

$=> (180^o - w) + (180^o - x) + 360^o - (y + z) = 180^o$

$=> x + y + z + w = 540^o$

The correct answer is option D.

**34.**

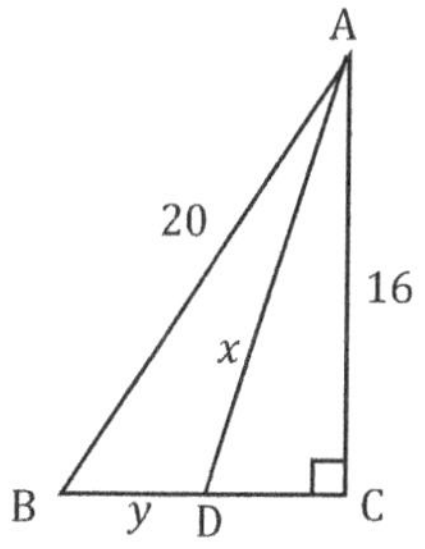


Since $\triangle$ABC is right-angled at C, we have:

$BC = \sqrt{AB^2 - AC^2} = \sqrt{20^2 - 16^2} = 12$

Since BD = $y$, we have: CD = $12 - y$

Thus, in right-angled $\triangle$ACD:

$AD^2 = AC^2 + CD^2$

$=> x^2 = 16^2 + (12 - y)^2 = 16^2 + 12^2 + y^2 - 24y$

$=> x^2 = 400 + y^2 - 24y$

$=> x = \sqrt{400 + y^2 - 24y}$

The correct answer is option E.

**35.**

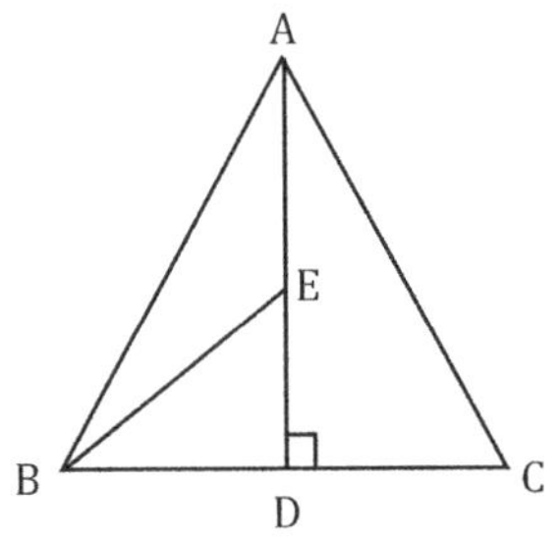


$\triangle ABC$ is an equilateral triangle, with each side of length 24.

Since $AD \perp BC$, we have:

$BD = CD = \frac{24}{2} = 12$

In right-angled $\triangle ADC$:

$AD = \sqrt{AC^2 - CD^2} = \sqrt{24^2 - 12^2} = 12\sqrt{3}$

Since E is the midpoint of AD, we have: $AE = ED = \frac{12\sqrt{3}}{2} = 6\sqrt{3}$

Thus, in right-angled $\triangle EDB$:

$BE = \sqrt{BD^2 + ED^2}$

$= \sqrt{12^2 + (6\sqrt{3})^2} = \sqrt{144 + 108} = \sqrt{252}$

$= 6\sqrt{7}$

The correct answer is option D.

**36.** The diagram for the above scenario is shown below:

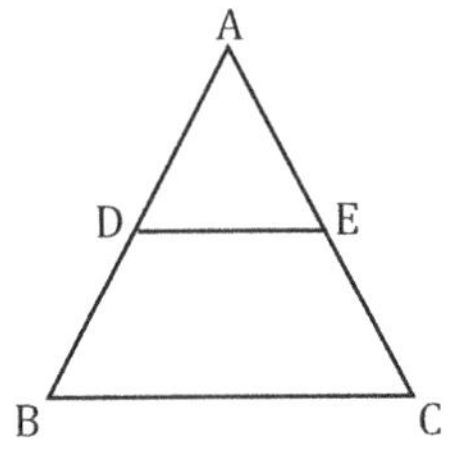


Since BCED is a trapezium, a pair of sides must be parallel.

 

Thus, DE is parallel to BC.

Thus, we have:

$\angle ADE = \angle ABC$ (corresponding angles)

$\angle AED = \angle ACB$ (corresponding angles)

Thus, $\triangle ADE$ is similar to $\triangle ABC$

$$=> \frac{\text{Area of } \triangle ADE}{\text{Area of } \triangle ABC} = \left(\frac{DE}{BC}\right)^2 = \left(\frac{3}{5}\right)^2 = \frac{9}{25}$$

$$=> \frac{\text{Area of } \triangle ADE}{\text{Area of BCED}} = \frac{9}{25-9} = \frac{9}{16}$$

The correct answer is option C.

**37.**

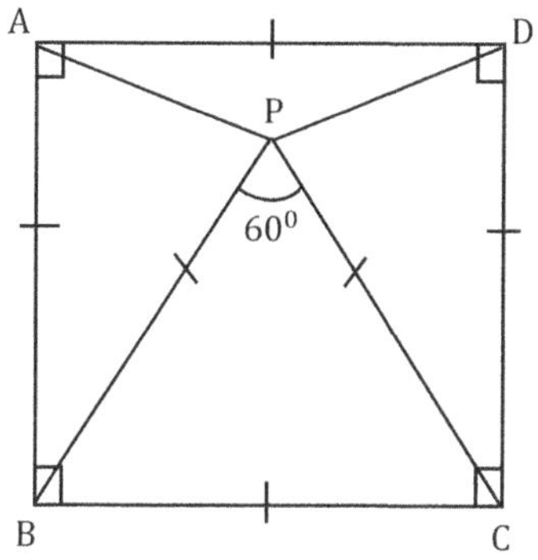


Since ABCD is a square, we have: AB = BC = CD = DA.

Also, $\angle DCB = \angle ABC = 90^\circ$

Also, since $\triangle BPC$ is equilateral, we have: BP = PC = CB.

Also, $\angle PCB = \angle PBC = \angle BPC = 60^\circ$

Thus: $\angle PCD = \angle PBA = 90^\circ - 60^\circ = 30^\circ$

Also, we have: $\triangle BPA$ and $\triangle CPD$ are isosceles.

Thus: $\angle PAB = \angle APB = \angle DPC = \angle PDC = \dfrac{180^\circ - 30^\circ}{2} = 75^\circ$

Thus, we have:

$\angle APD = 360^\circ - \angle APB - \angle DPC - \angle BPC = 360^\circ - 75^\circ - 75^\circ - 60^\circ$

$= 150^\circ$

The correct answer is option E.

**38.**

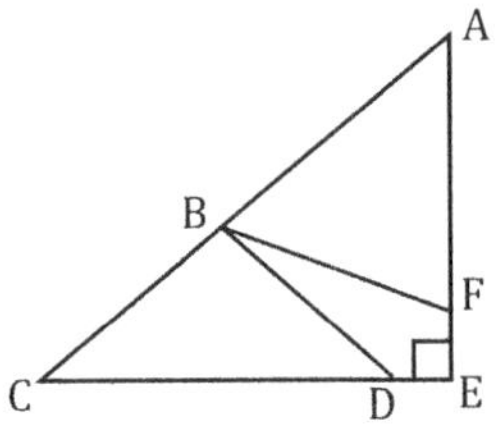


Since AB = AF in $\triangle$ABF, we have $\angle$ABF = $\angle$AFB.

Let $\angle$ABF = $\angle$AFB = $x$.

Similarly, let $\angle$CBD = $\angle$CDB = $y$ (since BC = BD in $\triangle$BCD).

Thus: $\angle$DBF = $(180^{\circ} - x - y)$.

Also, $\angle$CAE = $(180^{\circ} - 2x)$ and $\angle$ACE = $(180^{\circ} - 2y)$.

Thus, in right-angled $\triangle$AEC:

$(180^{\circ} - 2x) + (180^{\circ} - 2y) + 90^{\circ} = 180^{\circ}$

$=> x + y = 135^{\circ}$

Thus, we have:

$\angle DBF = (180^{\circ} - x - y) = 180^{\circ} - 135^{\circ}$

$= 45^{\circ}$

The correct answer is option C.

**39.** Let us draw lines CX and DY parallel to AB, as shown in the diagram below:

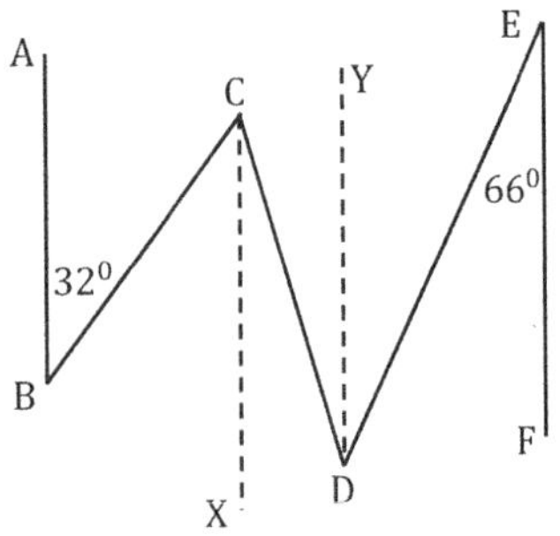


 

Thus, we have:

$\angle BCX = \angle ABC = 32^o$ (alternate angles)

$=> \angle XCD = 53^o - 32^o = 21^o$

$=> \angle CDY = \angle XCD = 21^o$ (alternate angles)

Again, $\angle YDE = \angle FED = 66^o$ (alternate angles)

Thus, we have:

$\angle CDE = \angle CDY + \angle YDE$

$= 21^o + 66^o = 87^o$

The correct answer is option D.

**40.**

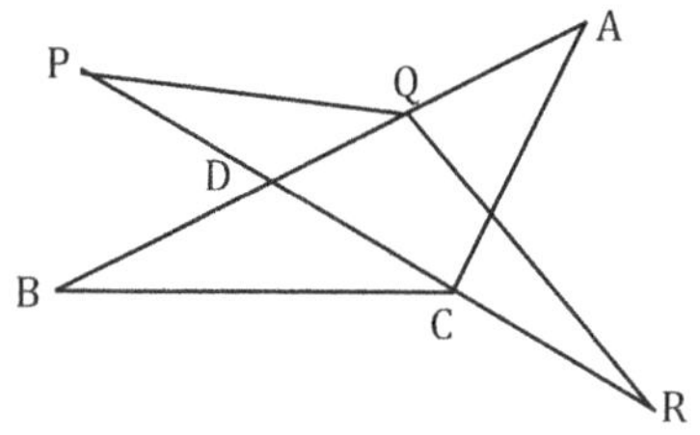


Let us consider $\triangle ADC$ and $\triangle RDQ$:

AD = RD (Since it is given that: AD = 2 * AQ = 2 * CR = RD)

DC = DQ (Given)

$\angle ADC = \angle RDQ$ (Same angle)

Thus, $\triangle ADC$ and $\triangle RDQ$ are congruent triangles

$=> \angle PRQ = \angle DRQ = \angle DAC = 40^o$

The correct answer is option C.

**41.** In $\triangle ABC$, we have: $AB^2+BC^2=AC^2$ => $\triangle ABC$ is right-angled at B.

The diagram is shown below:

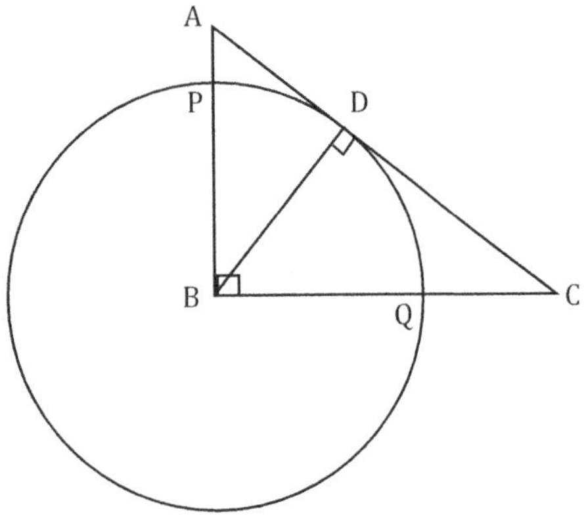


Area of $\triangle ABC$

$= \frac{1}{2}(AB)(BC) = \frac{1}{2}(AC)(BD)$

$=> \frac{1}{2} * 6 * 8 = \frac{1}{2} * 10 * BD$

$=> BD = 4.8 = BP = BQ$

Thus, we have:

$AP = AB - BP = 6 - 4.8 = 1.2$

$CQ = BC - BQ = 8 - 4.8 = 3.2$

Thus, the required ratio

$= \frac{AP}{CQ} = \frac{1.2}{3.2} = \frac{3}{8}$

The correct answer is option B.

**42.** The diagram is shown below:

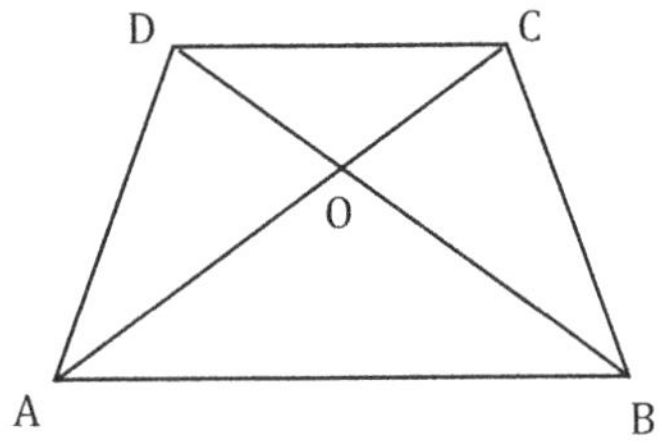


$\triangle COD$ is similar to $\triangle AOB$

(Since $\angle OCD = \angle OAB$ and $\angle ODC = \angle OBA$: alternate angles)

$=> \frac{CD}{AB} = \frac{OC}{OA} = \frac{OD}{OB} = \frac{1}{3}$

 

Also, we have:

$$\frac{\text{Area of }\triangle COD}{\text{Area of }\triangle AOB}=\left(\frac{CD}{AB}\right)^2=\left(\frac{1}{3}\right)^2=\frac{1}{9}$$

=> Area of $\triangle$AOB = 9 * (Area of $\triangle$COD) = 54

Again, for $\triangle$ADC, DO is drawn from the vertex which divides the side AC in parts AO and OC.

Thus, $\triangle$AOD and $\triangle$COD have the same height; hence, ratio of their area is equal to ratio of their corresponding bases.

$$=> \frac{\text{Area of }\triangle COD}{\text{Area of }\triangle AOD}=\frac{OC}{OA}=\frac{1}{3}$$

=> Area of $\triangle$AOD = 3 * (Area of $\triangle$COD) = 18

Again, for $\triangle$BCD, CO is drawn from the vertex which divides the side BD in parts BO and OD.

Thus, $\triangle$BOC and $\triangle$COD have the same height; hence, ratio of their area is equal to ratio of their corresponding bases.

$$=> \frac{\text{Area of }\triangle COD}{\text{Area of }\triangle BOC}=\frac{OD}{OB}=\frac{1}{3}$$

=> Area of $\triangle$ BOC = 3 * (Area of $\triangle$ COD) = 18

Thus, area of ABCD

= Area of $\triangle$AOB + Area of $\triangle$BOC + Area of $\triangle$COD + Area of $\triangle$AOD

= 54 + 18 + 6 + 18

= 96

The correct answer is option D.

**Alternate Approach**:

Refer to the following diagram:

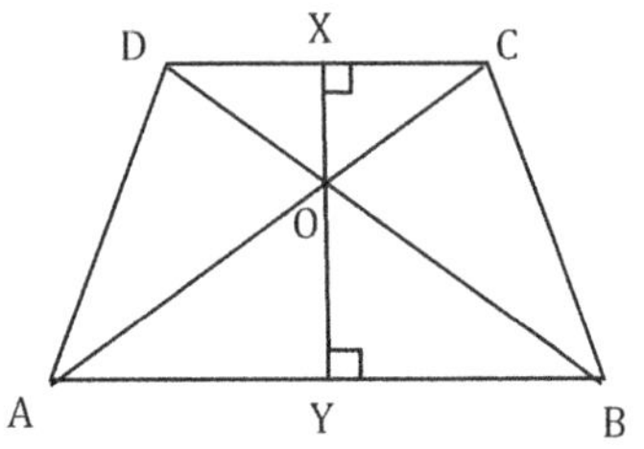


We know that,

Area of a trapezium = $\frac{1}{2} *$ (Sum of parallel sides) * height

$= \frac{1}{2} * (AB + CD) * XY$

$= \frac{1}{2} * (3*CD + CD) * (OX + OY)$

$= \frac{1}{2} * 4CD * (OX + OY) \ldots (1)$

Given that,

Area of $\triangle COD = \frac{1}{2} * CD * OX = 6$

$=> CD * OX = 12 \ldots (2)$

$\triangle COD$ is similar to $\triangle AOB$

(Since $\angle OCD = \angle OAB$ and $\angle ODC = \angle OBA$: alternate angles)

$=> \frac{CD}{AB} = \frac{OX}{OY} = \frac{1}{3}$ Thus, from eqn (1), we get,

Area of a trapezium = $\frac{1}{2} * 4CD * (OX + 3*OX) = \frac{1}{2} * 4CD * 4OX = 8CD * OX$

Thus, from eqn (2), we get,

Area of a trapezium = $8CD * OX = 8 * 12 = 96$

**43.** The diagram for the above scenario is shown below:

 

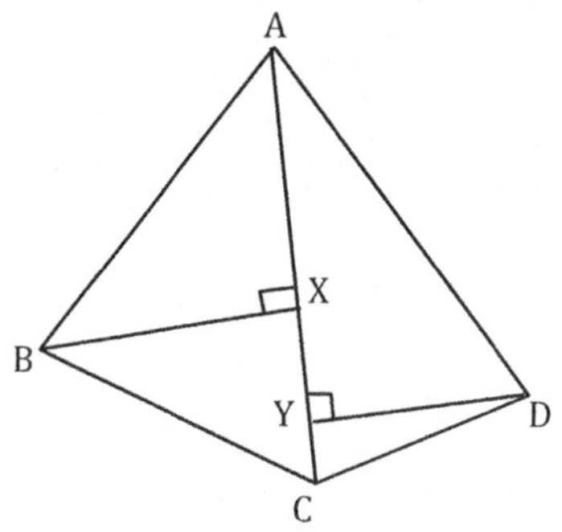


Here, AC = 16, BX = 12 and DY = 10.

Thus, area of ABCD

= Area of $\triangle$ABC + Area of $\triangle$ADC

$= \frac{1}{2}(BX)(AC) + \frac{1}{2}(DY)(AC)$

$= \frac{1}{2}(BX + DY)(AC)$

$= \frac{1}{2}(12 + 10) * 16$

= 176

The correct answer is option B.

**44.**

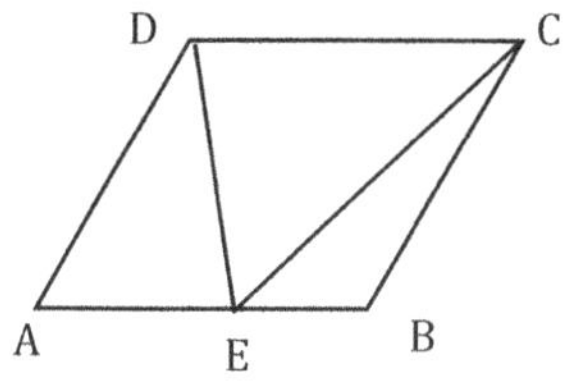


Let $\angle ADC = 2x$

Since ABCD is a parallelogram, sum of angles at adjacent vertices is $180^o$

=> $\angle BCD = (180^o - 2x)$

Since DE bisects $\angle$ADC, we have: $\angle EDC = \frac{2x}{2} = x$

Again, since CE bisects $\angle$BCD, we have: $\angle ECD = \frac{180^o - 2x}{2} = 90^o - x$

Thus, in $\triangle$DEC:

$\angle DEC = 180^0 - x - (90^0 - x) = 90^0$

The correct answer is option D.

**45.** In the diagram below, we have:

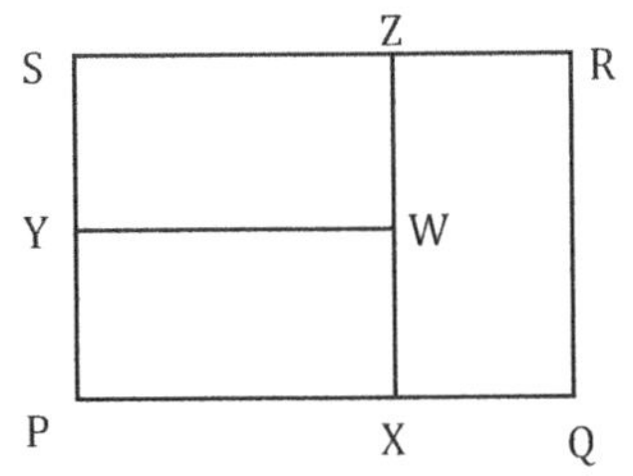


Rectangles SZWY, PYWX and QRZX are congruent

=> PX = QR and SY = YP = QX

Thus, we have:

QR = SY + YP = 2YP

PQ = PX + QX = QR + YP = 2YP + YP = 3YP

Thus, we have:

$\frac{PQ}{QR} = \frac{3YP}{2YP} = \frac{3}{2}$

The correct answer is option B.

**46.** Let us drop perpendiculars DX and CY on AB.

The diagram is shown below:

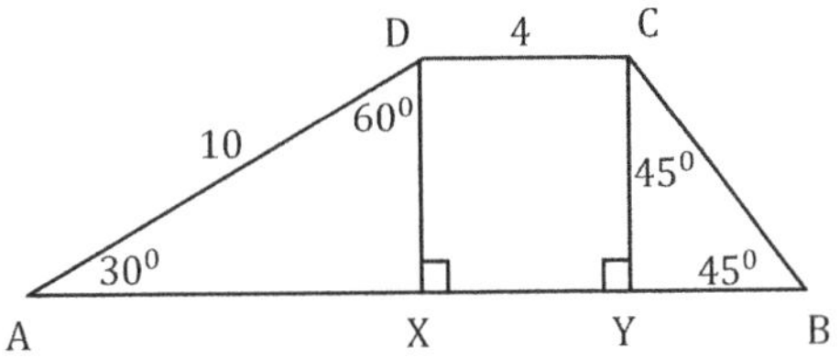


Since $\triangle$ADX is a 30-60-90 triangle:

$DX = \frac{AD}{2} = 5$

 

$AX = \sqrt{3}\,(DX) = 5\sqrt{3}$

Again, since $\triangle BCY$ is a 45-45-90 triangle:

$BY = CY = DX = 5$

Again, since DCYX is a rectangle:

$DC = XY = 4$

Thus: $AB = AX + XY + BY = 5\sqrt{3} + 4 + 5 = 9 + 5\sqrt{3}$

Thus, area of trapezium ABCD

$= \frac{1}{2}\,(AB + CD)\,(DX) = \frac{1}{2}\,(9 + 5\sqrt{3} + 4)\,(5)$

$= \frac{5}{2}(13 + 5\sqrt{3})$

The correct answer is option B.

**47.** Let us join DE.

The diagram is shown below:

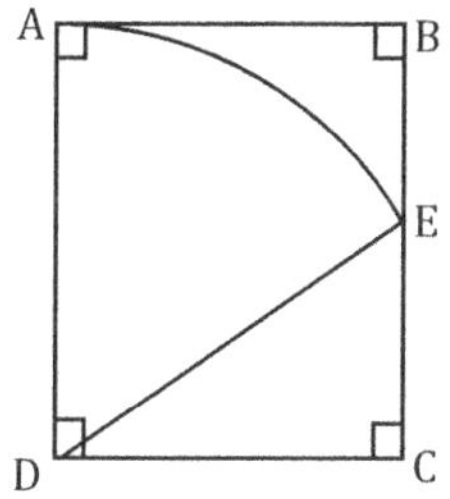


$DE = AD = \sqrt{2}$ (radius of the circle drawn with center at D).

Also, $CD = AB = 1$.

Thus, in right-angled $\triangle DCE$:

$CE = \sqrt{DE^2 - CD^2} = \sqrt{\left(\sqrt{2}\right)^2 - 1} = 1$

Thus: $BE = BC - CE = AD - CE$

$= \sqrt{2} - 1$

The correct answer is option A.

**48.** We know that the sum of interior angles of a polygon with $n$ sides is $(n - 2) * 180^o$.

Thus, for a pentagon, the sum of the interior angles $= (5 - 2) * 180^o = 540^o$.

Since the angles are distinct integers, and we need to maximize any one angle, we choose the other four angles to be the least possible values, i.e. $1^o, 2^o, 3^o$ and $4^o$.

Thus, the maximum possible measure of any interior angle should have been

$= 540^o - (1^o + 2^o + 3^o + 4^o) = 530^o$

However, any interior angle can never be greater than $360^o$.

Thus, the maximum possible measure any interior angle $= 359^o$ (the largest integer value less than $360^o$).

Note: Such an angle is a reflex angle and a possible diagram of such a pentagon is given below:

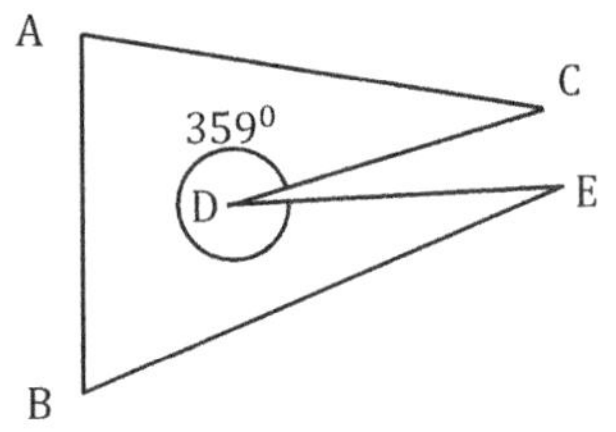


However, if it were mentioned that the pentagon is convex, i.e. each interior angle must be less than $180^o$, the answer would then have been $179^o$ (the largest integer value less than $180^o$).

The correct answer is option B.

**49.** Let us make some construction as shown in the diagram below:

We have:

 

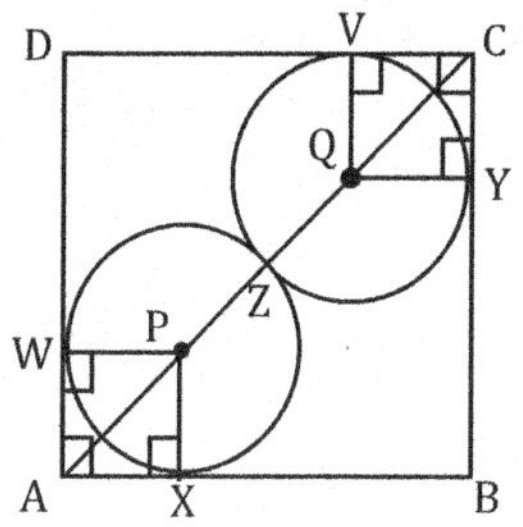


PX = PW = PZ = QZ = QY = QV = radius of the circle = 1

Thus, PWAX and QVCY are squares of side 1

Thus, PA = QC = $\sqrt{1^2 + 1^2} = \sqrt{2}$

Thus: AC = PA + PZ + QZ + QC

$= \sqrt{2} + 1 + 1 + \sqrt{2} = 2\left(\sqrt{2} + 1\right)$

Since AC is the diagonal of the square ABCD, we have:

Each side of the square ABCD = $\frac{AC}{\sqrt{2}} = \frac{2\left(\sqrt{2}+1\right)}{\sqrt{2}} = \sqrt{2}\left(\sqrt{2}+1\right) = 2 + \sqrt{2}$

The correct answer is option B.

**50.** Let us join OB, as shown in the diagram below.

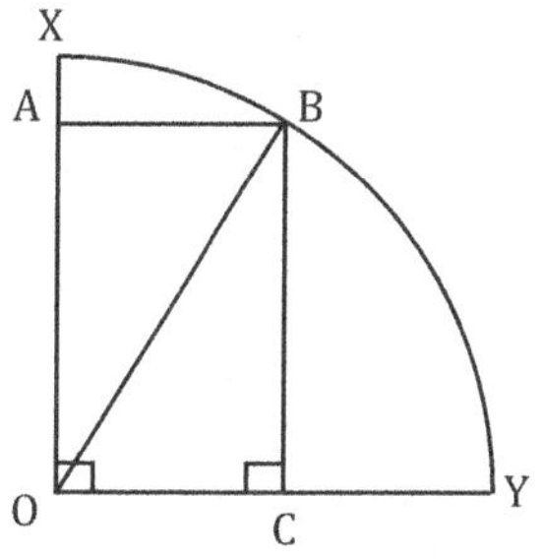


Let OA = BC = $2x$

=> OX = OB = OY = OA + AX = $2x + 2$

=> OC = $\frac{3}{5}$ OY = $\frac{3}{5}(2x + 2)$

Thus, in right-angled $\triangle$CBO:

$OB^2 = OC^2 + BC^2$

 

$$=> (2x + 2)^2 = \left(\frac{3}{5}(2x + 2)\right)^2 + (2x)^2$$

$$=> (2x + 2)^2 = \frac{9}{25}(2x + 2)^2 + (2x)^2$$

$$=> \left(1 - \frac{9}{25}\right)(2x + 2)^2 = (2x)^2$$

$$=> \frac{16}{25}(2x + 2)^2 = (2x)^2$$

Taking square roots on both sides (and ignoring the negative sign, since $x$ must be positive):

$$\frac{4}{5}(2x + 2) = 2x$$

$$=> 8x + 8 = 10x => x = 4$$

Thus, we have:

OB = Radius of the arc = $2x + 2 = 2 * 4 + 2 = 10$

The correct answer is option C.

**51.** The diagram for the above scenario is shown below:

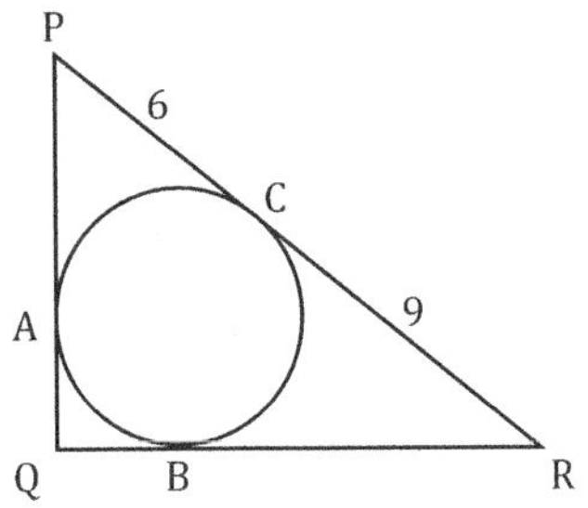


Since tangents drawn to a circle from a point are equal:

PA = PC = 6

BR = CR = 9

Also, let QA = QB = $x$

Thus: PQ = $(6 + x)$, QR = $(9 + x)$ and PR = 15

Since the perimeter is 36, we have:

$$(6 + x) + (9 + x) + 15 = 36 => x = 3$$

 

Thus, we have: PQ = 9, QR = 12 and PR = 15, which satisfy Pythagoras' theorem:

$PQ^2 + QR^2 = PR^2$

=> $\triangle$PQR is right-angled at Q

Thus, area of $\triangle PQR = \frac{1}{2}$ (PQ) (QR) $= \frac{1}{2}$ (9) (12)

= 54

The correct answer is option C.

**52.**

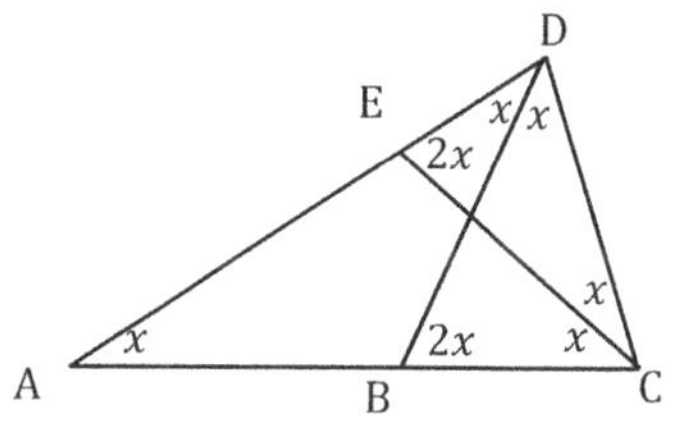


Let $\angle DAC = x$.

In $\triangle ABD$, AB = BD => $\angle DAB = \angle BDA = x$

=> $\angle DBC$ = Exterior angle for $\triangle ABD = x + x = 2x$

Again, in $\triangle AEC$, AE = EC => $\angle EAC = \angle ECA = x$

=> $\angle CED$ = Exterior angle for $\triangle AEC = x + x = 2x$

Again, in $\triangle DBC$, DB = DC => $\angle DBC = \angle DCB = 2x$

Similarly, in $\triangle DEC$, DC = EC => $\angle DEC = \angle EDC = 2x$

(Note: $\angle BDC = \angle EDC - \angle ADB = x$ and $\angle DCE = \angle DCB - \angle ECA = x$)

Thus, in $\triangle ACD$, we have:

$\angle DAC = x$, $\angle DCA = 2x$ and $\angle ADC = 2x$

=> $x + 2x + 2x = 180^\circ$

=> $x = 36^\circ$

The correct answer is option B.

 

**53.** Area of rectangle ABFE = AB * AE = 20 * 10 = 200.

Let us join CF, as shown in the diagram below:

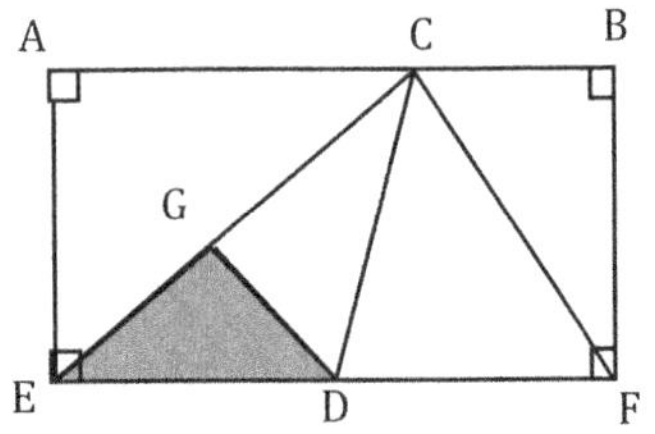


Thus, area of $\triangle$ECF

$= \frac{1}{2}$ * Base * Height

$= \frac{1}{2} *$ Area of rectangle ABFE = 100

Since in $\triangle$ECF, CD is a line drawn from the vertex to the opposite base such that ED = DF. Thus, CD is a median which divides the triangle in two equal areas. Thus, we have:

Area of $\triangle$CED = Area of $\triangle$CFD = $\frac{1}{2} *$ Area of $\triangle$ECF = 50

Since in $\triangle$CED, DG is a line drawn from the vertex to the opposite base such that EG = GC, we have:

Area of $\triangle$EGD = Area of $\triangle$CGD = $\frac{1}{2} *$ Area of $\triangle$CED = 25

The correct answer is option C.

**Alternate Approach**:

The questions can be solved intuitively too.

Since point C on AB is any random point, let us take it to our best advantage.

Assume that Point C is at the mid of AB. Thus, the diagram would look like the following.

 

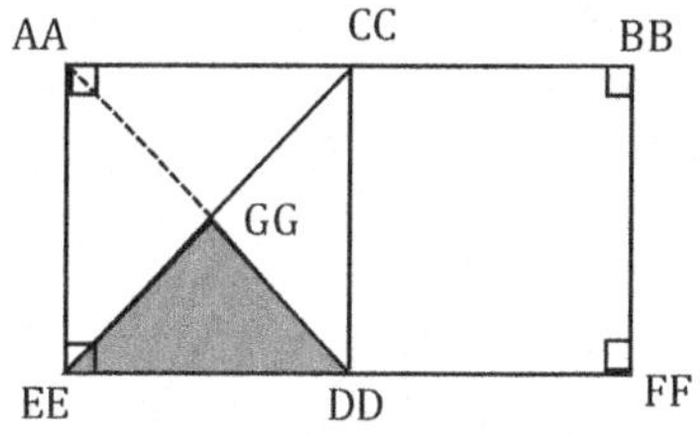


We see that $\triangle$EGD is one-fourth of square ACDE, which is one-half of rectangle ABFE having an area of 20 * 10 = 200.

Thus, the area of $\frac{1}{4} * \frac{1}{2} * 200 = 25$.

**54.** Volume of the cube = $(\text{Side})^3 = 6^3 = 216$ cm$^3$.

When the cube is completely submerged, the volume of water displaced by it will result in increase of water level in the rectangular vessel.

Let the increase in height of water level be $x$ cm.

Since dimensions of the base of the vessel are 15 cm by 12 cm, the volume of water displaced = $x * 15 * 12$

Thus, we have:

$x * 15 * 12 = 216$

$$=> x = \frac{216}{15 * 12} = \frac{18}{15} = 1.2 \text{ cm}$$

The correct answer is option B.

**55.** The diagram for the above scenario is shown below:

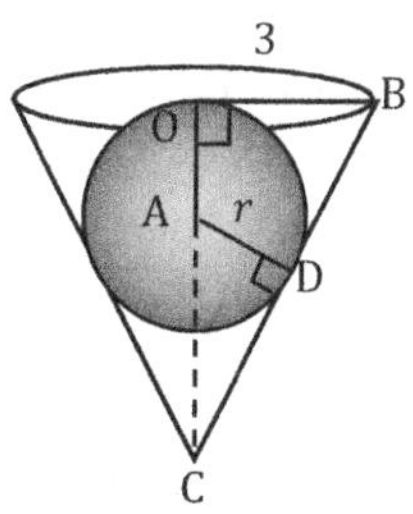


Since the sphere has to be the largest possible, it must touch the sides of the cone and also be at the same level as the base.

We have: OC = 4 and OB = 3.

Thus, we have: BC = $\sqrt{3^2 + 4^2} = 5$.

Let OA = $r$.

We join AD. Since AD is also the radius, it is perpendicular to the tangent BC.

In $\triangle$CAD and $\triangle$CBO:

$\angle ACD = \angle BCO$ and $\angle ADC = \angle BOC = 90^o$

=> $\triangle$CAD is similar to $\triangle$CBO

=> $\frac{AC}{BC} = \frac{AD}{OB}$ => $\frac{OC - OA}{5} = \frac{r}{3}$

=> $\frac{4 - r}{5} = \frac{r}{3}$

=> $12 - 3r = 5r$ => $r = \frac{3}{2}$

The correct answer is option C.

**56.** The possible diagrams for the above scenario are presented below:

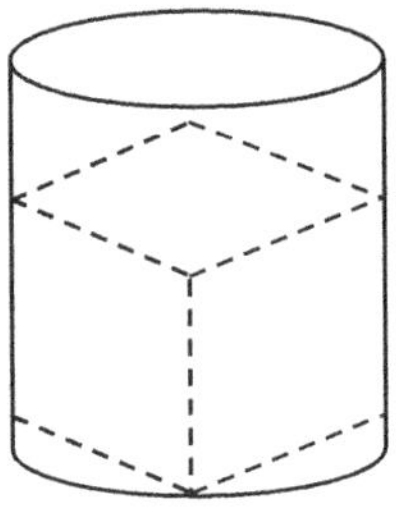

Case 1

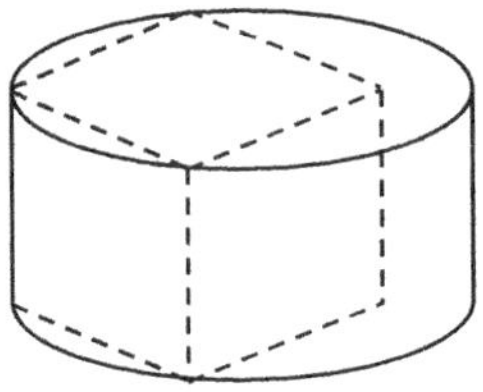

Case 2

In Case 1, the cube touches the sides of the cylinder, but leaves an empty space on top; while in Case 2, the cube fits in the height of the cylinder, but leaves an empty space along the sides.

We need to see first, which of the two cases is valid.

Since the height of the cylinder is 3, the maximum side of the cube can be 3.

Since the radius of the cylinder is 2, i.e. the diameter is 4; the maximum length of the diagonal of a face of the cube can be 4.

 

If the side of the cube be $a$, then the diagonal is $a\sqrt{2} => a\sqrt{2} = 4$

$=> a = 2\sqrt{2} \approx 2 * 1.4 = 2.8$

Thus, the maximum length of the side of the cube is the LESSER of the two: 3 and $2\sqrt{2}$, i.e. $2\sqrt{2}$

Thus, the volume of the largest cube = $\left(2\sqrt{2}\right)^3 = 16\sqrt{2}$

The correct answer is option A.

**57.** The box is open on one side, and we need to minimize the length of tape required.

Thus, we need to decide which side to keep open that would minimize the tape utilization.

The total length of tape required is the sum of the lengths of the edges of the box, except for the face that is open.

The dimensions of the box are 3 cm by 2.5 cm by 2 cm.

In a rectangular solid, there are a total of 12 edges.

Thus, each of the three distinct edges are present $\frac{12}{3} = 4$ times.

Considering all edges, the total length of tape

$= 4 * 3 + 4 * 2.5 + 4 * 2$

$= 30$ cm

There are three distinct faces of the box, of dimensions 3 cm by 2.5 cm, 3 cm by 2 cm, and 2.5 cm by 2 cm.

The perimeters of the above three distinct faces are:

- For the face having dimensions 3 cm by 2.5 cm: $2(3 + 2.5) = 11$ cm
- For the face having dimensions 3 cm by 2 cm: $2(3 + 2) = 10$ cm
- For the face having dimensions 2.5 cm by 2 cm: $2(2.5 + 2) = 9$ cm

Since we need to minimize the length of tape, we need to keep open the face having the LARGEST perimeter, i.e. the face having perimeter 11 cm.

Thus, minimum length of tape required

= 30 - 11

= 19 cm

The correct answer is option C.

**58.** The dimensions of the base of the rectangular reservoir = 120 m by 60 m.

Since the water rises up by 3 m, the volume of water filled

$= 120 * 60 * 3 = 21600\text{m}^3$

This volume of water is filled in 18 hours.

Thus, volume of water filled in 1 hour = $\frac{21600}{18} = 1200\ \text{m}^3$

Let the speed of water flowing through the pipe = $x$ meters per hour.

Area of the pipe cross-section = 2 * 2 = 4 $\text{m}^2$

Thus, volume of water flowing through the pipe in 1 hour = $4x\ \text{m}^3$

Thus, we have:

$4x = 1200$

$=> x = 300$

The correct answer is option D.

**59.** For each cut parallel to a face, two new faces are generated, as shown in the diagram below:

 

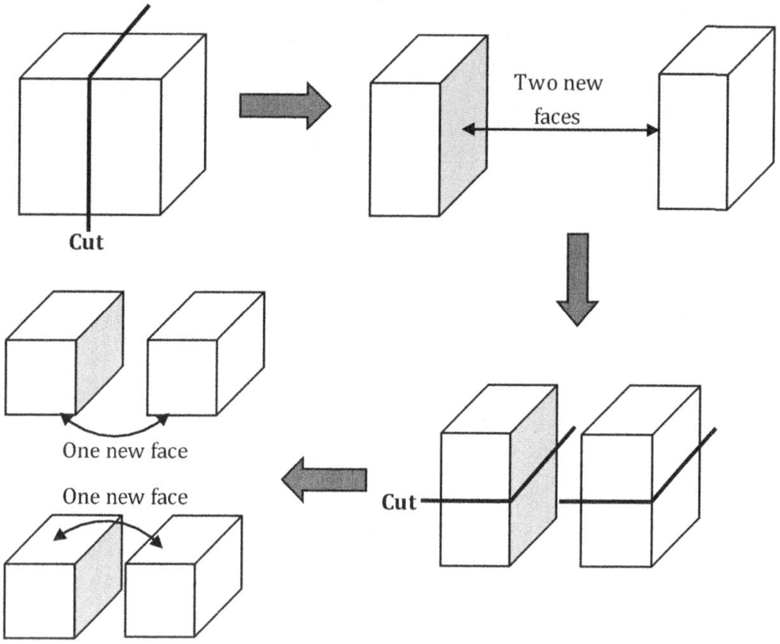


Since there are three cuts, there would be six new faces, all identical squares.

Initially, the cube had six faces, which are six identical squares.

Thus, the surface area increased by an area equal to that of the six faces.

Thus, required percent increase $= \frac{6}{6} * 100 = 100\%$

The correct answer is option C.

**60.** Let each side of the cube be $a$.

Let the radius and height of the cylinder be $b$.

Since the volumes are equal, we have:

$(\text{Side of the cube})^3 = \pi * (\text{radius of the cylinder})^2 * (\text{height of the cylinder})$

$\Rightarrow a^3 = \pi b^2 * b \Rightarrow a^3 = \pi b^3$

$\Rightarrow \frac{b}{a} = \frac{1}{\sqrt[3]{\pi}}$

Curved surface area of the cylinder $= 2\pi$ (radius of the cylinder) $*$ (height of the cylinder)

$= 2\pi b^2$

Total surface area of the cube $= 6 * (\text{Side of the cube})^2$

 

$= 6a^2$

Thus, the required ratio

$= \frac{2\pi b^2}{6a^2} = \frac{2\pi}{6}\left(\frac{b}{a}\right)^2$

$= \frac{\pi}{3}\left(\frac{1}{\sqrt[3]{\pi}}\right)^2 = \frac{\pi}{3} * \frac{1}{\pi^{\left(\frac{2}{3}\right)}} = \frac{\pi^{\left(1-\frac{2}{3}\right)}}{3}$

$= \frac{\sqrt[3]{\pi}}{3}$

The correct answer is option D.

### 5.1.2 Data Sufficiency

Standard options for Data Sufficiency questions are as follows.

A. Statement (1) ALONE is sufficient, but statement (2) ALONE is not sufficient to answer the question asked.

B. Statement (2) ALONE is sufficient, but statement (1) ALONE is not sufficient to answer the question asked.

C. BOTH statements (1) and (2) TOGETHER are sufficient to answer the question asked, but NEITHER statement ALONE is sufficient to answer the question asked.

D. EACH statement ALONE is sufficient to answer the question asked.

E. Statements (1) and (2) TOGETHER are NOT sufficient to answer the question asked, and additional data specific to the problem are needed.

**61.** From statement 1:

Let the angles be $x$, $y$ and $z$.

Thus: $x + y + z = 180$

Since the difference between exactly two pairs of angles of $\triangle ABC$ is $20^o$, let us have:

- Case 1: $x - y = 20$ and $z - y = 20$

  $\Rightarrow x = z = y + 20$

  $\Rightarrow (y + 20) + y + (y + 20) = 180$ (Since $x + y + z = 180$)

  $\Rightarrow y = \left(\frac{140}{3}\right)^o$

  $\Rightarrow x = z = 20 + \frac{140}{3} = \left(\frac{200}{3}\right)^o$

  Thus, none of the angles are $60^o$.

- Case 2: $x - y = 20$ and $y - z = 20$

  $\Rightarrow y = z + 20$ and $x = y + 20 = z + 40$

$=> (z + 40) + (z + 20) + z = 180$ (Since $x + y + z = 180$)

$=> z = 40^o$

$=> x = (z + 40) = 80^o$

$y = (z + 20) = 60^o$

Thus, one angle is $60^o$.

Thus, the answer to the question can be 'Yes' or 'No'.

Thus, there is no unique answer. - Insufficient

From statement 2:

We only know that the ratio of two sides of the triangle is $\sqrt{3} : 1$.

Only in a right-angled triangle, if the ratio of the sides is $\sqrt{3} : 1$, then one angle is $60^o$.

However, we have no information whether any angle is $90^o$. - Insufficient

Thus, from both statements together:

Even after combining both statements, we can have a triangle where no angle is $60^o$ and the ratio of the sides is $\sqrt{3} : 1$. - Insufficient

The correct answer is option E.

**62.** From statement 1:

We only know the length of a side of the rhombus.

Thus, the area cannot be determined. - Insufficient

From statement 2:

We only know the length of a diagonal of the rhombus.

Thus, the area cannot be determined. - Insufficient

Thus, from both statements together:

We need to determine the length of the other diagonal.

 

The area can then be determined as: Area = $\frac{1}{2} *$ Product of the diagonals

We know that in a rhombus, the diagonals bisect each other at right angles.

The diagram is shown below:

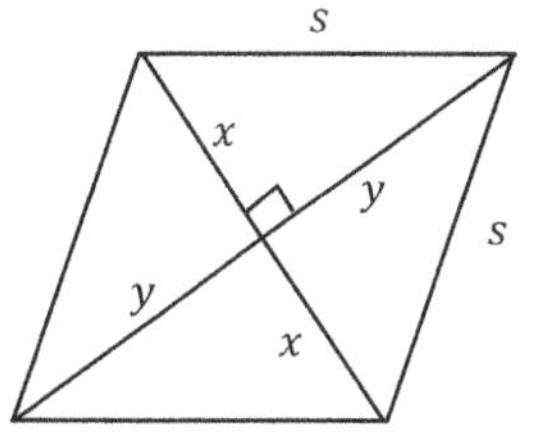


If the diagonals of a rhombus are $2x$ and $2y$ and the side is $s$, then from Pythagoras' theorem, we have:

$x^2 + y^2 = s^2$

Here, $s = 13$ and $x = \frac{10}{2} = 5$

$=> y = \sqrt{13^2 - 5^2} = 12$

Thus, the length of the other diagonal = 2 * 12 = 24

Thus, the area of the rhombus

$= \frac{1}{2} * 24 * 10 = 120$. – Sufficient

The correct answer is option C.

**63.** Let us draw PW, PX, PY and PZ perpendicular from point P to AB, BC, CD and DA, respectively.

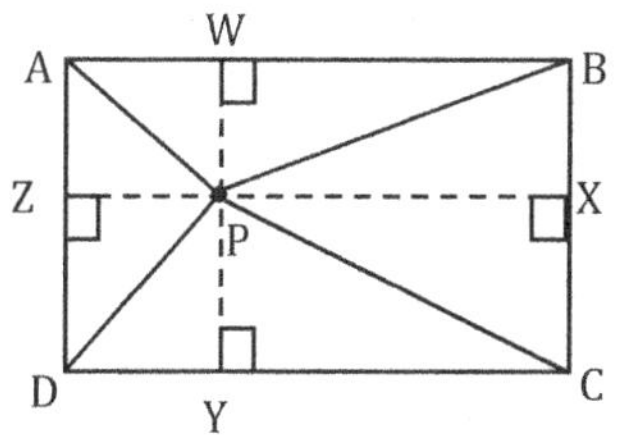


We have, from Pythagoras' theorem:

$AP^2 = AW^2 + WP^2 = DY^2 + BX^2 \ldots$(i)

$BP^2 = BW^2 + BX^2 \ldots$(ii)

$CP^2 = CX^2 + CY^2 = DZ^2 + BW^2$ ...(iii)

$DP^2 = DY^2 + DZ^2$ ...(iv)

Adding (i) and (iii):

$AP^2 + CP^2$

$= \left(DY^2 + BX^2\right) + \left(DZ^2 + BW^2\right)$

$= \left(DY^2 + DZ^2\right) + \left(BX^2 + BW^2\right)$

$= DP^2 + BP^2$

Thus, to find any of AP, BP, CP or DP, we need to know the values of the other three.

From statement 1:

We only know the length of two among AP, BP, CP and DP. - Insufficient

From statement 2:

We only know the length of one among AP, BP, CP and DP. - Insufficient

Thus, from both statements together:

$AP^2 + CP^2 = DP^2 + BP^2$

$=> AP^2 + 5^2 = 6^2 + 8^2$

$=> AP = \sqrt{6^2 + 8^2 - 5^2} = \sqrt{75} = 5\sqrt{3}$. - Sufficient

The correct answer is option C.

**Alternate Approach**:

From statement 1:

While maintaining BP = 8 and DP = 6, floating random point P inside the rectangle can have two positions, affecting the length of AP. Let see in the flowing diagram.

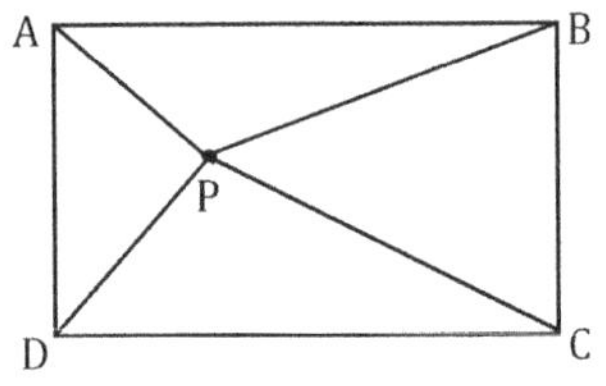


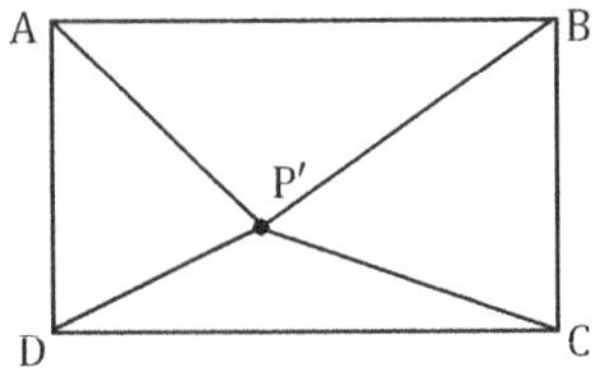

We see that AP < AP', thus we cannot get its unique value. – Insufficient

From statement 2:

On the similar reasoning, merely knowing the value of CP, point P can have infinite number of locations inside the rectangle. – Insufficient

Thus, from both statements together:

Since in the above figure, only one of CP or CP' can be 5, thus, we are assured of the location of the point P. Thus, we can get the unique value of AP.

**64.** From statement 1:

The diagram for the above scenario is shown below:

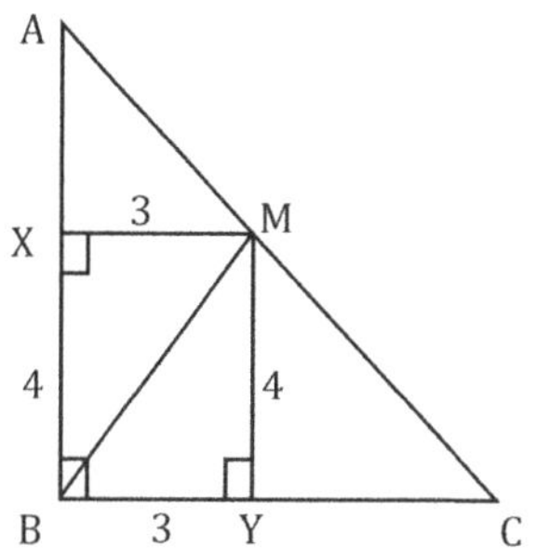


We have:

BM $=\sqrt{BY^2+MY^2} = \sqrt{MX^2+MY^2} = \sqrt{3^2+4^2} = 5$ In $\triangle AXM$ and $\triangle MYC$:

$\angle AXM = \angle MYC = 90^o$

$\angle AMX = \angle MCY$ (corresponding angles since MX is parallel to CB)

Thus, $\triangle AXM$ is similar to $\triangle MYC$ => $\frac{AX}{MY}=\frac{MX}{CY}$

=> $\frac{AX}{4}=\frac{3}{CY}$

However, the length of AX cannot be determined.

Hence, the length of AB cannot be determined. – Insufficient

From statement 2:

We have no information about the lengths of any side. – Insufficient

 

Thus, from both statements together:

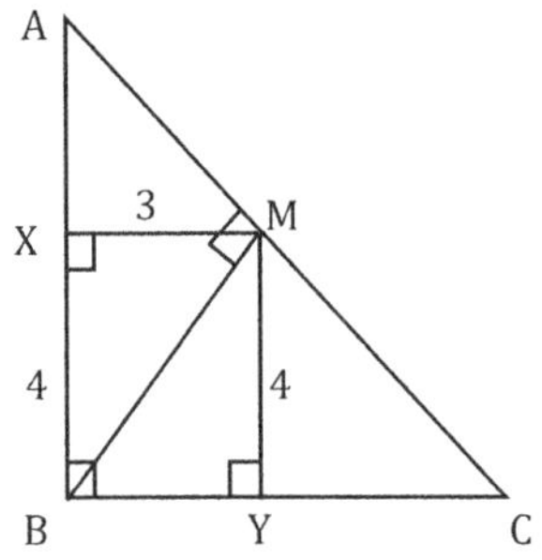


In $\triangle$ABM: Let $\angle$MAB = $x$

=> $\angle AMX = 90^{\circ} - x$

=> $\angle XMB = 90^{\circ} - (90^{\circ} - x) = x$

Thus, in $\triangle$AMB and $\triangle$MXB:

$\angle BAM = \angle BMX = x$

$\angle AMB = \angle MXB = 90^{\circ}$

Thus, $\triangle$AMB is similar to $\triangle$MXB => $\frac{AB}{MB} = \frac{MB}{XB}$

=> $\frac{AB}{5} = \frac{5}{4}$ => AB = $\frac{25}{4}$. - Sufficient

The correct answer is option C.

**65.** Let us draw a line EX perpendicular to AB.

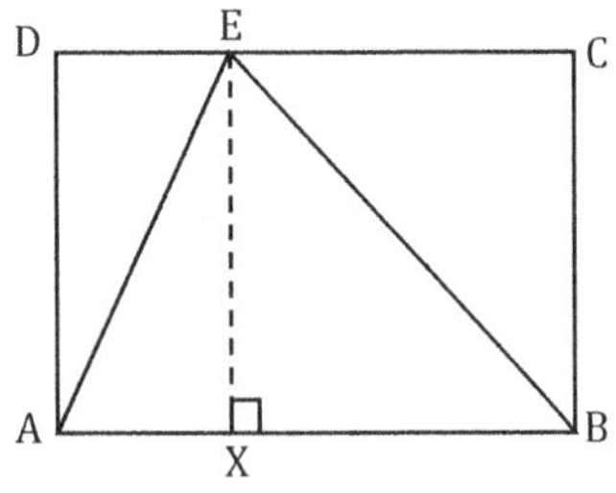


EXBC is a rectangle and EB is a diagonal:

Area $\triangle$BXE = Area $\triangle$BCE

Again, since EXAD is a rectangle and EA is a diagonal:

Area $\triangle$AXE = Area $\triangle$ADE

 

Thus, we have:

Area of ABCD = Area △ADE + Area △AXE + Area △BXE + Area △BCE

= 2(Area △ADE + Area △BCE)

From statement 1:

Area of △ADE is not known. – Insufficient

From statement 2:

Area of △BCE is not known. – Insufficient

Thus, from both statements together:

Area of ABCD = 2 * (30 + 20) = 100. – Sufficient

The correct answer is option C.

**Alternate Approach:**

Area of ABCD = Area of ADEX + Area of BCEX

=> AD $*$ DE + BC $*$ CE

From statement 1:

Area △BCE = $\frac{1}{2} * BC * CE = 30 => BC * CE = 60$

From statement 2:

Area △ADE = $\frac{1}{2} * AD * DE = 20 => AD * DE = 40$

Thus, from both statements together:

Required area = 100.

**66.** From statement 1:

We only know the measure of ∠QMR. – Insufficient

From statement 2:

We only know the measure of ∠QPR. – Insufficient

Thus, from both statements together:

We see that: $\angle QMR = 2\angle QPR$.

We know that in a circle, angle subtended by an arc at the center is double the angle subtended by the same arc at the circumference.

However, if the angle subtended by an arc at any point inside the circle is double that of the angle subtended at the circumference, that point need not be the center.

Let us see how, using the diagram below:

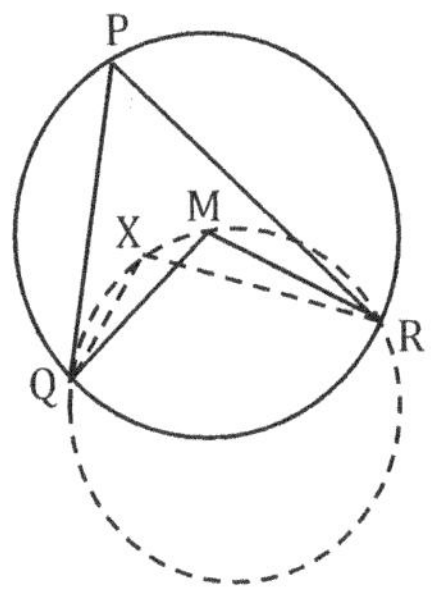


We have constructed a circle passing through Q, M and R.

(Note: We can always draw a circle passing through three points)

Let us take another point X on this newly constructed circle.

In the new circle, we have:

$\angle QXR = \angle QMR$, since both are subtended on the circumference by arc QR

We know that $\angle QMR = 2\angle QPR$

$\Rightarrow \angle QXR = 2\angle QPR$

Thus, logically, X could also have been the center of the initial circle.

In fact, there could be infinite points inside the given circle which would satisfy the conditions given in the two statements.

Thus, the answer to the question could be 'Yes' or 'No'. – Insufficient

The correct answer is option E.

 

**67.** We need to equate the volume of the cubical vessel and the volume of water remaining in the cylinder after some water had been drained out.

From statement 1:

We know the dimensions of the cylinder.

However, we have no information about the volume of water drained out. - Insufficient

From statement 2:

We have no information about the dimensions of the cylinder. - Insufficient

Thus, from both statements together:

Volume of the cylinder = $\pi(\text{Radius})^2$ (Height) $= \pi\ (3^2)\ (16) = 144\pi$.

We know that after the water was drained out, the water level formed a straight line joining the upper and lower rims.

Thus, the volume of water remaining is equal to the volume of the empty space above the water level.

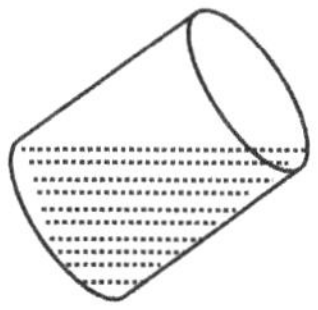

Thus, volume of water remaining $= \frac{1}{2} * 144\pi = 72\pi$.

Thus, we have:

Volume of the cube = $(\text{Side})^3 = 72\pi$ => Side of the cube = $\sqrt[3]{72\pi}$. - Sufficient

The correct answer is option C.

**68.** From statement 1:

We know that ABCD is a square.

However, since the position of X on CD is not known, we cannot determine the dimensions of $\triangle$PDX and $\triangle$QCX.

 

Thus, the measure of $\angle PXQ$ cannot be determined. – Insufficient

Note: In the diagram, it appears that P and Q are on the same level and hence, it seems that X is the midpoint of DC. However, since it has not been mentioned explicitly, we should not assume the same.

Another possible diagram could have been:

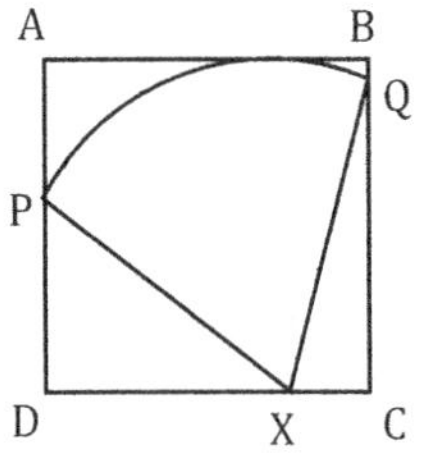


From statement 2:

We know that $\angle PXD = 60^o$.

However, there is no information about the nature of ABCD, whether it is any random quadrilateral or a special figure like a parallelogram, rectangle, rhombus or square. – Insufficient

Thus, from both statements together:

Since $\angle PDX = 90^o$, $\triangle PDX$ is a 30-90-60 triangle.

Let AB = BC = CD = DA = 2.

Since the arc touches the side of the square, the radius of the arc is also 2, i.e. XP = XQ = 2.

In $\triangle PDX$: $DX = \frac{PX}{2} = 1$.

Thus, CX = CD – DX = 2 – 1 = 1.

In $\triangle QCX$, we have:

$\angle QCX = 90^o$ and $CX = \frac{QX}{2}$

Thus, $\triangle QCX$ is also a 30-90-60 triangle

=> $\angle QXC = 60^o$

 

Thus, we have:

$\angle PXQ = 180^o - \angle PXD - \angle QXC$

$= 180^o - 60^o - 60^o$

$= 60^o$. – Sufficient

The correct answer is option C.

**69.** From statement 1:

We know the lengths of AD and DE.

However, we cannot determine the length of BE. – Insufficient

From statement 2:

We only know the length of one side of the rectangle. – Insufficient

Thus, from both statements together:

Let us draw a line EX perpendicular to AD, as shown in the diagram below:

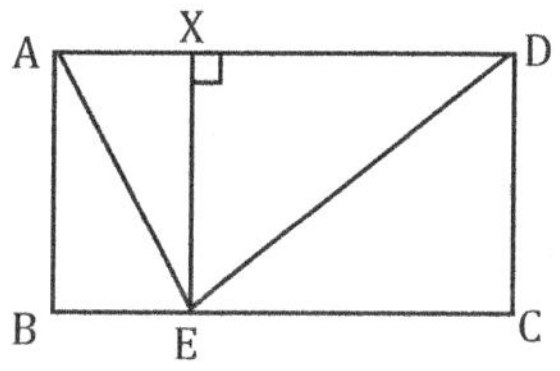


We have: EX = AB = 2.4

In $\triangle EXD$: $XD = \sqrt{DE^2 - EX^2} = \sqrt{4^2 - 2.4^2} = 3.2$

Thus, BE = AX = AD – XD = 5 – 3.2 = 1.8

The correct answer is option C.

**70.** From statement 1:

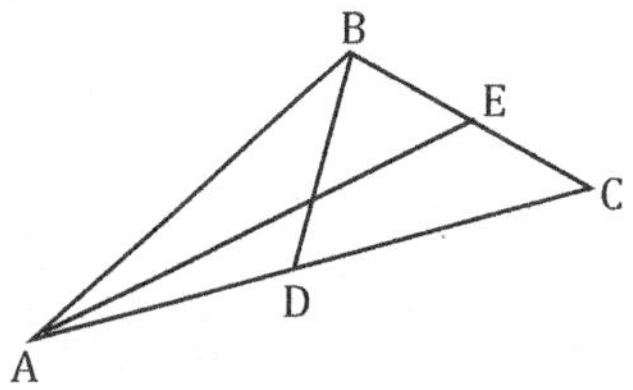


 

We know that AD = CD

Thus, $\triangle$BDA and $\triangle$BDC have the same height and equal base.

Thus, we have: Area $\triangle$BDC = Area $\triangle$BDA = $\dfrac{\text{Area } \triangle\text{ABC}}{2}$

However, we have no information about $\triangle$ABE. - Insufficient

From statement 2:

We know that BE = CE

Thus, $\triangle$ABE and $\triangle$ACE have the same height and equal base.

Thus, we have: Area $\triangle$ABE = Area $\triangle$ACE = $\dfrac{\text{Area } \triangle\text{ABC}}{2}$

However, we have no information about $\triangle$BDC. - Insufficient

Thus, from both statements together:

We have:

Area $\triangle$BDC = Area $\triangle$ABE

Thus, the ratio of their areas is 1. - Sufficient

The correct answer is option C.

**71.** From statement 1:

Let the radius of the smaller circles be $r$.

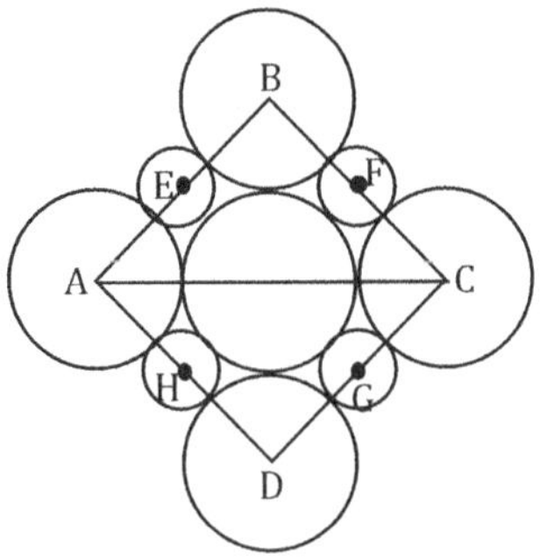


Let us join AC.

Thus, we have:

 

AB = BC = 2 + 2$r$ + 2 = 2$r$ + 4

AC = 2 + 2 + 2 + 2 = 8

In right-angled $\triangle$ABC:

$AB^2 + BC^2 = AC^2$

$=> (2r + 4)^2 + (2r + 4)^2 = 8^2$

$=> (r + 2)^2 = 8$

$=> r + 2 = 2\sqrt{2}$

$=> r = \left(2\sqrt{2} - 2\right) = 2(\sqrt{2} - 1)$. - Sufficient

Alternately, we could have done:

In right angled triangle ABC, AB = AC, thus: $\angle$ BAC = $\angle$ BCA = 45°.

Thus, AB = BC = $\frac{1}{\sqrt{2}} * \text{Hypotenuse} = \frac{1}{\sqrt{2}} * 8$

$=> 2r + 4 = \frac{1}{\sqrt{2}} * 8$

$=> 2r = \frac{8}{\sqrt{2}} - 4 => 4\sqrt{2} - 4 = 4(\sqrt{2} - 1) => r = 2(\sqrt{2} - 1)$ - Sufficient

From statement 2:

We know that AC = 8.

This is the same information derived from statement 1. - Sufficient

The correct answer is option D.

**72.** Area of shaded portion = Area of Quadrilateral ABCD − Area of 4 sectors

From statement 1:

Apparently, it seems that ABCD is a square having side 2 + 2 = 4. Thus, the shaded area is simply the area of the square, less the areas of the quadrants of the four circles.

However, ABCD need not be a square, as shown in the diagram below:

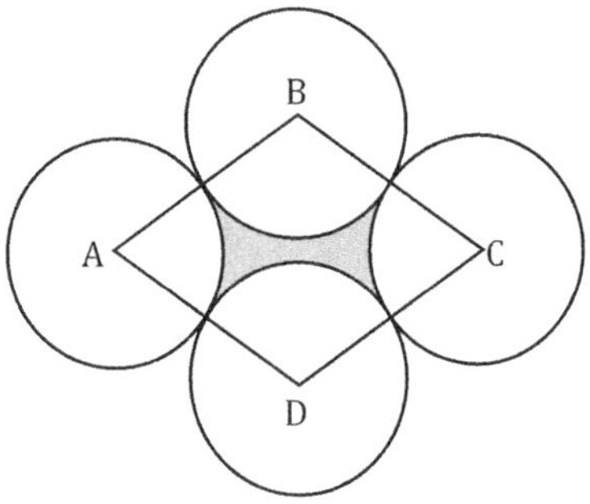


However, we still have:

AB = BC = CD = DA = 2 + 2 = 4

Thus, ABCD is a rhombus, not necessarily a square.

As diagonals and angles of this rhombus are unknown the area of ABCD cannot be determined.

Hence, the shaded area cannot be determined. - Insufficient

From statement 2:

Simply knowing that ABCD is a square cannot help us to determine the shaded area as we do not know the dimensions of the square or that of the circles. - Insufficient

Thus, from both statements together:

Shaded area

= Area of square ABCD - Areas of the quadrants of the four circles

$= (2 + 2)^2 - 4 * \left(\frac{\pi * 2^2 * 90}{360}\right)$

$= (16 - 4\pi)$. - Sufficient

The correct answer is option C.

**73.** From statement 1:

We only know the perimeter and not the individual sides.

Thus, the area cannot be determined. - Insufficient

 

From statement 2:

We only know the ratio of the sides. – Insufficient

Thus, from both statements together:

We know that the ratio of the lateral side to the base is 3 : 4.

Let the lateral side be $3a$ and the base be $4a$.

Since this is an isosceles triangle, we have two cases:

(1) The sides are $3a$, $3a$ and $4a$ => Perimeter = $10a = 110$ => $a = 11$

=> The sides are 33, 33 and 44.

(2) The sides are $3a$, $4a$ and $4a$ => Perimeter = $11a = 110$ => $a = 10$

=> The sides are 30, 40 and 40.

We can see that in both cases, the inequality that the sum of two sides of the triangle should be greater than the third side is satisfied.

Thus, there are two distinct isosceles triangles, as shown below:

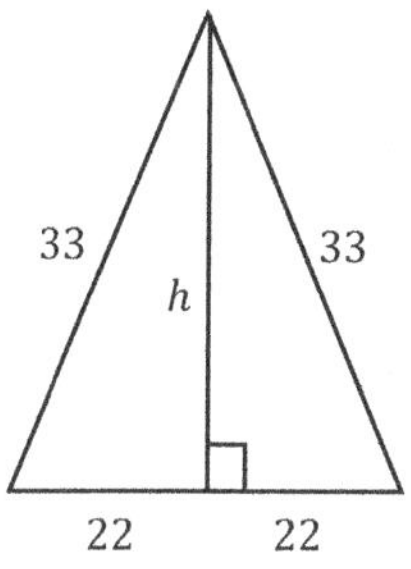


Here, $h = \sqrt{33^2 - 22^2} = 11\sqrt{5}$

Area $= \frac{1}{2} * 44 * 11\sqrt{5} = 242\sqrt{5}$

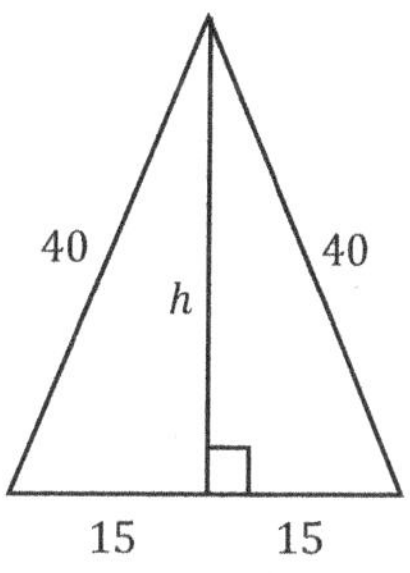


Here, $h = \sqrt{40^2 - 15^2} = 5\sqrt{55}$

Area $= \frac{1}{2} * 30 * 5\sqrt{55} = 75\sqrt{55}$

Thus, there is no unique value of the area of the triangle. – Insufficient

The correct answer is option E.

**74.** Let both the length of the unequal side and the altitude to the unequal side be $2a$.

The diagram for the above scenario is shown below:

 

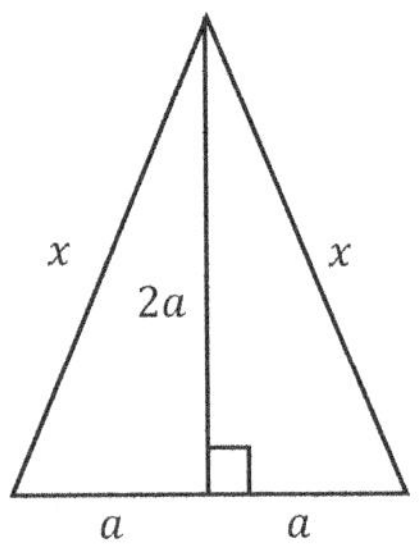


From statement 1:

Let the length of the equal sides be $x$.

Since the height to the unequal side bisects the side, we have, from Pythagoras' theorem: $x^2 = (2a)^2 + a^2$

$\Rightarrow x = a\sqrt{5}$

Thus, the perimeter of the triangle = $2x + 2a = 2a\sqrt{5} + 2a = 2a\left(\sqrt{5} + 1\right)$

Thus, we have:

$2a\left(\sqrt{5} + 1\right) = 6\left(\sqrt{5} + 1\right) \Rightarrow a = 3$

Thus, the length of the equal sides = $x = a\sqrt{5} = 3\sqrt{5}$. - Sufficient

From statement 2:

Area of the triangle = $\frac{1}{2} * \text{Base} * \text{Height} = \frac{1}{2}(2a)(2a) = 2a^2$

Thus, we have:

$2a^2 = 18 \Rightarrow a = 3$, which is the same information as obtained from statement 1.
- Sufficient

The correct answer is option D.

**75.** Let us join MP.

 

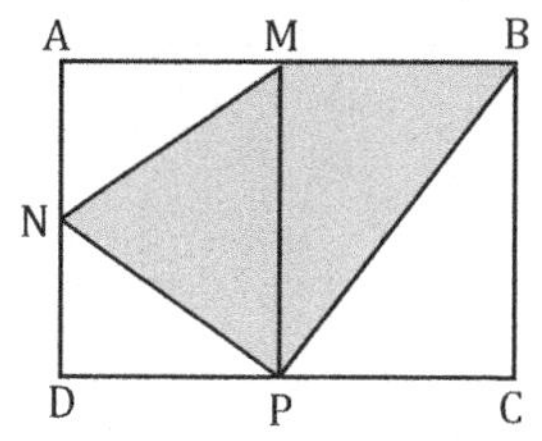


Thus, shaded area

= Area $\triangle$MNP + Area $\triangle$MPB

$= \left(\frac{1}{2} * MP * AM\right) + \left(\frac{1}{2} * MP * MB\right)$

$= \left(\frac{1}{2} * MP\right)(AM + MB)$

$= \frac{1}{2}(AD)(AB)$

$= \frac{1}{2}$ (Area of rectangle ABCD)

From statement 1:

Shaded area

$= \frac{1}{2}(14 * 8) = 56$. - Sufficient

From statement 2:

Shaded area

$= \frac{1}{2}(112) = 56$. - Sufficient

The correct answer is option D.

**76.** Let us join BD.

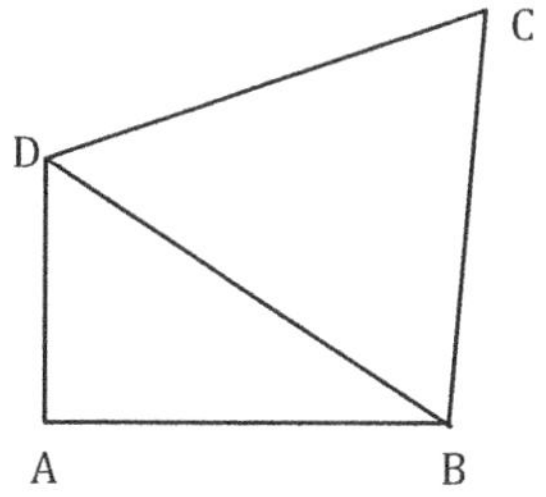


Area of ABCD = Area $\triangle$ADB + Area $\triangle$CBD

From statement 1:

$\triangle$ADB is right angled triangle with $\angle$ DAB = 90°.

Thus, area of $\triangle$ADB

$= \frac{1}{2}(AD)(AB) = \frac{1}{2} * 18 * 24 = 216.$

However, we cannot determine the area of $\triangle$CBD since the lengths of CD and CB are unknown.

Thus, the area of ABCD cannot be determined. - Insufficient

From statement 2:

We only know that CD = CB = 30.

Thus, area of ABCD cannot be determined. - Insufficient

Thus, from both statements together:

In $\triangle$ADB, from Pythagoras' theorem:

$BD = \sqrt{AD^2 + AB^2} = \sqrt{18^2 + 24^2} = 30.$

Thus, in $\triangle$CBD: CB = CD = BD = 30 => $\triangle$CBD is equilateral

=> Area of $\triangle$CBD $= \frac{\sqrt{3}}{4}\left(CB^2\right) = \frac{\sqrt{3}}{4}\left(30^2\right) = 225\sqrt{3}.$

Thus, area of ABCD = Area $\triangle$ADB + Area $\triangle$CBD

$= (216 + 225\sqrt{3})$. - Sufficient

The correct answer is option C.

**77.**

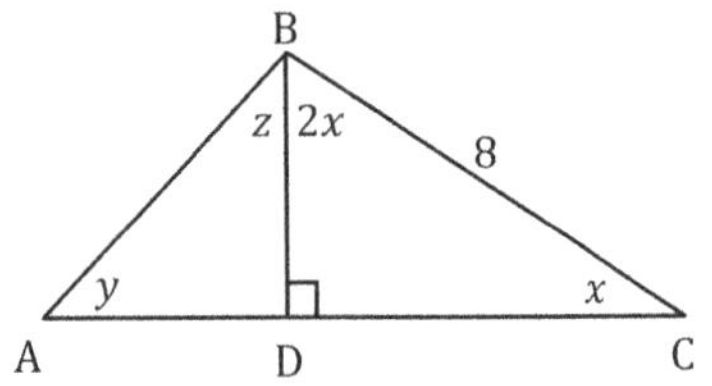


In $\triangle$BDC: $x + 2x = 180^0 - 90^0 = 90^0$

=> $x = 30^0$

Thus $\triangle$BDC is a 60-90-30 triangle

 

$=> BD = \frac{BC}{2} = 4$

Also, $DC = \sqrt{3}BD = 4\sqrt{3}$

$=> \text{Area } \triangle BDC = \frac{1}{2}(BD)(DC) = \frac{1}{2} * 4 * 4\sqrt{3} = 8\sqrt{3}$

In $\triangle ABD$: $y + z = 180^o - 90^o = 90^o \ldots$ (i)

From statement 1:

Since $y = z$, each is equal to $45^o$ (from (i) above).

Thus, $\triangle ABD$ is a 45-45-90 triangle

$=> AD = BD = 4$

$=> \text{Area } \triangle ABD = \frac{1}{2}(AD)(BD) = \frac{1}{2} * 4 * 4 = 8$

Thus: Area $\triangle ABC$ = Area $\triangle BDC$ + Area $\triangle ABD$

$= (8\sqrt{3} + 8) = 8(\sqrt{3} + 1)$. - Sufficient

From statement 2:

We know that $x = 30^o$.

Since $x + y = 75^o$, we have:

$y = 75^o - 30^o = 45^o$.

In $\triangle ABD$: $y + z = 180^o - 90^o = 90^o => z = 90^\circ - 45^o = 45^o$

This is the same information as obtained from statement 1. - Sufficient

The correct answer is option D.

**78.** From statement 1:

Let us draw EX perpendicular to AD, as shown in the diagram below.

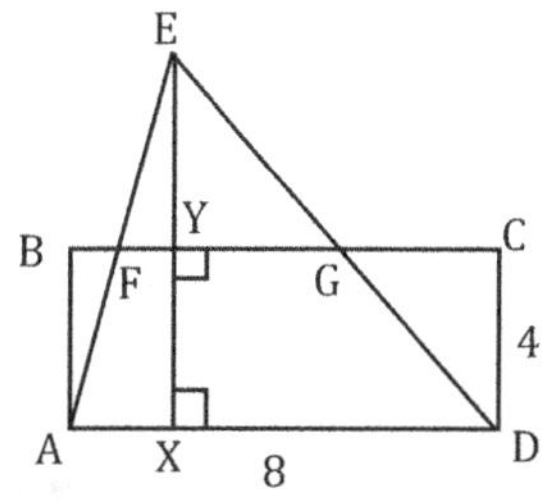

In $\triangle$EFG and $\triangle$EAD:

$\angle$EFG = $\angle$EAD and $\angle$EGF = $\angle$EDA (corresponding angles) with $\angle$E as the common angle.

Thus, $\triangle$EFG is similar to $\triangle$EAD

$=> \frac{FG}{AD} = \frac{EY}{EX}$

(Ratio of the sides is equal to the ratio of the heights for similar triangles)

$=> \frac{4}{8} = \frac{EY}{EY + 4} => EY = 4$

$=> EX = EY + XY = 4 + 4 = 8$

Thus: Area $\triangle$AED

$= \frac{1}{2}(AD)(EX)$

$= \frac{1}{2} * 8 * 8 = 32.$ - Sufficient

Note: $\triangle$BAF congruent to $\triangle$YEF, and $\triangle$CDG congruent to $\triangle$YEG.

=> Area $\triangle$AED = Area AFGD + $\triangle$YEF + $\triangle$YEG

= Area AFGD + $\triangle$BAF + $\triangle$CDG = Area of rectangle ABCD

From statement 2:

We only know the length of BF.

However, to find the length of EX, we need to determine FG, which is not possible.

- Insufficient

The correct answer is option A.

**79.** From statement 1:

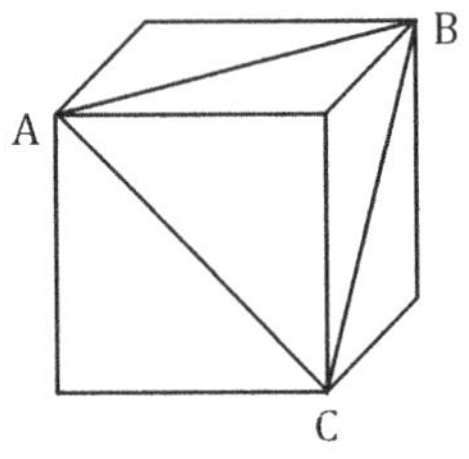


 

Let each edge of the rectangular solid (cube) be $x$.

Thus: AC, AB and BC are the face diagonals.

Since each face of the cube is a square of side $x$, each face diagonal is $x\sqrt{2}$.

Thus, $\triangle$ABC is an equilateral triangle.

Hence, $\angle ABC = 60^{\circ}$. – Sufficient

From statement 2:

The sum of the lengths of all the edges is not sufficient to determine the measure of $\angle ABC$. – Insufficient

The correct answer is option A.

**80.** From statement 1:

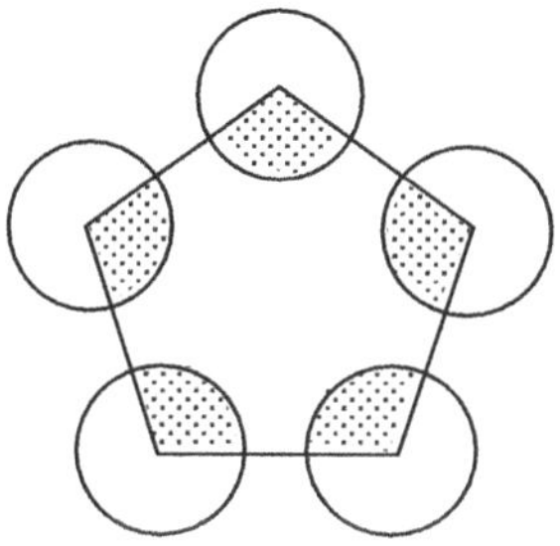

Let the angle subtended by the shaded sectors be $x$, $y$, $z$, $w$ and $v$.

Thus, shaded area

$$= \pi\left(1^2\right)\left(\frac{x}{360}\right) + \pi\left(1^2\right)\left(\frac{y}{360}\right) + \pi\left(1^2\right)\left(\frac{z}{360}\right) + \pi\left(1^2\right)\left(\frac{w}{360}\right) + \pi\left(1^2\right)\left(\frac{v}{360}\right)$$

$$= \pi\left(\frac{x+y+z+w+v}{360}\right)$$

In a pentagon, the sum of the interior angles

$= x + y + z + w + v$

$= (5-2) * 180^{\circ} = 540^{\circ}$

Thus, the shaded area

$$= \pi\left(\frac{x+y+z+w+v}{360}\right) = \pi\left(\frac{540}{360}\right)$$

 

$= \frac{3}{2}\pi$. - Sufficient

From statement 2:

The fact that the pentagon is regular is neither necessary nor sufficient to answer the question. - Insufficient

The correct answer is option A.

**81.** From statement 1:

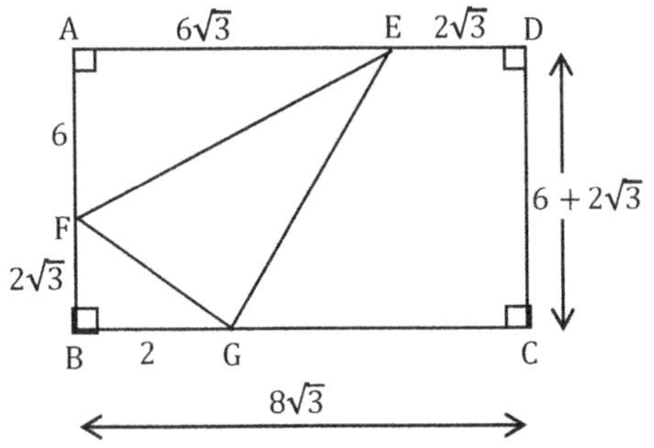


$AE = 8\sqrt{3} - 2\sqrt{3} = 6\sqrt{3}$

$BF = AB - AF = (6 + 2\sqrt{3}) - 6 = 2\sqrt{3}$

The completed diagram is shown:

In right-angled $\triangle FAE$: $EF = \sqrt{AF^2 + AE^2} = 12$

Thus, ratio of the sides of $\triangle FAE$ is:

$AE : EF : AF = 6\sqrt{3} : 12 : 6 = \sqrt{3} : 2 : 1$

Thus, $\triangle FAE$ is a 60-90-30 triangle with $\angle AFE = 60^o$.

Similarly, in right-angled $\triangle FBG$: $FG = \sqrt{BF^2 + BG^2} = 4$

Thus, ratio of the sides of $\triangle FBG$ is:

$BF : FG : BG = 2\sqrt{3} : 4 : 2 = \sqrt{3} : 2 : 1$

Thus, $\triangle FBG$ is a 30-90-60 triangle with $\angle BFG = 30^o$.

Thus, $\angle EFG = 180^o - 60^o - 30^o = 90^o$

Thus, in right-angled $\triangle EFG$:

 

$EG = \sqrt{EF^2+FG^2} = \sqrt{12^2 + 4^2} = 4\sqrt{10}$. - Sufficient

From statement 2:

We only know that $\angle EFG = 90^o$.

However, the lengths of the sides EF and FG are not known. - Insufficient

The correct answer is option A.

**82.** From statement 1:

Since perimeter of ABCD is 120, we have:

$AB = BC = CD = DA = \frac{120}{4} = 30$

However, we have no information about the sides of EFGH. - Insufficient

From statement 2:

Since perimeter of EFGH is 40, we have:

$EF = FG = GH = HE = \frac{40}{4} = 10$

However, we have no information about the sides of EFGH. - Insufficient

Thus, from both statements together:

Let us extend the sides EH and FG as shown in the diagram below:

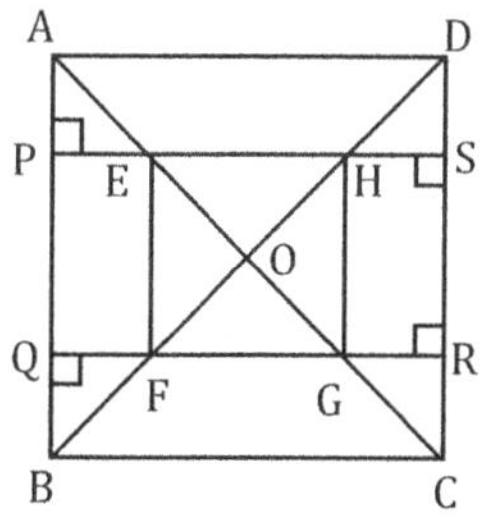


Since ABCD and EFGH share the same corner and the same diagonals, we have:

$PE = QF = SH = RG = \frac{AD - EH}{2} = 10$

Also, $PQ = EF = 10$

Thus, $AP = QB = \frac{AB - PQ}{2} = 10$

Thus, in right-angled $\triangle$APE:

AE = $\sqrt{AP^2+PE^2} = 10\sqrt{2}$

Thus, perimeter of AEFB = $10\sqrt{2} + 10\sqrt{2} + 10 + 30 = 20\left(\sqrt{2}+2\right)$. – Sufficient

The correct answer is option C.

**83.** From statement 1:

Since ABCD is an isosceles trapezium, AB = CD.

Since $\triangle$ABE and $\triangle$CFD are isosceles, we have: AB = BE = CF = CD.

Perimeter of ABCD

= AB + BC + CD + DA

By replacing AB by BE and CD by CF,

= BE + BC + CF + (EF + AE + FD)

= BE + BC + CF + EF + (AE + FD)

= Perimeter of BCFE + (AE + FD)

=> Perimeter of BCFE = Perimeter of ABCD – (AE + FD)

Since the perimeter of the new trapezium is 20 less than the perimeter of the original trapezium, we have:

AE + FD = 20

Thus, we have: AD = (AE + FD) + EF = 20 + EF

However, the length of EF is not known. – Insufficient

From statement 2:

We only know the ratio of BC and AD.

We have no information about the actual lengths of any side. – Insufficient

Thus, from both statements together:

Let us drop perpendiculars BX and CY as shown in the diagram below:

 

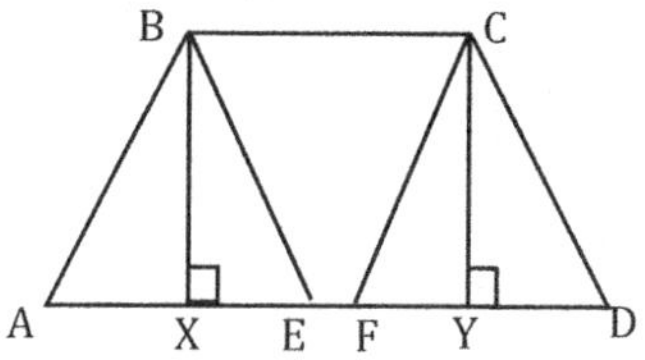


We know that:

AE + FD = 20

Since $\triangle$ABE and $\triangle$CFD are congruent => AE = FD = $\frac{20}{2}$ = 10.

Thus, AX = XE = DY = YF = $\frac{10}{2}$ = 5

Thus XY = BC = 5 + 5 + EF = 10 + EF

Since BC : EF = 5 : 3, we have:

$\frac{10 + EF}{EF} = \frac{5}{3}$

=> EF = 15

=> AD = 20 + EF = 35. – Sufficient

The correct answer is option C.

**84.** From statement 1:

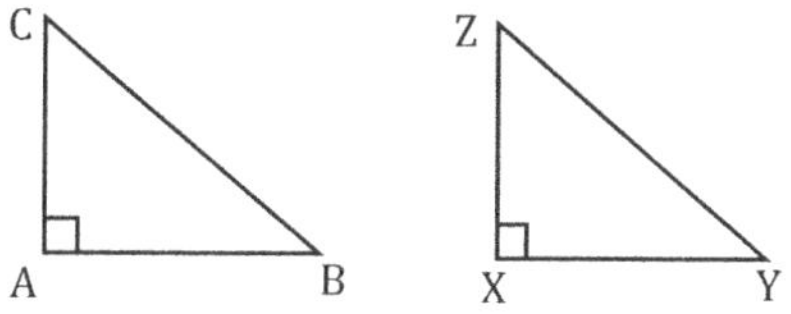


We only know the length of one side of each triangle. – Insufficient

From statement 2:

We know that $\frac{AC}{BC} = \frac{XY}{ZY}$; thus, $\triangle$ABC is similar to $\triangle$XZY.

However, we have no information about the lengths of the sides of the triangles.
– Insufficient

Thus, from both statements together:

$\triangle$ABC is similar to $\triangle$XZY

$$=> \frac{\text{Area } \triangle ABC}{\text{Area } \triangle XZY} = \left(\frac{AB}{XZ}\right)^2 = \left(\frac{4}{5}\right)^2 < 1$$

Thus, area of $\triangle$XZY is greater than that of $\triangle$ABC.

The answer to the question is 'No'. - Sufficient

The correct answer is option C.

**85.** From statement 1:

Let the heights of $\triangle$ABC be $h$ each.

Let the sides of $\triangle$ABC be $a$, $b$ and $c$.

Since the area of a triangle = $\frac{1}{2}$ * altitude * base, equating the area, we have:

$$\frac{1}{2}ah = \frac{1}{2}bh = \frac{1}{2}ch => a = b = c$$

Thus, $\triangle$ABC is an equilateral triangle, hence is acute angled. - Sufficient

From statement 2:

We know that the altitude drawn from vertex A on BC is equal to the median drawn through A.

The above holds true in both the scenarios shown in the diagram below:

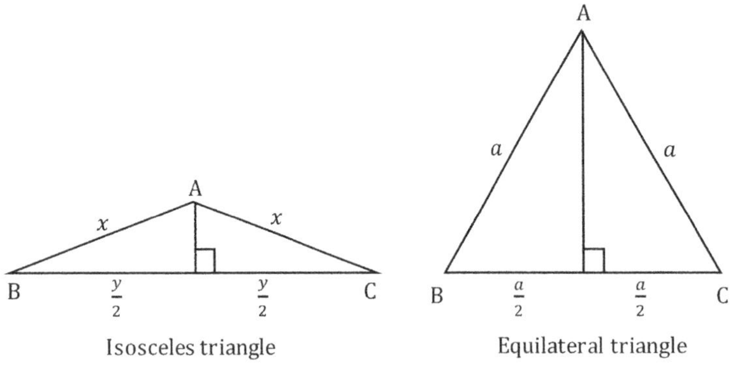


We can see that in the isosceles triangle, the altitude to the unequal side also bisects the side. So, if BC were the unequal side, then the altitude and median on BC would be the same. Since $\triangle$ABC is isosceles, we can have a situation where $\angle$BAC is an obtuse angle.

Also, in an equilateral triangle, the altitude and median are always the same for any of the three sides.

Thus, the triangle may be acute angled or obtuse angled. - Insufficient

The correct answer is option A.

**86.** From statement 1:

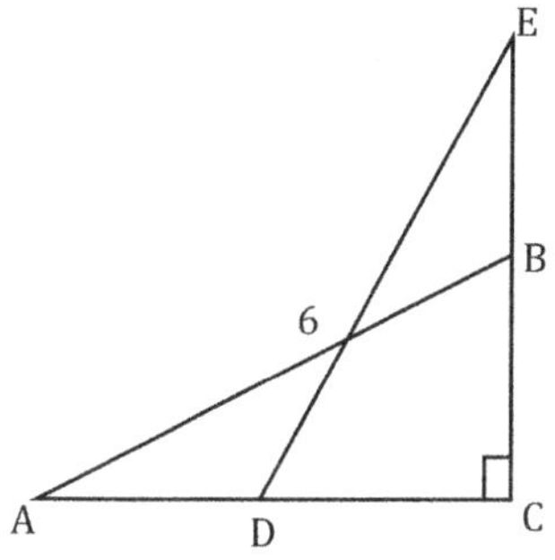


We have: BC = BE = 3.

In right-angled $\triangle ABC$: $AC = \sqrt{AB^2 - BC^2} = 3\sqrt{3}$

(Note: $BC = \frac{AB}{2} \Rightarrow \angle BAC = 30^o$)

However, the length of CD cannot be determined since the length of AD is unknown. - Insufficient

From statement 2:

We know that: $\angle BAC = 90^o - \angle EDC$

However, no dimensions of the sides are given. - Insufficient

Thus, from both statements together:

Since $\angle BAC = 90^o - \angle EDC$, and $\angle BAC = 30^o$, we have: $\angle EDC = 60^o$

$\Rightarrow \angle CED = 30^o$

Thus, in $\triangle EDC$: $CD = \frac{CE}{\sqrt{3}} = \frac{BC + BE}{\sqrt{3}} = \frac{6}{\sqrt{3}} = 2\sqrt{3}$. - Sufficient

The correct answer is option C.

**87.** From statement 1:

 

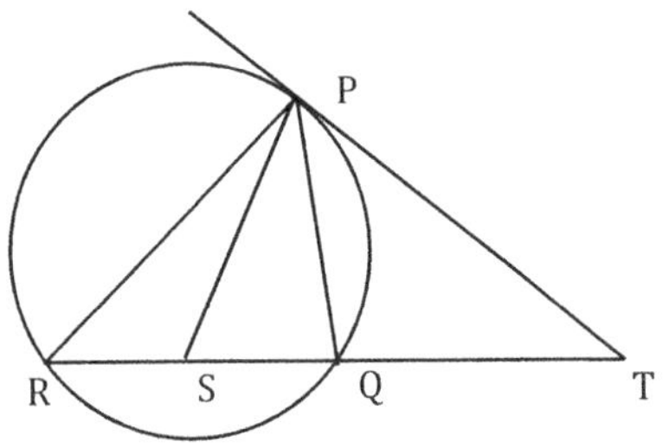


Let ∠RPS = $a$ and ∠PRS = $b$

For △PRS, exterior ∠PSQ = $a + b$

∠SPQ = ∠RPS = $a$ (Since PS bisects ∠QPR)

∠QPT = ∠QRP = $b$

(Since angles in alternate segments are equal, i.e. angle between a chord and tangent is equal to the angle subtended by the chord at the circumference)

=> ∠SPT = ∠SPQ + ∠QPT = $a + b$

=> ∠PST = ∠SPT

=> TP = TS

Thus, the answer to the question is 'Yes'. - Sufficient

From statement 2:

The answer cannot be determined using the fact that PR > PQ. - Insufficient

The correct answer is option A.

**88.** From the diagram it seems that AC is the radius and hence, has length 10.

However, the point to be noted is that C is 'just a point inside the circle', and not necessarily the center.

From statement 1:

We cannot determine the length of AC only knowing ∠DAB and the length of DC. - Insufficient

From statement 2:

 

We cannot determine the length of AC only knowing ∠DCB and the length of DC. – Insufficient

Thus, from both statements together:

In the diagram shown:

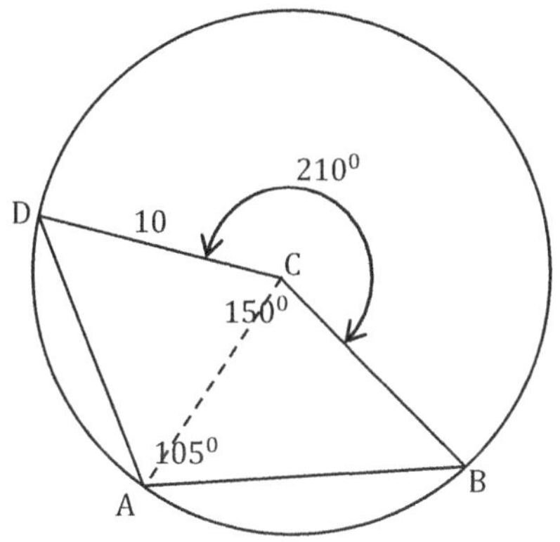


Reflex ∠DCB = 360° − 150° = 210°

$\angle DAB = 105^\circ = \frac{210^\circ}{2} = \frac{\text{Reflex DCB}}{2}$

We know that:

In a circle, the angle subtended by any arc at the center is double the angle subtended by the same arc at the circumference.

However, as we have discussed in a previous problem, if the angle subtended by any arc at a point in the circle is double the angle subtended by the same arc at the circumference, that point does not necessarily have to be the center.

Thus, C is not necessarily the center of the circle.

Thus, AC is not necessarily the radius of the circle.

Thus, the length of AC cannot be determined. – Insufficient

The correct answer is option E.

**89.** From statement 1:

Only using the area of $\triangle ABY$, we cannot determine the possible area of rectangle ABCD. - Insufficient

From statement 2:

We drop perpendiculars XZ and YW as shown in the diagram below:

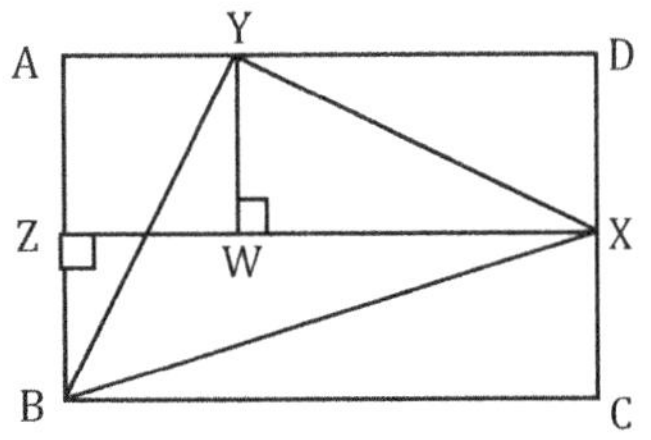


Area of rectangle BCXZ = 2 * Area $\triangle BXC$ = 18.

Area of rectangle DYWX = 2 * Area $\triangle DXY$ = 4.

Thus, we have:

Area of rectangle ABCD

= Area of rectangle BCXZ + Area of rectangle DYWX + Area of rectangle AYWZ

= 18 + 4 + Area of rectangle AYWZ

=> Area of rectangle ABCD > 22 - Sufficient

The correct answer is option B.

**90.** The pentagon ABCDE is not a regular pentagon since a regular pentagon has each interior angle equal to $\frac{(5-2) * 180^0}{5} = 108^0$.

Let us extend the sides AB, AE and CD as shown in the diagram below:

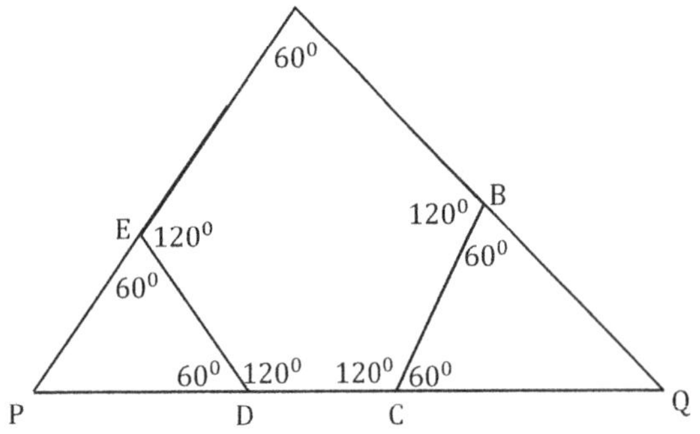


 

Thus, we have three equilateral triangles: $\triangle PED$, $\triangle QBC$ and $\triangle PAQ$.

Thus: BC = CQ = BQ and DE = PD = PE.

Also, AP = AQ = PQ

=> AE + PE = AB + BQ = PD + CD + CQ

Replacing PE by DE, BQ by BC, PD by DE, CQ by BC:

=> **AE + DE** = AB + BC = **DE + CD + BC**

From the first and the third terms of the above, we have:

AE = CD + BC

From statement 1:

Length of CD is not known. - Insufficient

From statement 2:

Length of BC is not known. - Insufficient

Thus, from both statements together:

AE = CD + BC = 2 + 6 = 8. - Sufficient

The correct answer is option C.

**91.** Let the lengths of the two smaller sides and the hypotenuse of the triangle be $a, b$ and $h$, respectively.

Thus, we have: $a^2 + b^2 = h^2$

To determine the area, we need to find the value of $\frac{1}{2}ab$.

From statement 1:

$a + b + h = 90$

$=> a + b = 90 - h$

Squaring both sides:

$a^2 + b^2 + 2ab = 8100 + h^2 - 180h$

Using $a^2 + b^2 = h^2$:

$2ab = 8100 - 180h \ldots$(i)

Since the value of $h$ is unknown, the answer cannot be determined. - Insufficient

From statement 2:

We know that: $h = 39 \ldots$(ii)

However, we cannot determine the value of $\frac{1}{2}ab$. - Insufficient

Thus, from both statements together:

From (i) and (ii):

$2ab = 8100 - 180 * 39 = 1080$

$=> \frac{1}{2}ab = \frac{1080}{4} = 270$. - Sufficient

The correct answer is option C.

**92.** From statement 1:

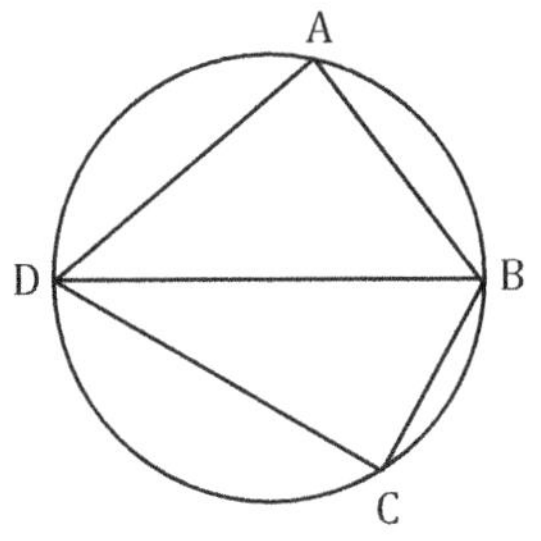


Since $\angle$DAB = 90°, DB is the diameter of the circle

=> $\angle$DCB = 90°

However, the measure of $\angle$DBC cannot be determined. - Insufficient

From statement 2:

We know that $\angle$BDC = 20°.

However, in $\triangle$BCD, the measure of $\angle$DCB is not known. - Insufficient

Thus, from both statements together:

In $\triangle$BCD: $\angle$DCB = 90° and $\angle$BDC = 20°

 

=> $\angle DBC = 180^\circ - (90^\circ + 20^\circ) = 70^\circ$. - Sufficient

The correct answer is option C.

**93.** From statement 1:

Let us join RQ and RP, as shown in the diagram below:

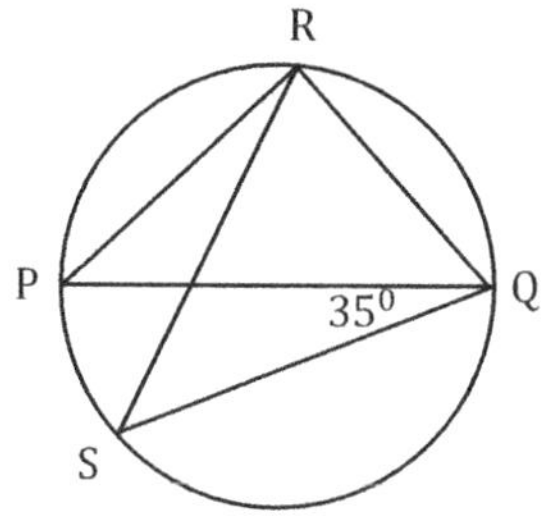


Since PQ is the diameter, $\angle PRQ = 90^\circ$.

Also: $\angle PRS = \angle PQS = 35^\circ$ (both are angles subtended by arc PS)

Thus: $\angle QRS = 90^\circ - 35^\circ = 55^\circ$. - Sufficient

From statement 2:

Let us join RQ and RP, as shown in the diagram below:

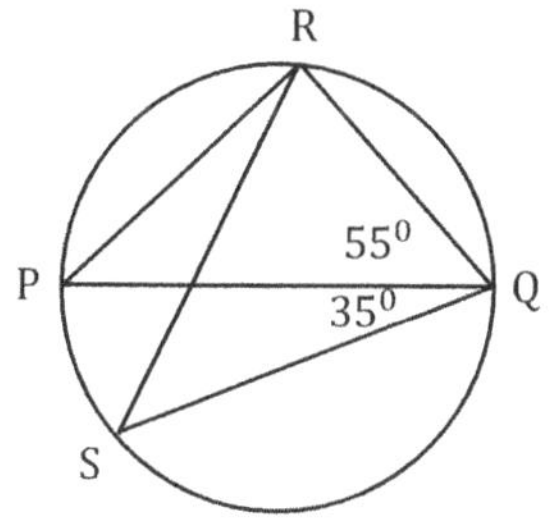


We know: $\angle PQR = 55^\circ$

However, we cannot determine the measure of $\angle QRS$. - Insufficient

The correct answer is option A.

**94.** Since PQ is the diameter, $\angle PRQ = 90^\circ$.

From statement 1:

$\angle PRS = \angle PQS = 22^\circ$ (both are angles subtended by arc PS)

Thus: $\angle QRS = 90^o - 22^o = 68^o$.

However, we cannot determine the measure of $\angle QPR$. - Insufficient

From statement 2:

We know: $\angle SQR = 90^o$

Thus, RS is a diameter of the circle.

However, we cannot determine the measure of $\angle QPR$. - Insufficient

Thus, from both statements together:

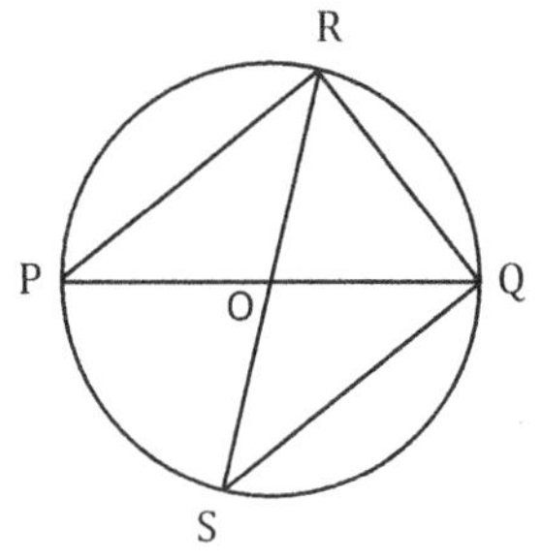


Since RS and PQ are diameters, O is the center of the circle

=> OP = OR = OQ = OS (radii of the circle)

Thus, in $\triangle POR$, PO = RO => $\angle RPO = \angle PRO$ (isosceles triangle)

Thus: $\angle PQS = \angle PRS = \angle QPR = 22^o$. - Sufficient

The correct answer is option C.

**95.** From statement 1:

Let us join the centers of the circles to X, P, Q and Y as shown in the diagram below:

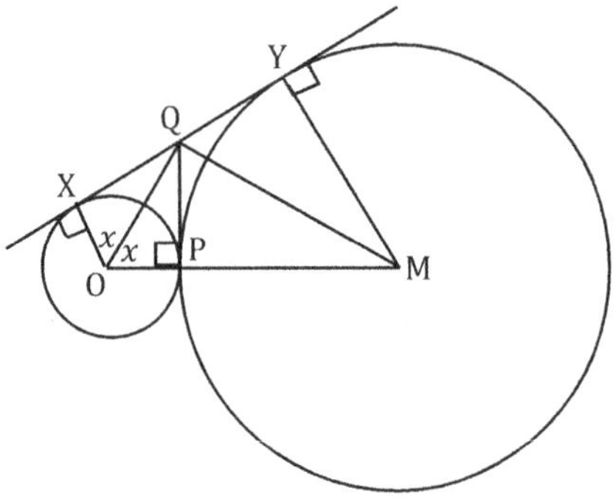


 

$\triangle$OQX and $\triangle$OQP are congruent, and so are $\triangle$MQP and $\triangle$MQY.

Let $\angle QOX = \angle QOP = x$

$=> \angle OQX = \angle OQP = (90 - x)$

$=> \angle MQP = \angle MQY = \dfrac{180 - 2(90 - x)}{2} = x$

$=> \angle QMP = \angle QMY = (90 - x)$

=> $\triangle$OQP is similar to $\triangle$QMP

$=> \dfrac{QP}{MP} = \dfrac{OP}{QP}$

Since the ratio of radii is given as 1 : 3, we have:

$\dfrac{QP}{3} = \dfrac{1}{QP} => QP = \sqrt{3}$

Thus, in right-angled $\triangle$OQP, we have: OP : QP = $1 : \sqrt{3}$

=> $\triangle$OQP is a 60-60-90 triangle

$=> \angle PQO = 30^o$

$=> \angle PQX = 2 * 30^o = 60^o$. - Sufficient

From statement 2:

Since QX and QP are tangents to the same circle, we have QX = QP.

Similarly, since QY and QP are tangents to the same circle, we have QY = QP.

Thus, we have: QP = QX = QY.

Thus, there is no additional information that can be used to determine the answer. - Insufficient

The correct answer is option A.

**96.** From statement 1:

The value of $x$ cannot be determined. - Insufficient

From statement 2:

The value of $x$ cannot be determined. - Insufficient

 

Thus, from both statements together:

Let each side of the cube be $a$ inches.

Thus, surface area of the cube

$= 6a^2 = x^3$

$=> a^2 = \frac{x^3}{6}$

Also, volume of the cube

$= a^3 = x^3$

$=> a^2 = x^2$

Thus, we have:

$x^2 = \frac{x^3}{6}$

$=> x = 6$. - Sufficient

The correct answer is option C.

**97.** Since EB and FC are the bisectors of $\angle$DEF and $\angle$AFE, respectively, we have:

$\angle AFC = \angle DEB = \frac{90^o}{2} = 45^o$.

Thus, $\triangle$AFC and $\triangle$DEB are right-angled isosceles triangles

=> AC = DB = AF = DE.

From statement 1:

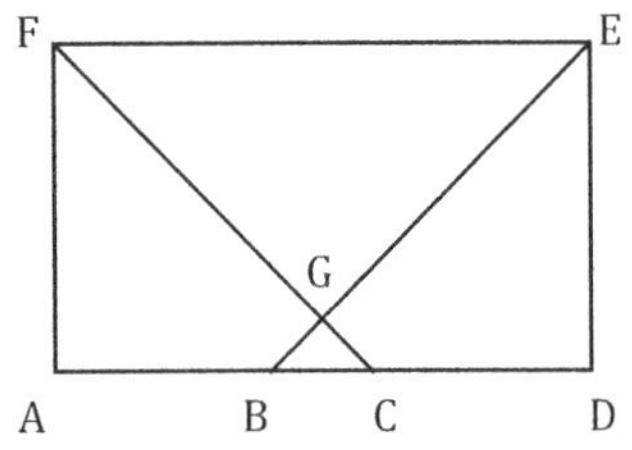


Since AF = 4, we have:

AC = DB = 4.

However, the area of $\triangle$GBC cannot be determined. - Insufficient

 

From statement 2:

The area of $\triangle GBC$ cannot be determined only knowing the length of AD. - Insufficient

Thus, from both statements together:

AD = AC + DB - BC

=> 6 = 4 + 4 - BC

=> BC = 2.

In $\triangle GBC$, $\angle GCB = \angle GBC = 45^o$ (since $\triangle AFC$ and $\triangle DEB$ are right-angled isosceles triangles)

=> $\angle BGC = 90^o$

Also, GB = GC.

Thus, we have:

$GB^2 + GC^2 = BC^2$

=> $2GB^2 = 2^2$

=> $GB = GC = \sqrt{2}$

=> Area $\triangle GBC = \frac{1}{2}$ (GB) (GC)

$= \frac{1}{2} * \sqrt{2} * \sqrt{2} = 1.$ - Sufficient

The correct answer is option C.

**98.**

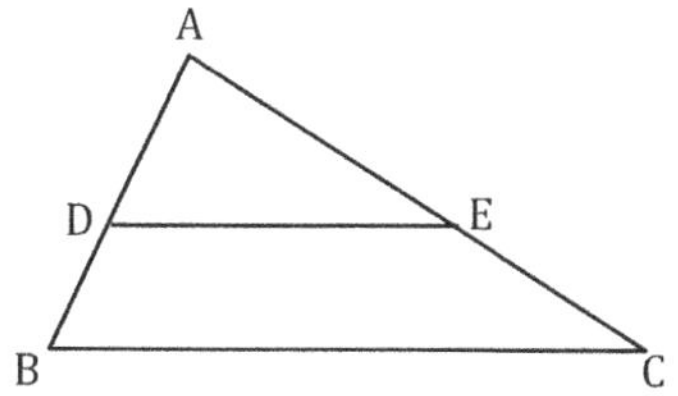


Since DE is parallel to BC, we have, for $\triangle ADE$ and $\triangle ABC$:

$\angle ADE = \angle ABC$ and $\angle AED = \angle ACB$ (corresponding angles)

=> $\triangle ADE$ is similar to $\triangle ABC$

=> $\frac{\text{Area } \triangle ADE}{\text{Area } \triangle ABC} = \left(\frac{DE}{BC}\right)^2 \ldots$ (i)

From statement 1:

We know that:

Ratio of areas of $\triangle ABC$ and $\triangle ADE$ is 2.

Also, BC = 2.

Thus, from (i), we have:

$\frac{1}{2} = \left(\frac{DE}{2}\right)^2$ => DE = $\sqrt{2}$. - Sufficient

From statement 2:

The actual value of the area of $\triangle ABC$ is neither necessary nor sufficient to answer the question. - Insufficient

The correct answer is option A.

**99.** We know that:

In triangles $\triangle ABC$ and $\triangle DEF$, $\angle ABC = \angle DEF$ and $\angle ACB = \angle DFE$

=> $\triangle ABC$ is similar to $\triangle DEF$

=> $\frac{AB}{DE} = \frac{AC}{DF} \ldots$ (i)

From statement 1:

We cannot determine the numerical value of the length of DF just knowing the expressions for the lengths of AB and AC. - Insufficient

From statement 1:

We cannot determine the numerical value of the length of DF just knowing the expressions for the lengths of DE and DF. - Insufficient

Thus, from both statements together:

 

From (i), we have:

$$\frac{10x-2}{2x+2} = \frac{6x}{x+2}$$

$$=> \frac{2(5x-1)}{2(x+1)} = \frac{6x}{x+2}$$

$$=> \frac{5x-1}{x+1} = \frac{6x}{x+2}$$

$$=> 5x^2 + 9x - 2 = 6x^2 + 6x$$

$$=> x^2 - 3x + 2 = 0$$

$$=> (x-1)(x-2) = 0$$

$$=> x = 1 \text{ OR } 2$$

Thus, we have:

- If $x = 1$: DF $= x + 2 = 3$
- If $x = 2$: DF $= x + 2 = 4$

Thus, the numerical value of the length of DF is not unique. - Insufficient

The correct answer is option E.

**100.** From statement 1:

We know that the perimeter of the rectangle is 24.

The area of a quadrilateral with perimeter 24 is the maximum if the quadrilateral is a square, i.e. each side $= \frac{24}{4} = 6$.

Thus, the area of quadrilateral with perimeter 24 having the maximum area is the area of a square of side 6, i.e. $6^2 = 36$.

Thus, the area of the rectangle is 4 less than the area of the square.

Thus, area of the rectangle = 36 - 4 = 32. - Sufficient

From statement 2:

We know that the rectangle can be divided into exactly two identical squares by drawing a line joining the midpoints of two opposite sides.

The scenario is represented by the diagram shown:

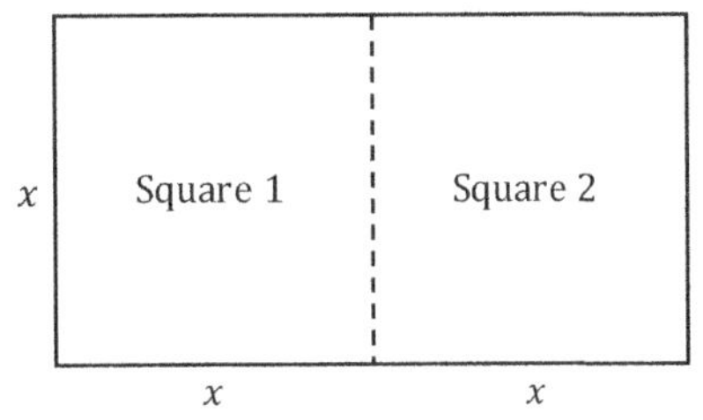


Thus, the perimeter of the rectangle

$= 2 * (x + 2x) = 6x$

Thus, we have:

$6x = 24 => x = 4$

Thus, the sides of the rectangle are: $x = 4$ and $2x = 8$.

Thus, the area of the rectangle = 4 * 8 = 32. - Sufficient

The correct answer is option D.

**101.**

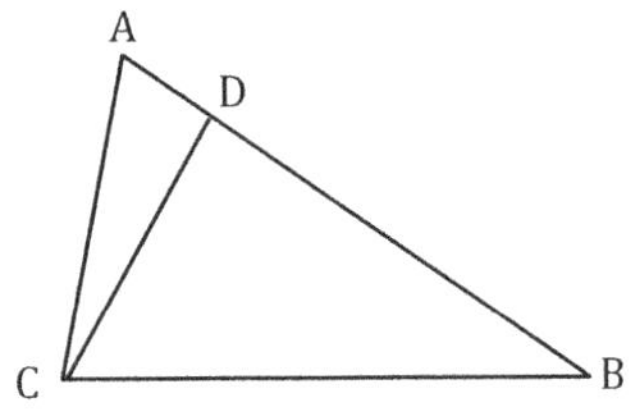


In $\triangle$ACB and $\triangle$CDB:

$\angle$CAB = $\angle$DCB (given) and $\angle$ABC = $\angle$CBD (common angle)

Thus, $\triangle$ACB and $\triangle$CDB are similar to each other

$$=> \frac{AC}{CD} = \frac{AB}{CB} = \frac{CB}{DB} \ldots \text{(i)}$$

From statement 1:

We know that: BC = 12 and BD = 9.

Thus, from (i), we have:

 

$\frac{AB}{CB} = \frac{CB}{DB} \Rightarrow \frac{AB}{12} = \frac{12}{9}$

$\Rightarrow AB = \frac{12^2}{9} = 16$. – Sufficient

From statement 2:

We cannot determine the length of AB only knowing the length of CD. – Insufficient

The correct answer is option A.

**102.** CD and BF can be easily proved equal if we could prove that $\triangle DAC$ and $\triangle FAB$ are congruent.

From statement 1:

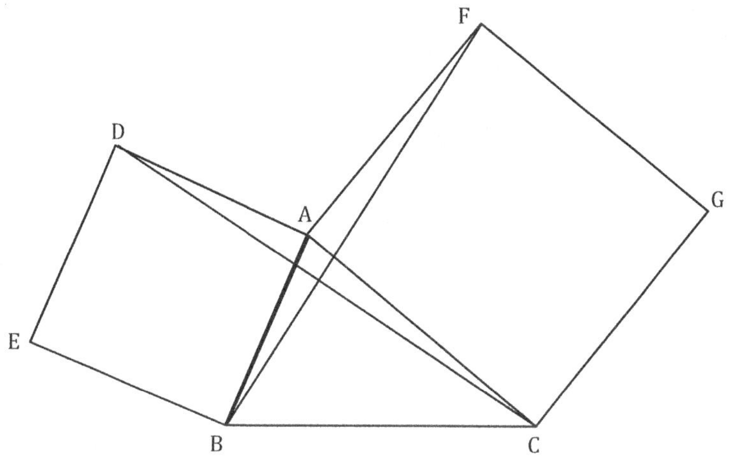


Since ABED and ACGF are squares, we have: $\angle DAB = \angle FAC = 90^o$

$\Rightarrow \angle DAC = \angle DAB + \angle BAC = \angle FAC + \angle BAC = \angle FAB$

However, we cannot conclusively say that the corresponding two sides between which the above angle is included are equal.

Thus, we cannot conclude that $\triangle DAC$ and $\triangle FAB$ are congruent.

Thus, we cannot conclude that CD and BF are equal.

Thus, there is no unique answer. – Insufficient

From statement 2:

We know that $\triangle ABC$ is an isosceles triangle.

However, we do not have any information about which two sides of the triangle are equal.

If AC = BC or AB = BC, i.e. AB and AC are not equal, we cannot prove that $\triangle$DAC and $\triangle$FAB are congruent.

Even if AB = AC, then for $\triangle$DAC and $\triangle$FAB, we have only one pair of sides equal.

To prove congruency, we need to have at least another pair of sides equal and one angle equal, which is not possible to conclude in this case.

Thus, we cannot conclude that $\triangle$DAC and $\triangle$FAB are congruent.

Thus, we cannot conclude that CD and BF are equal.

Thus, there is no unique answer. – Insufficient

Thus, from both statements together:

Since from the second statement it is not clear which two sides of $\triangle$ABC are equal, we cannot conclude that $\triangle$DAC and $\triangle$FAB are congruent.

Thus, we cannot conclude that CD and BF are equal.

Thus, there is no unique answer. – Insufficient

The correct answer is option E.

Note: If we had known that AB = AC and that ABED and ACGF are squares, we could prove that $\triangle$DAC and $\triangle$FAB are congruent and hence, we could conclude that CD equals BF.

**103.** From statement 1:

We only know DE = DF.

However, the positions of E and F are not fixed, as shown in the diagram:

 

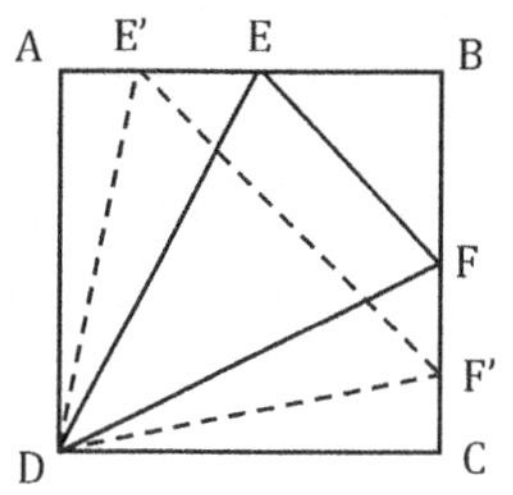


Hence, the answer cannot be determined. - Insufficient

From statement 2:

We know that E and F are the midpoints of AB and CB, respectively.

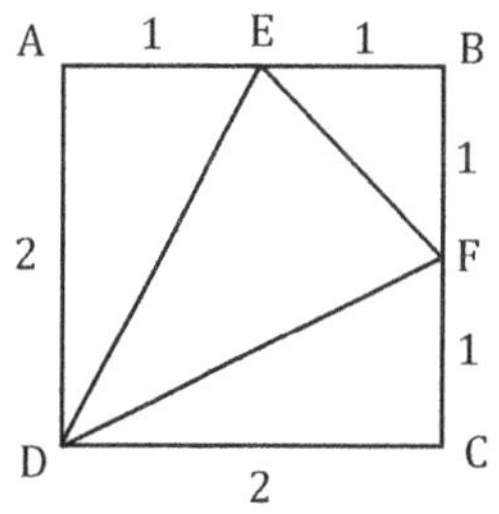


Assuming AB = BC = CD = DA = 2, we have:

AE = CF = 1.

=> Area $\triangle$ADE = Area $\triangle$CDF = $\frac{1}{2} * 2 * 1 = 1$.

Also, area $\triangle$BEF = $\frac{1}{2} * 1 * 1 = \frac{1}{2}$.

Area of square ABCD = 2 * 2 = 4.

Thus, area $\triangle$DEF = $4 - 1 - 1 - \frac{1}{2} = \frac{3}{2}$.

Thus, the required ratio

$= \frac{\left(\frac{3}{2}\right)}{4} = \frac{3}{8}$. - Sufficient

The correct answer is option B.

**104.** From statement 1:

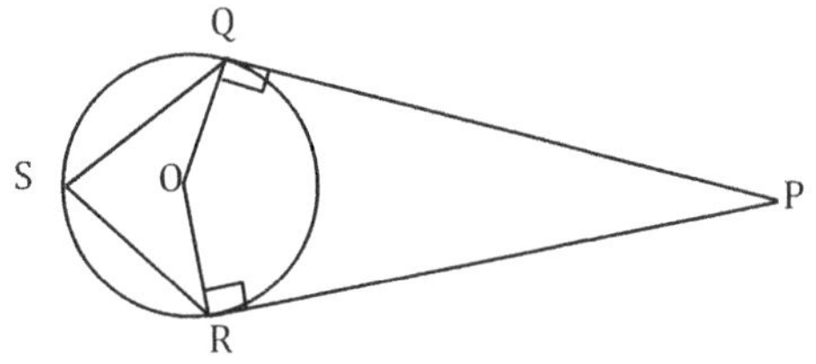


Let the center of the circle be at O.

Let us join QO and RO, as shown in the diagram:

Since the radius at the point of where a tangent meets the circle is perpendicular to the tangent, we have:

$\angle OQP = \angle ORP = 90^o$

Since $\angle QPR = 60^o$, in quadrilateral OQPR:

$\angle QOR = 360^o - (90^o + 90^o + 60^o) = 120^o$.

Since angle subtended by an arc at the circumference is half the angle subtended by the same arc at the center, we have:

$\angle QSR = \frac{120^o}{2} = 60^o$. - Sufficient

From statement 2:

We have no information about the measure of any angle. - Insufficient

The correct answer is option A.

**105.** From statement 1:

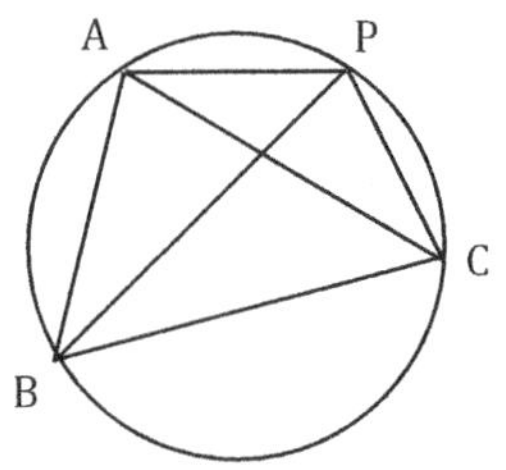


We cannot determine the measure of $\angle BPC$ only knowing the measure of $\angle ABC$. - Insufficient

From statement 2:

 

We know that Arc AB = Arc AC = Arc BC

Thus: AB = AC = BC.

Thus, in $\triangle ABC$: $\angle ABC = \angle ACB = \angle BAC = \frac{180^o}{3} = 60^o$.

Also, we have: Arc AP = $\frac{1}{2}$ (Arc AB)

(Note: It does NOT imply, however, that AP = $\frac{1}{2}$AB)

Let O be the center of the circle.

Thus, we have: $\angle ACB = \frac{1}{2}\angle AOB$

(Since angle subtended by an arc at the circumference is half the angle subtended by the same arc at the center)

Also, $\angle ACP = \frac{1}{2}\angle AOP$

Since Arc AP = $\frac{1}{2}$ (Arc AB), we have: $\angle AOP = \frac{1}{2}\angle AOB$

(Since angle subtended by an arc at the center is directly proportional to the length of the arc)

Thus, we have: $\angle ACP = \frac{1}{2}\angle AOP = \frac{1}{2} * \frac{1}{2}\angle AOB = \frac{1}{2} * \frac{1}{2} * 2\angle ACB = \frac{1}{2}\angle ACB$

$=> \angle ACP = \frac{1}{2} * 60^o = 30^o$. - Sufficient

The correct answer is option B.

**106.** From statement 1:

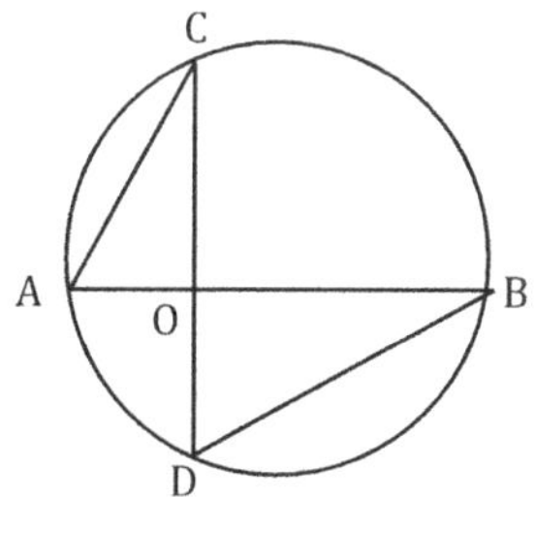


Let $\angle BAC = x$

In $\triangle AOC$: $\angle ACO = \angle COB - x$

(Since the exterior angle of a triangle equals the sum of opposite interior angles)

=> $\angle ABD = \angle ACD = \angle COB - x$

(Since angles subtended by the same arc AD at different points on the circumference are equal)

=> $\angle BAC + \angle ABD$

$= x + (\angle COB - x)$

$= \angle COB = 90^{o}$. – Sufficient

From statement 2:

If AB is the diameter, then there is no definite pattern in the values of $\angle BAC$ and $\angle ABD$.

We have seen above, that $\angle BAC + \angle ABD = \angle COB$.

Since in this case, $\angle COB$ cannot be determined, the answer cannot be determined either. – Insufficient

The correct answer is option A.

**107.** From statement 1:

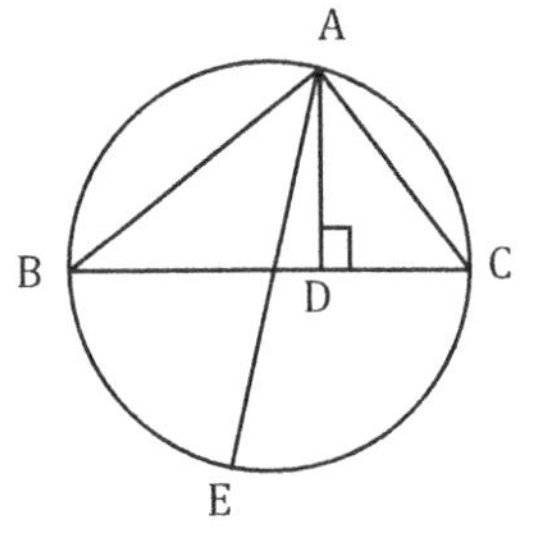


AB and AC are two chords in a circle of length 40 and 30, respectively.

From this information alone, the length of the diameter cannot be calculated. – Insufficient

From statement 2:

Only knowing the length of AD, the diameter cannot be calculated. – Insufficient

Thus, from both statements together:

 

In right-angled $\triangle ABD$:

$BD = \sqrt{AB^2 - AD^2} = \sqrt{40^2 - 24^2} = \sqrt{(40-24)(40+24)} = \sqrt{16 * 64} = 32.$

In right-angled $\triangle ACD$:

$CD = \sqrt{AC^2 - AD^2} = \sqrt{30^2 - 24^2} = \sqrt{(30-24)(30+24)} = \sqrt{6 * 54} = 18.$

=> $BC = 32 + 18 = 50.$

Thus, we observe that:

$BC^2 = AB^2 + AC^2$ => $\angle BAC = 90^o$

=> BC is the diameter.

Thus, we have: AE = BC = 50. - Sufficient

The correct answer is option C.

**108.** From statement 1:

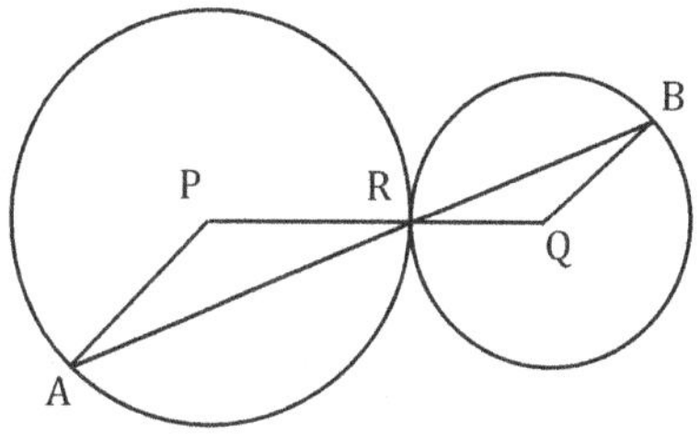


In $\triangle QBR$: QB = QR (radii)

=> $\angle QRB = \angle QBR = 30^o$

=> $\angle PRA = \angle QRB = 30^o$ (vertically opposite angles)

In $\triangle PAR$: PA = PR (radii)

=> $\angle PAR = \angle PRA = 30^o$. - Sufficient

From statement 2:

In $\triangle QBR$: QB = QR (radii)

=> $\angle QRB = \angle QBR = \frac{1}{2}(180^o - \angle BQR) = \frac{180^o - 120^o}{2} = 30^o.$

This is the same information as given in statement 1. - Sufficient

The correct answer is option D.

**109.** From statement 1:

There is no information about the number of sides of the polygon. - Insufficient

From statement 2:

There is no value with which, when equated, the value of $x$ can be determined. - Insufficient

Thus, from both statements together:

Number of sides = $(x - 3)$.

We know that sum of interior angles = $[n - 2] * 180^o$; where $n$ = number of sides

Thus, sum of interior angles = $[(x - 3) - 2] * 180^o$

Thus, we have:

$[(x - 3) - 2] * 180 = 9x^2$

$=> x^2 - 20x + 100 = 0$

$=> (x - 10)^2 = 0$

$=> x = 10$. - Sufficient

The correct answer is option C.

**110.** Let the number of sides be $n$.

From statement 1:

Sum of interior angles = $(n - 2) * 180^o$.

Sum of exterior angles = $360^o$.

Thus, we have:

$(n - 2) * 180^o = 4 * 360^o$

$=> n - 2 = 8$

$=> n = 10$. - Sufficient

From statement 2:

Since the polygon has $n$ sides, it also has $n$ vertices.

The number of lines that can be drawn connecting any two of the $n$ vertices = $C_2^n = \frac{n(n-1)}{2}$.

Amongst the above lines, there are $n$ sides also included.

Thus, the number of diagonals = $\frac{n(n-1)}{2} - n = \frac{n(n-3)}{2}$.

Thus, we have:

$\frac{n(n-3)}{2} - n = 25$

$=> n^2 - 5n - 50 = 0$

$=> (n - 10)(n + 5) = 0$

Since the number of sides of a polygon cannot be negative, we have:

$n = 10$ . - Sufficient

The correct answer is option D.

## 5.2 Co-ordinate geometry

### 5.2.1 Problem Solving

**111.** Since the three points are collinear, i.e. lie on the same straight line, the lines formed by any two of the three points must have equal slope.

Thus, slope of the line joining $(1, 1)$ and $(a, 0)$ is the same as slope of the line joining $(1, 1)$ and $(0, b)$

$=> \frac{1-0}{1-a} = \frac{1-b}{1-0}$

$=> \frac{1}{1-a} = \frac{1-b}{1}$

$=> 1 = 1 - a - b + ab$

$=> a + b = ab$

The correct answer is option D.

Though this problem can be solved through distance formulae, we are not sure about the order of the three points in the plane as the points (1, 1), $(a,\ 0)$ and $(0,\ b)$ may not lie in this order. Moreover, we will also have deal with square roots when applying the distance formulae, which is cumbersome.

**112.** The three vertices are shown in the diagram below.

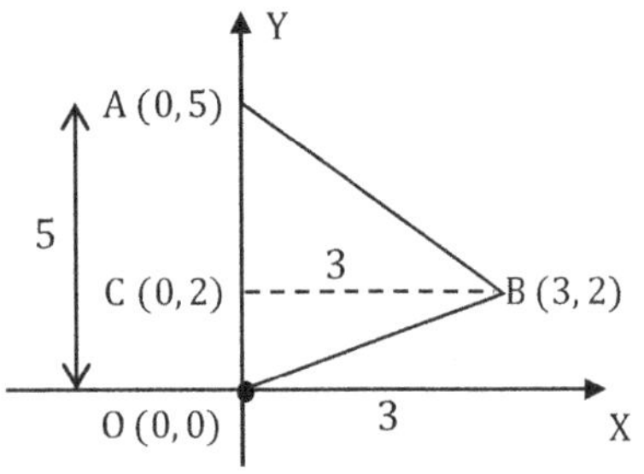


It can be seen above that both points A (0, 5) and O (0, 0) lie on the Y axis.

Taking AO to be the base of the triangle, BC is the height.

Thus, area of the triangle

 

$= \frac{1}{2} * \text{Base} * \text{Height}$

$= \frac{1}{2} * 5 * 3$

$= 7.5$

The correct answer is option E.

**113.** Let us first calculate the lengths of the three sides of the triangle:

- $AB = \sqrt{(7-3)^2 + (9-(-7))^2} = \sqrt{16+256} = \sqrt{272}$
- $BC = \sqrt{(3-(-3))^2 + (-7-3)^2} = \sqrt{36+100} = \sqrt{136}$
- $CA = \sqrt{(-3-7)^2 + (3-9)^2} = \sqrt{100+36} = \sqrt{136}$

Thus, we see that: $AB^2 = BC^2 + CA^2$

Thus, Pythagoras' theorem is satisfied and the hypotenuse of the triangle is AB.

Thus, $\angle C$, i.e. the angle opposite the hypotenuse must be $90^o$.

Note: Had we noticed that: AB + BC = CA, then $\angle C = 0^o$; whereas, had it been AC + BC = AB, then $\angle C = 180^o$ (both situations are the degenerate case of a triangle becoming a straight line).

The correct answer is option E.

**114.**

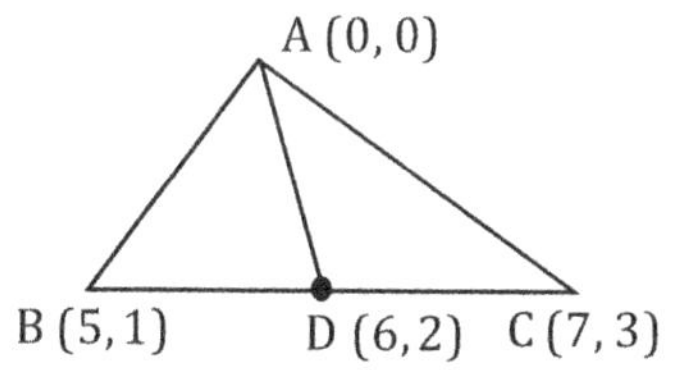


Let D be the midpoint of BC, thus AD is the median.

Coordinates of D $= \left(\frac{5+7}{2}, \frac{1+3}{2}\right) = (6,\ 2)$

Thus, the length of AD $= \sqrt{(6-0)^2 + (2-0)^2} = \sqrt{40}$

The correct answer is option D.

 

**115.**

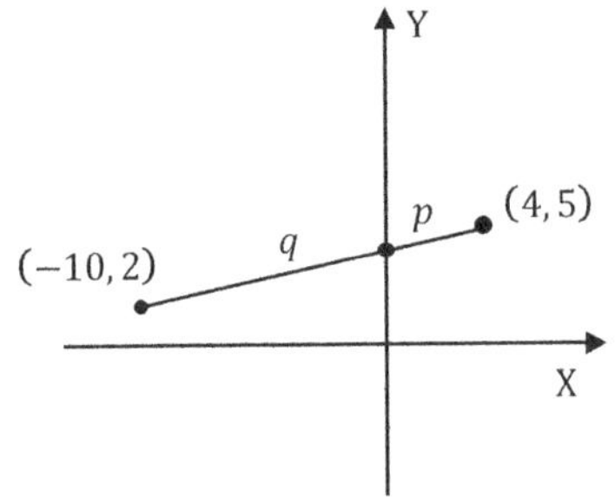


Let the Y axis intersect the line joining (4, 5) and (−10, 2) in the ratio $p : q$.

Thus, the value of the coordinates of the point of intersection

$$= \left(\frac{4p - 10q}{p+q}, \frac{5p + 2q}{p+q}\right)$$

Since the intersecting point lies on the Y-axis, we have:

$$\frac{4p - 10q}{p+q} = 0 \Rightarrow 4p = 10q$$

$$\Rightarrow p : q = 5 : 2$$

The correct answer is option B.

**116.** The equation of any line parallel to $2x - 3y + 5 = 0$ is $2x - 3y + k = 0$.

Since the line passes through (1, 1), we have:

$$2 * 1 - 3 * 1 + k = 0$$

$$\Rightarrow k = 1$$

Thus, the equation of the line is: $2x - 3y + 1 = 0$

Since we need to know the X intercept, we substitute $y = 0$

$$\Rightarrow 2x - 0 + 1 = 0$$

$$\Rightarrow x = -\frac{1}{2}$$

Thus, the X intercept is $\left(-\frac{1}{2}\right)$.

The correct answer is option B.

**117.** Let the names of the vertices with their coordinates be: P $(a + b, a - b)$, Q $(2a + b, 2a - b)$ and R $(a - b, a + b)$.

 

Let the coordinates of the fourth vertex be S $(m, n)$.

In a parallelogram, the diagonals bisect each other.

Thus, the midpoint of the diagonal PR and that of the diagonal QS are the same point.

Thus, we have:

$$\left(\frac{(a+b)+(a-b)}{2}, \frac{(a-b)+(a+b)}{2}\right) \equiv \left(\frac{(2a+b)+(m)}{2}, \frac{(2a-b)+(n)}{2}\right)$$

$$=> (a, a) \equiv \left(\frac{2a+b+m}{2}, \frac{2a-b+n}{2}\right)$$

$$=> a = \frac{2a+b+m}{2} => m = -b$$

AND

$$a = \frac{2a-b+n}{2} => n = b$$

Thus, the coordinates of the fourth vertex are: $(-b, b)$

The correct answer is option A.

**118.** Since the three points are collinear, i.e. lie on the same straight line, the lines formed by any two of the three points must have equal slope.

Thus, slope of the line AB is the same as slope of the line AC

$$=> \frac{3-1}{(2m+1)-(m+1)} = \frac{2m-1}{(2m+2)-(m+1)}$$

$$=> \frac{2}{m} = \frac{2m-1}{m+1}$$

$$=> 2m + 2 = 2m^2 - m$$

$$=> 2m^2 - 3m - 2 = 0$$

$$=> (2m+1)(m-2) = 0$$

$$=> m = -\frac{1}{2}, 2$$

Since $m$ is an integer, we have: $m = 2$

The correct answer is option D.

 

**119.** Let us calculate the lengths of the sides of the quadrilateral.

- AB $= \sqrt{(8-5)^2 + (8-3)^2} = \sqrt{34}$
- BC $= \sqrt{(8-3)^2 + (8-5)^2} = \sqrt{34}$
- CD $= \sqrt{(3-0)^2 + (5-0)^2} = \sqrt{34}$
- AB $= \sqrt{(0-5)^2 + (0-3)^2} = \sqrt{34}$

Thus, all four sides are equal.

The quadrilateral can either be a square or a rhombus. Since only for a square, the adjacent sides are perpendicular to each other, we can calculate their slopes and deduce whether the quadrilateral is a square or a rhombus.

Let us determine the slopes of AB and BC.

- Slope of AB $= \frac{8-3}{8-5} = \frac{5}{3}$
- Slope of BC $= \frac{8-5}{8-3} = \frac{3}{5}$

Thus, product of the slopes of AB and BC $\left(\frac{5}{3} * \frac{3}{5} = 1\right)$ is NOT '$-1$'.

Thus, the quadrilateral has equal sides but its adjacent sides are not perpendicular.

Hence, the quadrilateral is a rhombus.

The correct answer is option C.

**120.** Let the equation of the line be $ax + by = c$

Since it passes through $(-4, 1)$, we have:

$-4a + b = c \ldots$(i)

To determine the X intercept of the line, we substitute $y = 0$: $ax = c \Rightarrow x = \frac{c}{a}$ ...(ii)

To determine the Y intercept of the line, we substitute $x = 0$: $by = c \Rightarrow y = \frac{c}{b}$ ...(iii)

 

Since the X intercept and Y intercept are equal, we have:

$\frac{c}{a} = \frac{c}{b} => a = b \ldots$(iv)

Thus, from (i) and (iv), we have:

$-4a + a = c => a = b = -\frac{c}{3} => c = -3a = -3b$

Thus, the equation is:

$ax + ay = -3a$

$=> x + y + 3 = 0$

Alternately, one could work with each option and verifying whether:

- The line passes through $(-4,\ 1)$
- The line makes equal intercepts on the X and Y axes.

However, it would be a tad time consuming!

The correct answer is option D.

**121.** Since the lines $3y + 4x = 1$, $y = x + 5$ and $5y + bx = 3$ are concurrent, they all pass through the same point.

Let us solve the first two equations to find the point of intersection.

Substituting $y = x + 5$ in the first equation, we have:

$3\,(x + 5) + 4x = 1$

$=> x = -2$

$=> y = x + 5 = 3$

Thus, the coordinates of the point of intersection are $(-2,\ 3)$.

Substituting the values of $x$ and $y$ of the above point in the third equation, we have:

$5 * 3 + b * (-2) = 3$

$=> b = 6$

The correct answer is option E.

**122.** We have:

$$\frac{x}{a} + \frac{y}{b} = 1 => \frac{y}{b} = -\frac{x}{a} + 1$$

$$=> y = \left(-\frac{b}{a}\right) x + b$$

Thus, the slope of the above line is $\left(-\frac{b}{a}\right)$

Also, we have:

$$\frac{x}{p} + \frac{y}{q} = 1 => \frac{y}{q} = -\frac{x}{p} + 1$$

$$=> y = \left(-\frac{q}{p}\right) x + q$$

Thus, the slope of the above line is $\left(-\frac{q}{p}\right)$

Since the two given lines are perpendicular to one another, the product of their slopes is '−1.'

$$=> \left(-\frac{b}{a}\right) * \left(-\frac{q}{p}\right) = -1$$

$$=> bq = -ap$$

$$=> ap + bq = 0$$

The correct answer is option B.

**123.** We have:

- For $0 \le x < 0.5$ : $f(x) = 0$
- For $x = 0.5$, $f(x) = 0.5$
- For $0.5 < x < 1.5$, $f(x) = 1$
- For $x = 1.5$, $f(x) = 1$
- For $1.5 < x \le 2$, $f(x) = 2$

The graph for the function is shown below (using bold lines):

 

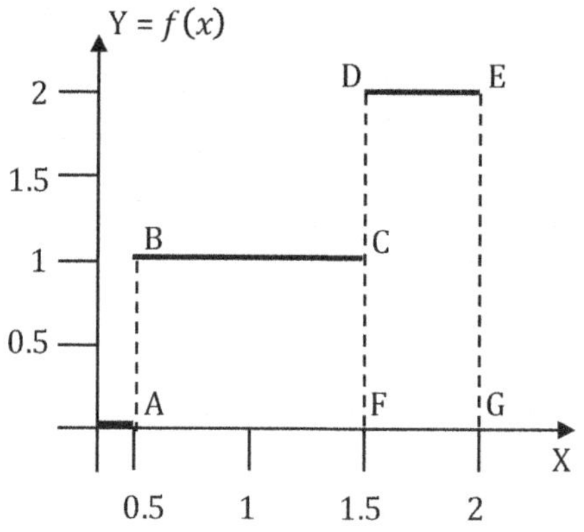


Thus, the required area = Area of rectangle ABCF + Area of rectangle FDEG

$= (1 * 1) + (2 * 0.5) = 2$

The correct answer is option D.

**124.** We have:

$\frac{x}{3} + \frac{y}{4} = 1 \Rightarrow 4x + 3y - 12 = 0$

Let the point on the X axis whose perpendicular distance from the above straight line is 3, be $(p, 0)$.

We know that:

Perpendicular distance of $(x_1, y_1)$ from $ax + by - k = 0$, is $\left|\frac{ax_1 + by_1 - k}{\sqrt{a^2 + b^2}}\right|$

Thus, we have:

$\left|\frac{4p + 0 - 12}{\sqrt{4^2 + 3^2}}\right| = 3 \Rightarrow |4p - 12| = 15$

$\Rightarrow 4p - 12 = \pm 15$

$\Rightarrow 4p = 15 + 12 \Rightarrow p = \frac{27}{4}$

OR

$4p = 12 - 15 \Rightarrow p = -\frac{3}{4}$

Thus, the coordinates of the required points are $\left(\frac{27}{4}, 0\right)$ and $\left(-\frac{3}{4}, 0\right)$.

The correct answer is option D.

 

**125.** We know that:

Perpendicular distance of $(x_1, y_1)$ from $ax + by - k = 0$, is $\left|\frac{ax_1 + by_1 - k}{\sqrt{a^2 + b^2}}\right|$

Thus, the perpendicular distance of $(0, 0)$ from $3x+4y+15 = 0$, is $\left|\frac{0 + 0 + 15}{\sqrt{3^2 + 4^2}}\right| = \frac{15}{5} = 3$

Thus, we have an isosceles triangle whose equal sides are 5 each and the altitude to the unequal side, i.e. OA = 3, as shown in the diagram below:

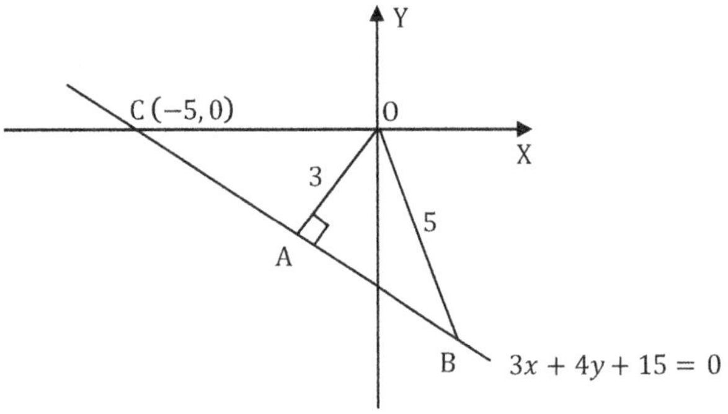


In the equation $3x + 4y + 15 = 0$, we see that the X intercept (the value of $x$ when $y = 0$) is:

$3x + 0 + 15 = 0 => x = -5$

Thus, OC = 5, i.e. OC is one of the sides of the isosceles triangle.

In right-angled triangle OAC, we have:

$OC^2 = OA^2 + AC^2 => AC = \sqrt{5^2 - 3^2} = 4$

Since in an isosceles triangle, the altitude to the unequal side bisects that side, we have:

AC = AB = 4

=> BC = 8

Thus, area of the triangle OCB

$= \frac{1}{2} * \text{Base} * \text{Height}$

$= \frac{1}{2} * BC * OA = \frac{1}{2} * 8 * 3$

$= 12$

 

The correct answer is option C.

**126.** Note: The equation $x^2 + y^2 = 9 = 3^2$ represents a circle having center at origin (0, 0) with radius 3.

Since we need to determine the lattice points (points whose coordinates can take integral values) on the circle and inside it, we need to find the set of all points $(x, y)$, such that:

$x^2 + y^2 \leq 9$

This can be done in a tabular manner as shown below:

| $x$ | $y$ | **# of lattice points** |
|---|---|---|
| 0 | $y^2 \leq 9 => y = 0, \pm 1, \pm 2, \pm 3$ | 7 |
| 1 | $y^2 \leq 8 => y = 0, \pm 1, \pm 2$ | 5 |
| −1 | $y^2 \leq 8 => y = 0, \pm 1, \pm 2$ | 5 |
| 2 | $y^2 \leq 5 => y = 0, \pm 1, \pm 2$ | 5 |
| −2 | $y^2 \leq 5 => y = 0, \pm 1, \pm 2$ | 5 |
| 3 | $y^2 \leq 0 => y = 0$ | 1 |
| −3 | $y^2 \leq 0 => y = 0$ | 1 |
| **Total** | | **29** |

The 29 points are shown below:

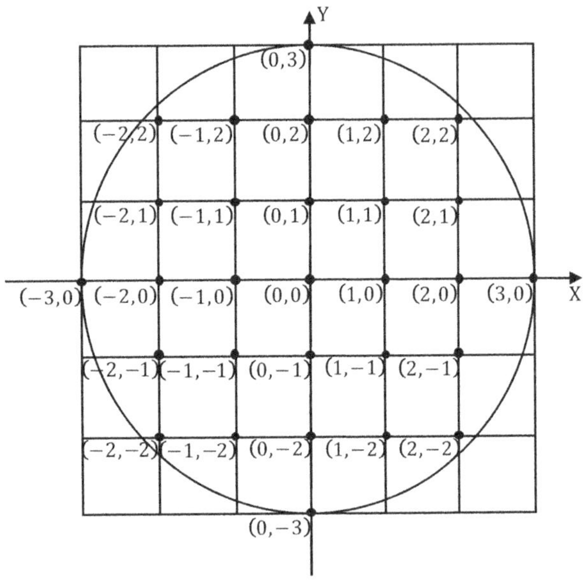


The correct answer is option B.

**127.** We know that the Y intercept (the value of $y$ when $x = 0$) is positive.

The value of the Y intercept is: $y = 0 + 0 + b = b$

Thus, we have: $b$ is positive

Also, since the quadratic intersects the X axis at two points to the right of the origin, it implies that both roots are positive.

Let the roots be $p$ and $q$, where both of them are positive numbers.

Thus, we have:

$x^2 + ax + b = (x - p)(x - q) = x^2 - (p + q)x + pq$

Comparing the terms, we have:

$a = -(p + q)$

Since $p$ and $q$ are positive, $a$ must be negative.

Thus, the equation of the straight line: $y = bx + a$

$=> y =$ (a positive quantity) $* x +$ (a negative quantity) Since the Y intercept of this line is obtained by substituting $x = 0$, we have:

 

$y = 0 +$ (a negative quantity)

Thus, the Y intercept of the straight line is NEGATIVE.

Also, in the equation $y = mx + c$, the value of $m$, i.e. the coefficient of $x$ denotes the slope.

Thus, the slope of the straight line is POSITIVE.

The correct answer is option B.

**Alternate Approach**:

We can assume convenient values for $a$ & $b$ for the graph $y = x^2 + ax + b$, keeping in mind that the graph intersects the X axis at two points to the right of the origin.

Let us assume that the coordinates of the two intersecting points are: $(1, 0)$ & $(2, 0)$.

Let's check whether these two assumed values result in a positive Y-intercept. If it does, we can be assured that we have assumed correct values.

- For the first point, $(1, 0) : y = x^2 + ax + b \Rightarrow 0 = 1^2 + a * 1 + b \Rightarrow a + b = -1$ $\ldots$(i)
- For the second point, $(2, 0) : y = x^2 + ax + b \Rightarrow 0 = 2^2 + a * 2 + b \Rightarrow 2a + b = -4$ $\ldots$(ii)

Solving (i): $a + b = -1$ and (ii): $2a + b = -4$, we get $a = -3$ & $b = 2$ (positive Y-intercept)

Thus, the equation of the straight line: $y = bx + a \Rightarrow y = 2x - 3$

It is clear that the line has a positive slope $(2)$ and a negative Y-intercept $(-3)$.

**128.** Since AB is one side of the square, let us calculate the length of that side.

$AB = \sqrt{(-3 - 0)^2 + (0 - 4)^2} = 5$

In a square with side $a$, the length of the diagonal is given by $a\sqrt{2}$.

Thus, the length of the diagonal of square ABCD = $5\sqrt{2}$

 

The correct answer is option C.

**129.** We know that:

Perpendicular distance of $(x_1, y_1)$ from $ax + by - k = 0$, is $\left|\frac{ax_1 + by_1 - k}{\sqrt{a^2 + b^2}}\right|$

Thus, the perpendicular distance of $(0, 0)$ from $3x+4y-60 = 0$, is $\left|\frac{0 + 0 - 60}{\sqrt{3^2 + 4^2}}\right| = \frac{60}{5} = 12$

Since the length of the rope is also 12, the cow would graze an area which is a quadrant of a circle having center at (0, 0) and radius 12, which would be a tangent to the line $3x + 4y = 60$.

The diagram is presented below:

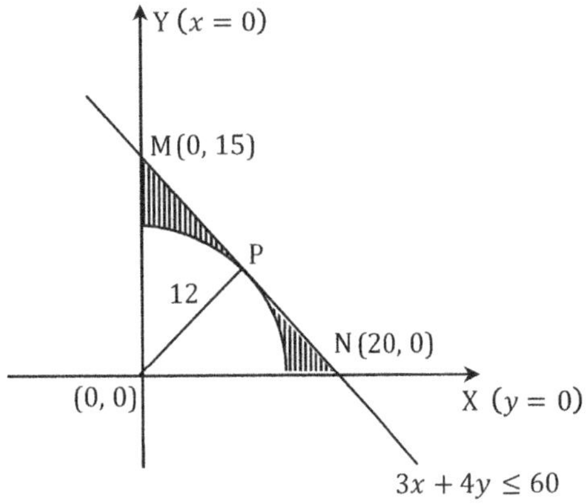


The shaded area is the area that cannot be grazed by the cow.

Thus, the area that can be grazed $= \frac{1}{4} * \pi * 12^2 = \frac{1}{4} * 3 * 144 = 108$

To find the area of the triangle, we need to determine the X intercept and Y intercept of the line $3x + 4y = 60$:

X intercept $(y = 0)$: $3x + 0 = 60 \Rightarrow x = 20$

Y intercept $(x = 0)$: $0 + 4y = 60 \Rightarrow y = 15$

Thus, total area = Area of the triangle MON $= \frac{1}{2} * 20 * 15 = 150$

Thus, area that cannot be grazed

 

$= 150 - 108$

$= 42$

The correct answer is option A.

**130.** Let us analyze the lines:

$y = 2x$: Both X and Y intercepts are '0' and the line passes through the origin

$x + y = 6$: Both X and Y intercepts are '6'.

Let us determine the point of intersection of these two lines.

Substituting $y = 2x$ in $x + y = 6$, we have:

$x + 2x = 6 => x = 2$

$=> y = 2x = 4$

Thus, the coordinates of the point of intersection are $(2, 4)$.

The diagram is shown below:

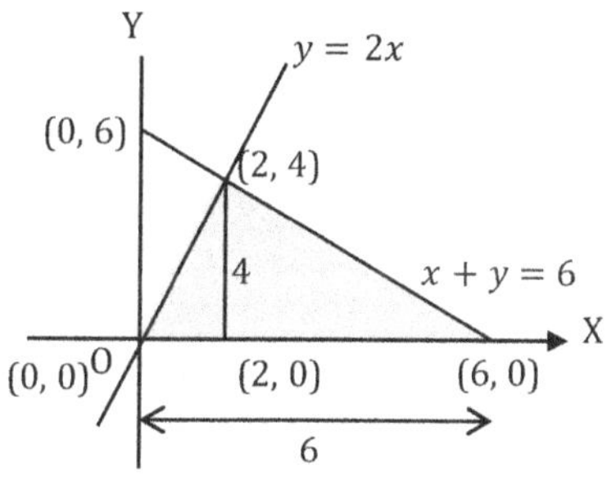


The shaded area is the area of the region bounded by the lines $y = 2x$, $x + y = 6$ and the X axis.

Thus, the required area

$= \frac{1}{2} * \text{Base} * \text{Height}$

$= \frac{1}{2} * 6 * 4$

$= 12$

The correct answer is option C.

 

### 5.2.2 Data Sufficiency

**131.** From statement 1:

Let us analyze the situation using a diagram:

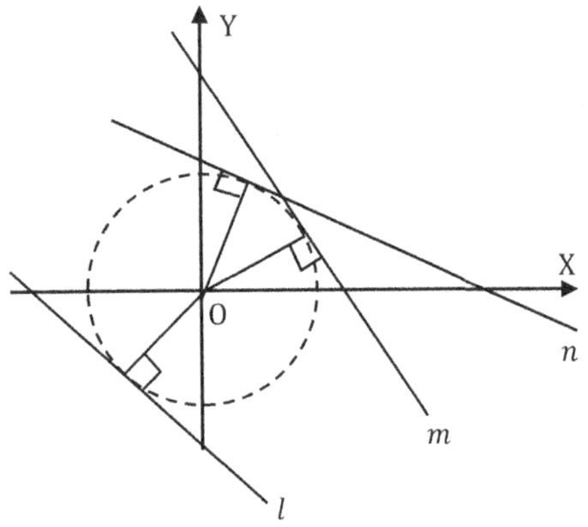


We have a circle with radius 3, having center at origin (shown by dotted lines).

Any line which is a tangent to the circle will be 3 units away from the origin.

Three such lines, $l$, $m$ and $n$ are shown, which have different Y intercepts.

Thus, the Y intercept cannot be uniquely determined. – Insufficient

From statement 2:

Let us analyze the situation using a diagram:

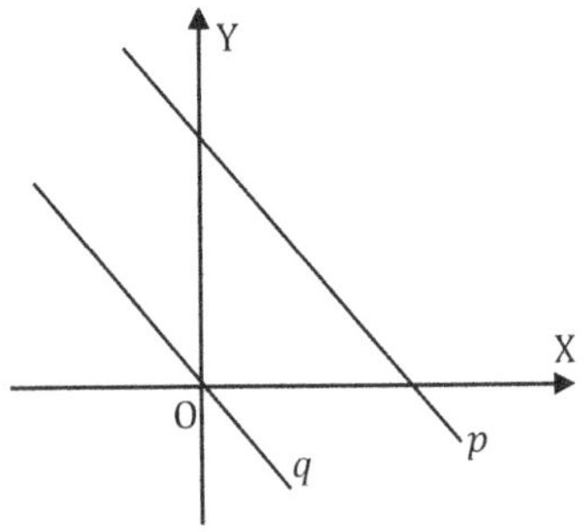


Two parallel lines $p$ and $q$ have been shown, both having the same slope '$-1$', but having different Y intercepts.

Thus, the Y intercept cannot be uniquely determined. – Insufficient

Thus, from both statements together:

 

Let us analyze the situation using a diagram:

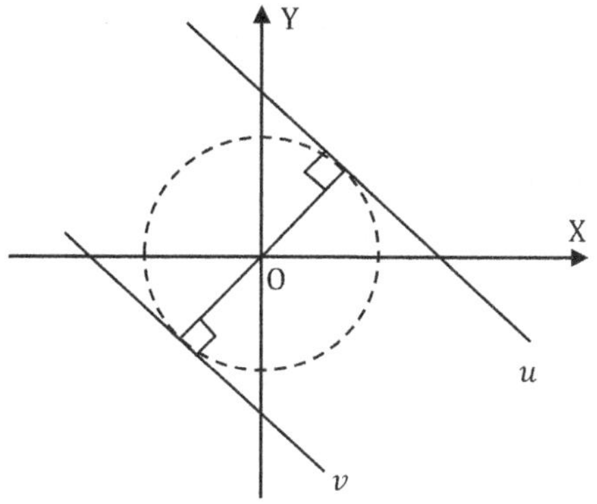


We have a circle with radius 3, having center at origin (shown by dotted lines).

Two parallel lines, $u$ and $v$ are shown, which have slope '$-1$'.

However, their Y intercepts are different. – Insufficient

The correct answer is option E.

Note: Since this is a DS problem, we need not calculate the possible values of the Y intercepts. However, you may try to find the value of the Y intercept using the concept of 45-45-90 triangle, which would give the values as $\pm 3\sqrt{2}$.

**132.** From statement 1:

The equation of the line:

$2x + 3y + 6 + k\,(9x - y + 12) = 0$

$\Rightarrow (2 + 9k)\,x + (3 - k)\,y + (6 + 12k) = 0$

$\Rightarrow y = -\left(\frac{2 + 9k}{3 - k}\right)x - \left(\frac{6 + 12k}{3 - k}\right)$

Thus, the slope of the line $= \left(-\frac{2 + 9k}{3 - k}\right)$

Slope of the line $7x + 5y - 4 = 0 \Rightarrow y = -\frac{7}{5}x + \frac{4}{5}$ is $\left(-\frac{7}{5}\right)$.

Since the lines are perpendicular to one another, the product of their slopes is '$-1$.'

$\Rightarrow \left(-\frac{2 + 9k}{3 - k}\right) * \left(-\frac{7}{5}\right) = -1$

 

$=> 7(2 + 9k) = -5(3 - k)$

$=> 14 + 63k = -15 + 5k$

$=> k = \left(-\frac{1}{2}\right)$ - Sufficient

From statement 2:

The Y intercept of the line $x + ky = 4$ is obtained by substituting $x = 0$:

$0 + ky = 4 => y = \frac{4}{k}$

$=> \frac{4}{k} = -8$

$=> k = \left(-\frac{1}{2}\right)$ - Sufficient

The correct answer is option D.

**133.** From statement 1:

We only know that the line passes through the points $(3, -6)$ and $(a, b)$.

However, from this alone, the value of $(a - b)$ cannot be determined. - Insufficient

From statement 2:

There is no mention of $a$ and $b$. - Insufficient

Thus, from both statements together:

Slope of the line passing through the points $(3, -6)$ and $(a, b) = \left(\frac{-6 - b}{3 - a}\right)$

Slope of the line $3x - 3y + 5 = 0 => y = x + \frac{5}{3}$ is '1'.

Since both lines are parallel, their slopes are equal:

$\frac{-6 - b}{3 - a} = 1 => -6 - b = 3 - a$

$=> a - b = 9$ - Sufficient

The correct answer is option C.

**134.** From statement 1:

Since the end-points of a diameter have coordinates (−3, −2) and (5, 2), the length of the diameter

$= \sqrt{(-3-5)^2 + (-2-2)^2}$

$= 4\sqrt{5}$

Thus, the radius $= \frac{1}{2} * 4\sqrt{5} = 2\sqrt{5}$

Thus, the area of the circle $= \pi * (2\sqrt{5})^2 = 20\pi$. - Sufficient

Since this is a DS question, there is no need to calculate the length (radius) and then area. Once you are satisfied that if you get the value of radius (length), you get the area, there is no need to literally calculate it.

From statement 2:

We cannot find the area only knowing the coordinates of the center of the circle. - Insufficient

The correct answer is option A.

**135.** From statement 1:

Let us analyze the situation using a diagram:

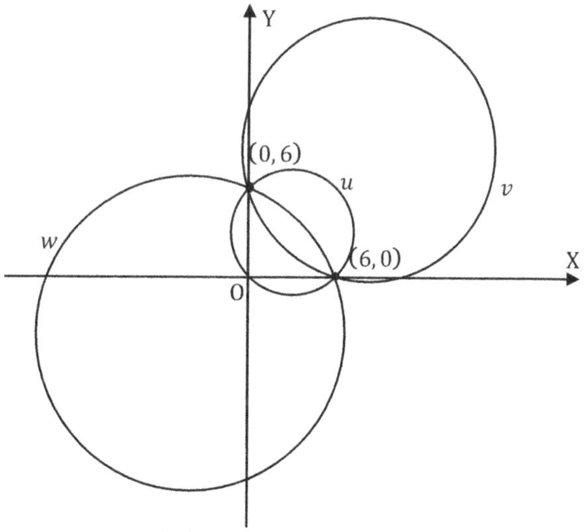


Three circles, $u$, $v$ and $w$ are shown, all of which pass through the points (6, 0) and (0, 6), but have different radii, and hence, have different area.

Thus, the area of the circle cannot be uniquely determined. - Insufficient

From statement 2:

We cannot find the area only knowing that the circle passes through $(0,\ 0)$. - Insufficient

Thus, from both statements together:

We know that the circle passes through $(0,\ 6)$, $(6,\ 0)$ and $(0,\ 0)$.

It can be seen from the diagram used for the explanation for 'statement A' that only circle $u$ passes through the three points.

Thus, the circle which passes through the three points can be uniquely determined.

Thus, the area of the circle can be uniquely determined. - Sufficient

The correct answer is option C.

Note: Since this is a DS problem, we need not calculate the value of the area.

For your information:

You may notice that the three points $(0,\ 6)$, $(6,\ 0)$ and $(0,\ 0)$ form a right-angled triangle.

Thus, the center of the circle lies on the line joining $(0,\ 6)$ and $(6,\ 0)$.

Thus, the center of the circle $= \left(\frac{0+6}{2}, \frac{6+0}{2}\right) = (3,\ 3)$.

Thus, radius of the circle is the distance of the center from the origin $= \sqrt{3^2+3^2} = 3\sqrt{2}$.

Thus, area $= \pi * \left(3\sqrt{2}\right)^2 = 18\pi$.

To assure a finite location and radius of a circle, you need the coordinates of three points, thus, both the statements combined together solves the purpose.

**136.** From statement 1:

We cannot find the coordinates of the center of the circle only knowing that the circle passes through (1, 2) and (5, 4). – Insufficient

From statement 2:

We cannot find the coordinates of the center of the circle only knowing that the center lies on the line $y = 2x + 7$. – Insufficient

Thus, from both statements together:

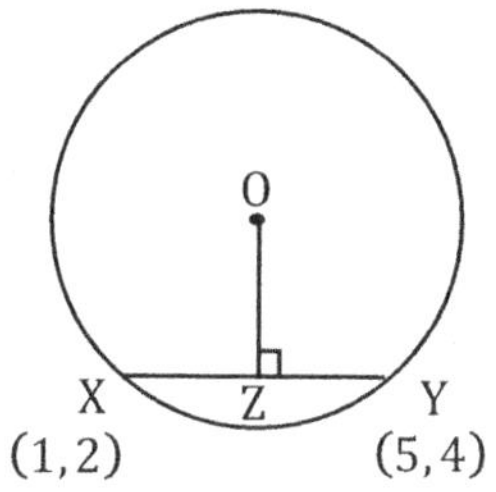


We know that in a circle, a perpendicular from the center to a chord bisects the chord i.e. OZ bisects XY.

Thus, coordinates of Z $= \left(\frac{1+5}{2}, \frac{2+4}{2}\right) = (3,\ 3)$.

Slope of the line XY $= \frac{4-2}{5-1} = \frac{3}{4}$

Since OZ ⊥ XY, product of the slopes of OZ and XY is '−1'.

Thus, slope of OZ $= \left(-\frac{4}{3}\right)$.

Thus, OZ passes through (3, 3) and has slope $\left(-\frac{4}{3}\right)$.

Thus, equation of the line OZ:

$\frac{y-3}{x-3} = -\frac{4}{3} \Rightarrow 3y - 9 = -4x + 12$

$\Rightarrow 3y + 4x = 21 \ldots$(i)

However, 'O' lies on the line $y = 2x + 7 \ldots$(ii)

Solving (i) and (ii), we can get the coordinates of 'O'. – Sufficient

The correct answer is option C.

Note: Since this is a DS problem, we need not solve the two equations.

 

For your information, let us solve (i) and (ii).

Substituting $y$ from (ii) in (i):

$3(2x + 7) + 4x = 21 \Rightarrow x = 0 \Rightarrow y = 7$

Thus, the coordinates of the center of the circle are $(0, 7)$.

**137.** From statement 1:

Since the lines $2y + kx = 16$, $y = x + 5$ and $ky + x = 9$ are concurrent, they all pass through the same point.

Let us solve the first two equations to find the point of intersection.

Substituting $y = x + 5$ in the first equation, we have:

$2(x + 5) + kx = 16 \Rightarrow x(k + 2) = 6$

$\Rightarrow x = \frac{6}{k+2}$

$\Rightarrow y = x + 5 = \frac{6}{k+2} + 5 = \frac{5k+16}{k+2}$

Thus, the coordinates of the point of intersection are $\left(\frac{6}{k+2}, \frac{5k+16}{k+2}\right)$.

Substituting the values of $x$ and $y$ of the above point in the third equation, we have:

$k\left(\frac{5k+16}{k+2}\right) + \frac{6}{k+2} = 9 \Rightarrow \frac{5k^2 + 16k + 6}{k+2} = 9$

$\Rightarrow 5k^2 + 7k - 12 = 0$

$\Rightarrow (5k + 12)(k - 1) = 0$

$\Rightarrow k = -\frac{12}{5}$ OR 1. - Insufficient

From statement 2:

The value of $k$ cannot be determined only knowing that it is an integer. - Insufficient

Thus, from both statements together:

$k = 1$. - Sufficient

 

The correct answer is option C.

**138.** From statement 1:

Slope of the line $4x + 3y + 5 = 0 \Rightarrow y = -\frac{4}{3}x - \frac{5}{3}$ is $\left(-\frac{4}{3}\right)$.

Thus, slope of a line perpendicular to the above line = $\frac{3}{4}$.

Slope of the line passing through the points $(a, 2a)$ and $(-2, 3) = \left(\frac{3-2a}{-2-a}\right)$.

Thus, we have:

$\left(\frac{3-2a}{-2-a}\right) = \frac{3}{4}$

$\Rightarrow 12 - 8a = -6 - 3a$

$\Rightarrow a = \left(\frac{18}{5}\right)$. - Sufficient

From statement 2:

The value of $a$ cannot be determined simply knowing that it is positive. - Insufficient

The correct answer is option A.

**139.** Let the coordinates of the point be $(p, q)$.

We need to determine the value of $q$.

From statement 1:

We know that:

Perpendicular distance of $(p, q)$ from $ax + by - k = 0$, is $\left|\frac{ap + bq - k}{\sqrt{a^2 + b^2}}\right|$.

Since the perpendicular distance of the point $(p, q)$ from the line $4x - 3y = 12$ is 3, we have:

$\left|\frac{4p - 3q - 12}{\sqrt{4^2 + 3^2}}\right| = 3 \Rightarrow |4p - 3q - 12| = 15$

$\Rightarrow 4p - 3q - 12 = \pm 15$

$\Rightarrow 4p - 3q = 12 \pm 15$

 

$=> 4p - 3q = 27$ OR $-3 \ldots$(i)

There are two unknowns in the above equation.

Thus, the values of $p$ and $q$ cannot be uniquely determined. - Insufficient

From statement 2:

Since the point lies on the Y axis, we have:

$p = 0 \ldots$(ii)

However, the value of $q$ cannot be determined. - Insufficient

Thus, from both statements together:

From equations (i) and (ii), we have:

$0 - 3q = 27$ OR $-3$

$=> q = -9$ OR $1$

Thus, the value of $q$ cannot be uniquely determined. - Insufficient

The correct answer is option E.

**Alternate approach:**

The scenario is shown in the diagram below:

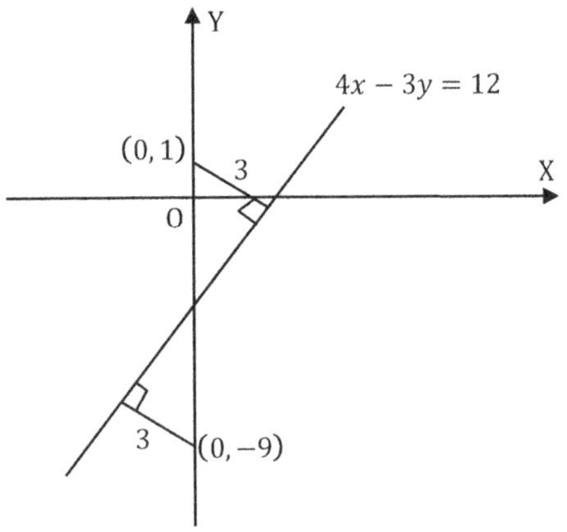


It can be easily observed, that there would be 'two' points on the Y axis which have a perpendicular distance of 3 units from the given line.

Hence, the answer cannot be uniquely determined.

**140.** From statement 1:

Since the slope of AD is 2, we have:

$\frac{6-0}{q-2} = 2 \Rightarrow 6 = 2q - 4$

$\Rightarrow q = 5 \ldots$(i)

Thus, the coordinates of D are (5, 6).

However, the coordinates of C are not known.

Hence, the length of BC cannot be determined. - Insufficient

From statement 2:

Since the slope of CD is $\frac{1}{2}$, we have:

$\frac{6-p}{q-11} = \frac{1}{2} \Rightarrow 12 - 2p = q - 11$

$\Rightarrow 2p + q = 23 \ldots$(ii)

There are two unknowns in the above equation.

Thus, the values of $p$ and $q$ cannot be uniquely determined.

Thus, the coordinates of C are not known.

Hence, the length of BC cannot be determined. - Insufficient

Thus, from both statements together:

From equations (i) and (ii):

$2p + 5 = 23$

$\Rightarrow p = 9$

Thus, the coordinates of C are (11, 9).

Thus, the length of BC

$= \sqrt{(11-9)^2 + (9-0)^2}$

$= \sqrt{85}$ - Sufficient

The correct answer is option C.

**Alternate approach:**

This question can be solved intuitively.

To get the length of BC, we need the coordinates of B and C; they are $(9, 0)$ & $(11, p)$, respectively. If we get the value of $p$, we get the answer.

From statement 1, with the application of slope formula, we get the UNIQUE value of $q$. The value of $q$ would be unique as the slope formulae does not have any squared term!

From statement 2, again with the application of slope formula, we get the UNIQUE value of $p$.

Since the coordinates of C and D are: $(11, p)$ & $(q, 6)$ and $p$ & $q$ are known, we would get the UNIQUE value of BC.

**141.** Let the coordinates of the point P be $(m, n)$.

We need to determine the value of $n$.

From statement 1:

It can be seen in the diagram below that there are two possible positions of point P (P and P') so that triangle APB is right-angled at P.

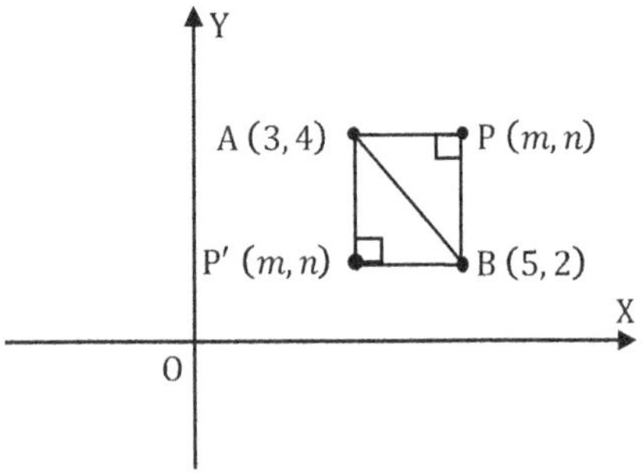


The X coordinate of P is the same as that of B and the Y coordinate of P is the same as that of A.

Thus, the coordinates of P are $(5, 4) => n = 4$

The X coordinate of P' is the same as that of A and the Y coordinate of P' is the same as that of B.

 

Thus, the coordinates of P' are (4, 5) => $n = 5$

Thus, there is no unique value of $n$. – Insufficient

From statement 2:

We only know that the area of triangle APB is 2.

Since no coordinates are mentioned, we cannot determine the coordinates of P. – Insufficient

Thus, from both statements together:

As in statement A, for the position P OR P', the area of triangle APB

$= \frac{1}{2}(AP)(PB) = \frac{1}{2} * 2 * 2 = 2$

Thus, the coordinates of P are not unique.

Thus, there is no unique value of $b$. – Insufficient

The correct answer is option E.

**142.** From statement 1:

Since the segment of the line intercepted between the axes is bisected at (2, 3), the position of the line is as shown below:

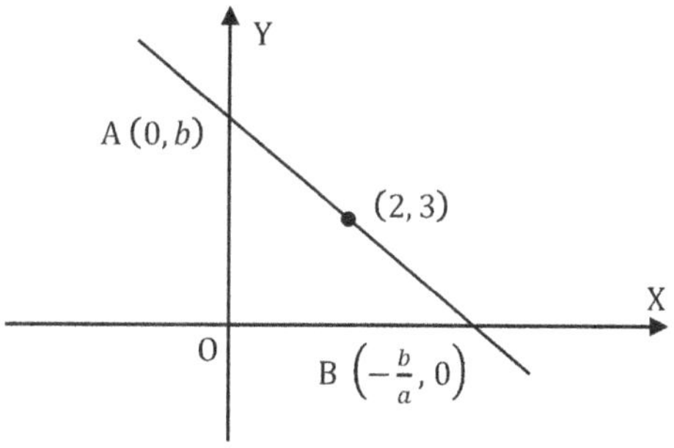


Since the equation of the line is $y = ax + b$, we have:

- The X intercept: $y = 0 \Rightarrow x = -\frac{b}{a}$
- The Y intercept: $x = 0 \Rightarrow y = b$

Since (2, 3) is the midpoint of the line AB, we have:

- $2 = \frac{\left(-\frac{b}{a} + 0\right)}{2} => \frac{b}{a} = -4 => b = -4a$
- $3 = \frac{(0 + b)}{2} => b = 6$

Thus, from the above two equations, we have:

$-4a = 6 => a = -\frac{3}{2}$

Thus, we have:

$a + b = -\frac{3}{2} + 6 = \left(\frac{9}{2}\right)$. - Sufficient

From statement 2:

We know that the line $y = ax + b$ passes through the point $\left(1, \frac{9}{2}\right)$.

Thus, we have:

$\frac{9}{2} = a * 1 + b$

$=> a + b = \left(\frac{9}{2}\right)$ - Sufficient

The correct answer is option D.

**143.** From statement 1:

The diagram is shown below:

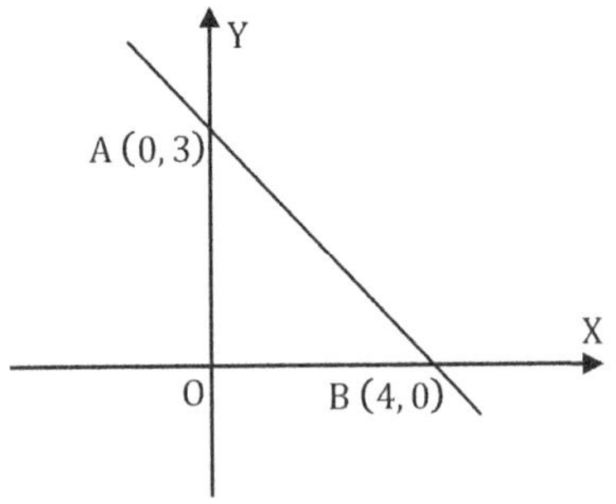


Thus, the slope of the line

$= \frac{3 - 0}{0 - 4} = \left(-\frac{3}{4}\right)$. - Sufficient

From statement 2:

The area of the triangle bounded by a line with the X and Y axes

 

$= \frac{1}{2}$ (X intercept) (Y intercept) $= 6$

=> (X intercept) (Y intercept) $= 12$

There are infinite possible values of the X and Y intercept. Two of them are shown below:

- X intercept = 1, i.e. coordinates are (1, 0), and Y intercept = 12, i.e. coordinates are (0, 12)
  => Slope $= \frac{12 - 0}{0 - 1} = -12$
- X intercept = 4, i.e. coordinates are (4, 0), and Y intercept = 3, i.e. coordinates are (0, 3)
  => Slope $= \frac{3 - 0}{0 - 4} = \left(-\frac{3}{4}\right)$

Thus, there is no unique value of the slope. - Insufficient

The correct answer is option A.

**144.** From statement 1:

The diagram is shown below:

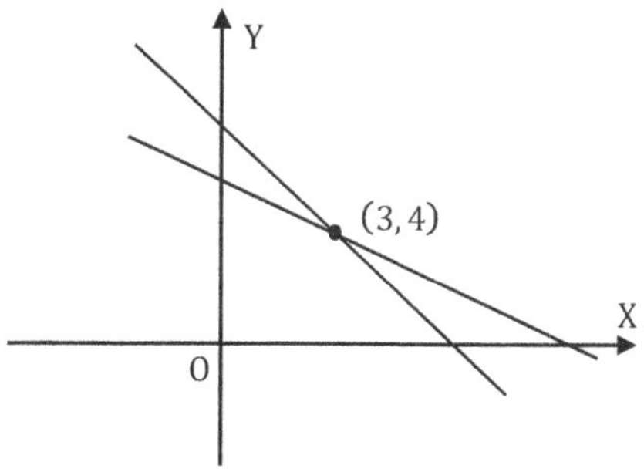


There could be infinite lines passing through the point (3, 4).

Hence, the slope of the line cannot be determined. - Insufficient

From statement 2:

The diagram is shown below:

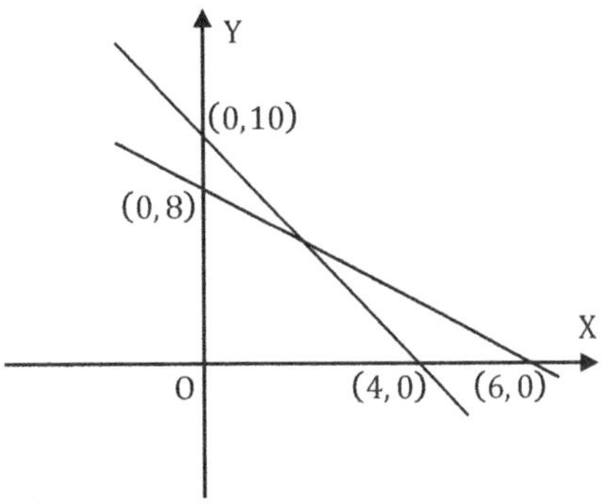


Two of the infinitely possible lines are shown in the diagram.

One line intersects the X and Y axes at (4, 0) and (0, 10), respectively, while the other line intersects the X and Y axes at (6, 0) and (0, 8), respectively.

In both cases, the sum of their intercepts is 14.

Hence, the slope of the line cannot be determined. - Insufficient

Thus, from both statements together:

Let the line intersects the X and Y axes at $(a,\ 0)$ and $(0,\ b)$, respectively.

Thus, we have:

$a + b = 14$

$\Rightarrow a = 14 - b \ldots$(i)

Since the line also passes through (3, 4), the slope of the line joining $(a,\ 0)$ and (3, 4) is the same as the slope of the line joining $(0,\ b)$ and (3, 4)

$\Rightarrow \dfrac{4-0}{3-a} = \dfrac{4-b}{3-0} \Rightarrow 12 - 4a - 3b + ab = 12$

$\Rightarrow 4a + 3b = ab \ldots$(ii)

Substituting the value of $a$ from (i) in (ii):

$4(14 - b) + 3b = (14 - b)\,b$

$\Rightarrow 56 - b = 14b - b^2$

$\Rightarrow b^2 - 15b + 56 = 0$

$\Rightarrow (b - 7)(b - 8) = 0$

 

$\Rightarrow b = 7$ OR $8$

$\Rightarrow a = 14 - b = 7$ OR $6$

Thus, the line can have two sets of intercepts:

- $(7, 0)$ and $(0, 7) \Rightarrow$ Slope $= -1$
- $(6, 0)$ and $(0, 8) \Rightarrow$ Slope $= -\frac{4}{3}$

Hence, the slope of the line cannot be uniquely determined. – Insufficient

The correct answer is option E.

**145.** From statement 1:

Since the line passing through $(3, k)$ and $(4, 7)$ has a slope of $k$, we have:

$\frac{7-k}{4-3} = k \Rightarrow 7 - k = k$

$\Rightarrow k = \left(\frac{7}{2}\right)$. – Sufficient

From statement 2:

Since the line passing through $(1, k)$ and $(k, 6)$ is parallel to the line $y = x$, the slope of the lines must be equal

$\Rightarrow \frac{k-6}{1-k} = 1 \Rightarrow k - 6 = 1 - k$

$\Rightarrow k = \left(\frac{7}{2}\right)$. – Sufficient

The correct answer is option D.

**146.** From statement 1:

The line $2x + y = 8$ and its reflection about the Y axis (dotted line) is shown in the diagram below:

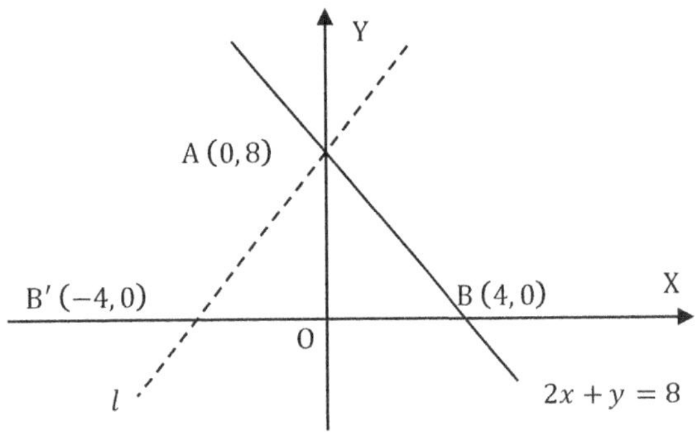


For the line $2x + y = 8$, we have:

- The X intercept: $y = 0 => x = 4$
- The Y intercept: $x = 0 => y = 8$

In the diagram, triangles AOB and AOB' are congruent, hence OB = OB'

=> The coordinates of B' are $(-4,\ 0)$

Thus, the slope of the reflected line AB' $= \frac{0-8}{-4-0} = 2$. - Sufficient

Note: For reflection of a line about Y axes, the slope of the line becomes negative, the Y intercept remains unchanged and the X intercept becomes negated in value.

From statement 2:

The line $2x + y + 8 = 0$ and its reflection about the X axis (dotted line) is shown in the diagram below:

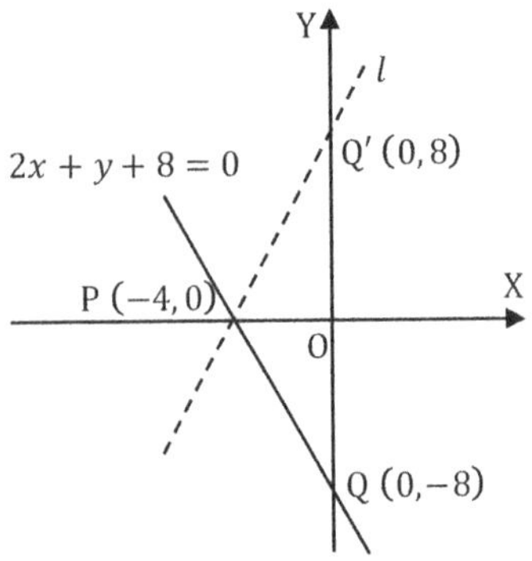


For the line $2x + y + 8 = 0$, we have:

- The X intercept: $y = 0 => x = -4$

 

- The Y intercept: $x = 0 => y = -8$

In the diagram, triangles POQ and POQ' are congruent, hence OQ = OQ'

=> The coordinates of Q' are (0, 8)

Thus, the slope of the reflected line PQ' = $\frac{0-8}{-4-0}$ = 2. - Sufficient

Note: For reflection of a line about X axes, the slope of the line becomes negative, the X intercept remains unchanged and the Y intercept becomes negated in value.

The correct answer is option D.

**147.** From statement 1:

The diagram showing the points and the line $y = x$ is shown below:

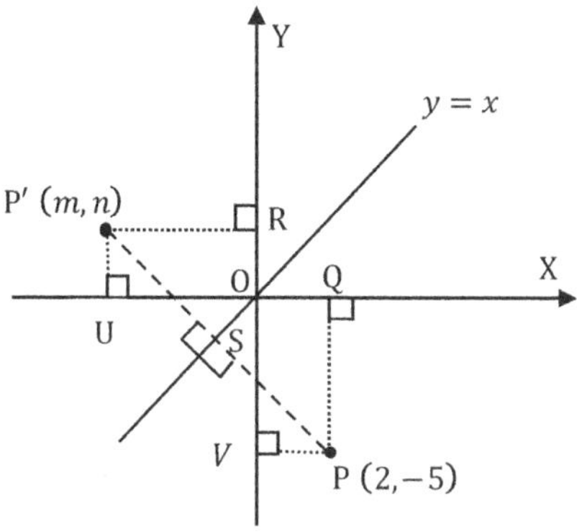


The reflection of the point P $(2, -5)$ is shown as P′ $(m, n)$.

It can be clearly seen in the diagram that:

|P'R| = |PQ| = 5 and |P'U| = |PV| = 2

Thus, the coordinates of P' are $(-5, 2)$.

Thus, sum of the coordinates of P' = $2 - 5 = -3$. - Sufficient

Note: For reflection of a point about $y = x$, the X and Y coordinate values of the point get interchanged.

From statement 2:

The diagram showing the points and the line $y + x = 0$ or $y = -x$ is shown below:

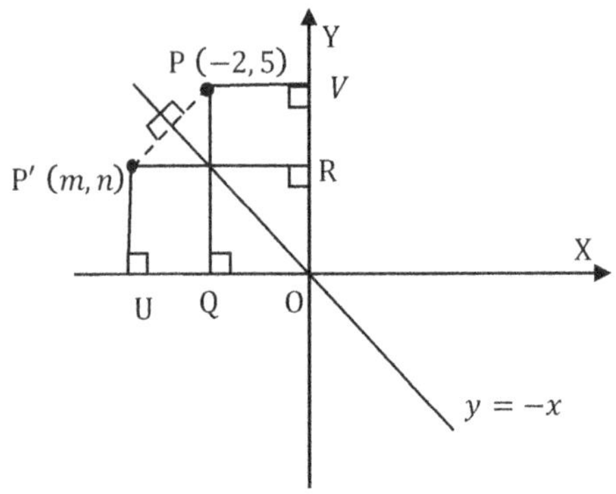


We can proceed in the same way as discussed under statement A.

Thus: |P'R| = |PQ| = 5 and |P'U| = |PV| = 2

Thus, the coordinates of P' are $(-5, 2)$.

Thus, sum of the coordinates of P' = 2 − 5 = −3. - Sufficient

Note: For reflection of a point about $y + x = 0$, the X and Y coordinate values of the point get interchanged and both also get negated.

The correct answer is option D.

**148.** From statement 1:

The lines are shown in the diagram below:

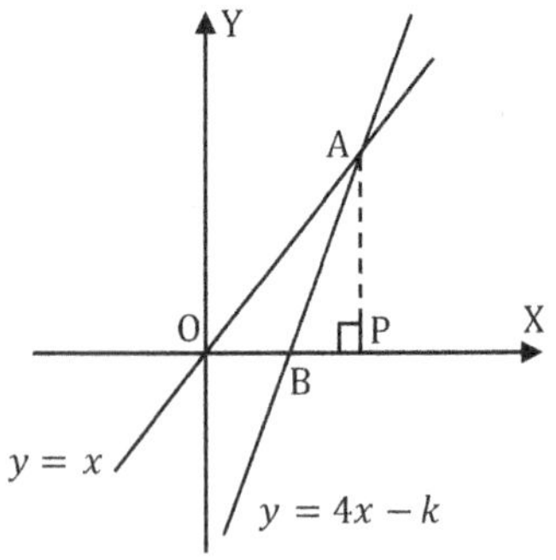


The triangle formed, whose area is given as 6, is triangle OAB.

Area of the triangle = $\frac{1}{2}$ (OB) (AP).

OB is the X intercept of the line $y = 4x - k$.

Thus, substituting $y = 0$ in the equation of the line, we have:

 

$x = \frac{k}{4}$ => OB $= \frac{k}{4}$

To determine AP, we need to solve for the Y coordinate of the point A.

Solving the equations $y = x$ and $y = 4x - k$, we have:

$y = 4y - k => y = \frac{k}{3}$ => AP $= \frac{k}{3}$

Since the area of the triangle OAB is 6, we have:

$\frac{1}{2}\left(\frac{k}{4}\right)\left(\frac{k}{3}\right) = 6 => k^2 = 144$

$=> k = \pm 12$

Since $k$ is positive, we have:

$k = 12$. - Sufficient

From statement 2:

The fact that $y = 4x - k$ makes a positive intercept with the X axis is obvious since the value of $k$ is given as positive.

The value of $k$ cannot be determined from this statement. - Insufficient

The correct answer is option A.

**149.** Let the coordinates of M be $(p,\ q)$.

We need to determine the value of $(p + q)$.

From statement 1:

There is no information about the location of point M. - Insufficient

From statement 2:

Since AM = BM, we have:

$\sqrt{(p-1)^2 + (q-1)^2} = \sqrt{(p-4)^2 + (q-4)^2}$

Squaring both sides:

$(p^2 - 2p + 1) + (q^2 - 2q + 1) = (p^2 - 8p + 16) + (q^2 - 8q + 16)$

$=> 6p + 6q = 30$

 

$=> p + q = 5$. - Sufficient

The correct answer is option B.

Note: One might be tempted to think that, since M is on AB and AM = BM, M must be the midpoint of AB, thus marking C as the correct answer, which is not!

In this case, it does not matter whether P lies or does not lie on AB. However, even if one assumes that, the same result ensues.

**150.** If $m$ satisfies the equation $m^2 - 5m + 6 = 0$, we have:

$m^2 - 5m + 6 = 0 => (m - 2)(m - 3) = 0$

$=> m = 2$ OR $3$

From statement 1:

The possible situations where a line makes equal intercepts of equal magnitude on the X and Y axes are shown in the diagram below:

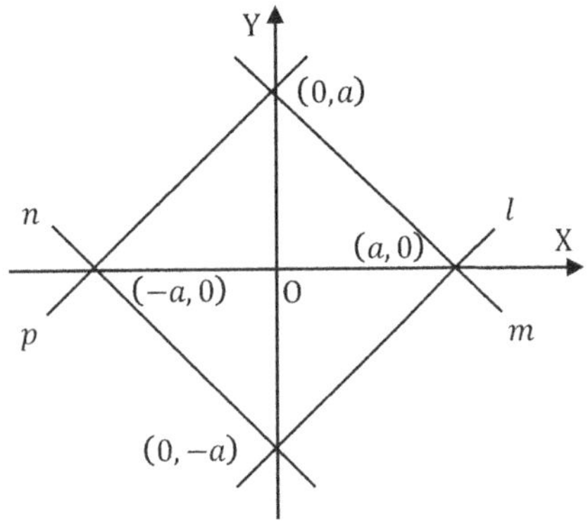


For the lines $p$ and $l$, the slope is '1', while for the lines $n$ and $m$, the slope is '$-1$'.

Thus, the value of $m = 1$ OR $-1$.

Thus, the values of $m$ do not match the values of $m$ required to satisfy the equation $m^2 - 3m + 2 = 0$.

Thus, the answer to the question is 'No'. - Sufficient

From statement 2:

We only know that the line passes through the point $(1, 1)$.

 

A line passing through (1, 1) may or may not have slope of 2 or 3.

Hence, the answer cannot be uniquely determined. – Insufficient

The correct answer is option A.

# Chapter 6

# Speak to Us

## Have a Question?

Please email your questions to info@manhattanreview.com. We will be happy to answer you. Your questions can be related to a concept, an application of a concept, an explanation of a question, a suggestion for an alternate approach, or anything else you wish to ask regarding the GMAT.

Please mention the page number when quoting from the book.

## GMAC - Quants Resources

- *Official Guide 13*: It is the best resource to prepare for the GMAT. It is a complete GMAT book. It comes with a Diagnostic test, which helps you measure your capability beforehand. The book contains an access code to avail GMATPrep Software.
- *GMATPrep Software*: If you buy OG13, you get a free online resource from the GMAC—the test-maker. Apart from practice questions and explanation, it also has two genuine Computer Adaptive tests; you can also buy four additional CATs and few practice questions upon the payment.

Made in the USA
Las Vegas, NV
21 September 2025

28373993R00168